SHAMANS OF THE HIMALAYAS

Anu Malhotra is one of India's leading film-makers, having won eighteen national/international awards, including the Nari Shakti Puraskar from the president of India and the UN AIDS Global Award. Her insightful documentaries, trendsetting television programming and impactful communication projects, produced and directed by her, have been broadcast on premier Indian and international television channels over the past three decades.

Besides her enormous repertoire of filming work, Anu is also an acclaimed photographer and writer. Her unique multimedia exhibition of photographs, documentaries and artifacts titled *Soul Survivors* was showcased at the National Museum, New Delhi, the Conference of the Parties COP28, and at Bikaner House, where Anu's first published book, *Soul Survivors*, was released in 2018. Her *Hindustan Times* column, *Travels with My Camera*, and other travel articles in popular magazines were much appreciated.

"I have always sought to capture India's rich cultural heritage and vibrant living traditions through my films and books. It has been my mission to document unique cultures that are fast disappearing, to encourage us to learn from and preserve their traditional wisdom."

– Anu Malhotra

SHAMANS OF THE HIMALAYAS

ANU MALHOTRA

Om Books International

Reprinted in 2025

Om Books International

Corporate & Editorial Office
A-12, Sector 64, Noida 201 301
Uttar Pradesh, India
Phone: +91 120 477 4100
Email: editorial@ombooks.com
Website: www.ombooksinternational.com

Sales Office
107, Ansari Road, Darya Ganj,
New Delhi 110 002, India
Phone: +91 11 4000 9000
Email: sales@ombooks.com
Website: www.ombooks.com

ISBN: 978-93-6395-290-4

Printed in India

10 9 8 7 6 5 4 3 2

I dedicate this book to all the Goors, Devis, Devtas and the people of Kullu Valley

Contents

Preface

The journey . . . is . . . the destination!

My earliest memories of "journey" are embedded in my childhood, when my parents would pack up my brother and me in our tiny sky-blue Fiat and set off to faraway places. We travelled by road from Jorhat to Delhi, from Delhi to Srinagar, from Madras to Bangalore, Mysore, and Ooty. Those journeys took days, with leisurely stops at scenic areas to picnic or sightsee; we ate at dhabas and visited friends living in towns en route. I grew to relish such adventurous journeys, so when I had the opportunity to traipse around India, filming for my travel shows, *Namaste India* and *Indian Holiday* (in the late 1990s), I was ecstatic!

For me, the journey is the destination. Each journey brings with it a treasure trove of new experiences: from tracking tigers and lions in the jungles of Kanha and Gir, scuba diving in Lakshadweep to motor-biking in the Himalayas; from smoking ceremonial opium and dancing with the Konyak head-hunters, drinking rice beer with the Apa Tani to witnessing shamans conducting divinations and exorcisms, they have all been wonderful and transformative journeys. The diversity and paradoxes that I have encountered across this incredible country never fail to amaze me. Exploring the wild and uncharted, interacting with unique cultures and experiencing our amazing living traditions almost made me feel like I was a time traveller. It is incredible how distant eras can be preserved in local cultural memory and tradition. I made it my mission to document for posterity some of our India's unique cultures and living traditions which I realised were under threat of disappearing without much record.

After 2000, I focused on exploring some of India's indigenous cultures in the documentary format, which allowed me to spend longer periods filming, thereby giving me a deeper insight into my quest. I began with producing and directing a series of seven documentary films, titled *Tribal Wisdom*,[1] followed by others.

The months and years that I spent filming the Apa Tani of Arunachal Pradesh, the Konyak of Nagaland and the Maharaja of Jodhpur were some of my most memorable and precious learning experiences. And then *Shamans of the Himalayas* happened! Although I had spent fifteen years exploring this diverse country, it was a revelation to discover a worldview that was so alien to anything that I had experienced earlier.

Cut off for much of its history from most of the outside world by its natural mountain barriers and a lack of proper roads and communication, the people of the Kullu Valley evolved a complex culture based on a unique series of interlinking mythic and magico-religious belief systems. The community is bound together by a commonly perceived reality, a social unity reinforced by the wisdom of traditional forms of worship, lifestyle and culture.

Their belief system is intrinsic to the mythic imagination of an ancient system that is rooted in the natural world and predated not just by rigid, conventional science but also by organised religion. The people of this valley have come to combine the local

---

1 *Tribal Wisdom* is a series of seven one-hour films documenting the unique culture and the intrinsic wisdom reflected in the customary lifestyle of various isolated tribes of India. This rare coverage of different indigenous groups explores their sustainable lifestyle, social fabric, vibrant culture and unique traditions.

with the orthodox cult, resulting in the widespread worship of a number of local animistic deities in addition to divinities of the more mainstream religions. The local Goors, or shamans, are at the core of the community's spiritual and social existence.

As I have discovered over the years of filming travel programmes and documentaries, while the diversity of our geographical landscapes is all encompassing, it is the multiplicity of India's diverse cultures that is astounding. And to truly understand this complexity, one has to deep dive into it. It is only by spending enough time immersively with a community that I could comprehend the nuances of their culture and way of life. It took me three years of researching, filming, transcribing dozens of interviews, and editing to make my four-part documentary series, *Shamans of the Himalayas*, and another four to write this book!

The main reason for my initial interest in documenting some of India's unique cultures was not just to record them for posterity, but also as a personal quest to understand why, contrary to our modern myth of "progress" and "development", these village communities seemed far happier and content than most of us living in cities! So, what do traditional societies have that we do not, which accounts for their more spiritual orientation to, and greater happiness within, the world?

The word "city" is, in a way, a metaphor for the urban myth of modern living—that bigger is better, that more is greater, that faster is automatically fitter for purpose, and that the system is there to be followed. "Traditional" is a way of mind rather than a place. And the essence of a "traditional" society is based on real community and caring. What we lose above all as we grow from children to adults, and from tribal to city dwellers, is our connection to the sacred, to the community and to nature.

The people from indigenous communities that I have met in my travels and documentation in the villages of Himachal Pradesh and across the country have a deep respect for nature which was reflected in their eco-centric lifestyle. They were self-sustained societies that enjoyed clean air, pure water, sunshine, physical work with earth and its resources, connecting to the natural rhythms of the seasons, and eating a wholesome diet with moderate consumption. Even the members of the older generation were usually productively employed and living robustly until a ripe old age. Until the turn of the previous century, most of these village communities lived like a cohesive whole, where orphans, widows, the aged and the infirm were well cared for. In the past couple of decades, the intrusion of so-called "materialistic development" and contemporary city values have, of course, taken its toll diluting their rich belief and value systems.

As we teeter on the precipice of irrevocable planetary crisis, struggling with climate change, loss of critical forest reserves and biodiversity, soil erosion and pollution of air and water, it is undeniable that the dominant mode of life and livelihood—in simpler words, the Western lifestyle, based on super-consumption—is destructive and unsustainable. This exploitative and dominating attitude towards nature is alien to indigenous or tribal societies. Only now are we beginning to realise that such communities provide a living expression of sustainable living, and can provide a possible alternative to our consumerist lifestyles.

Studies of social change, political evolution, and literary and cultural history have all observed the growing sense of isolation in individuals, and the loss of a sense of belonging, moorings, a sense of community, and togetherness. Further, religious and sectarian tensions over the past ten years have brought home to us, in no uncertain terms, that we have to look beyond the nation-state, political ideologies, religious faiths, and economic theories to cultural traits that bind people in communities.

New ways of looking at the sources of people's togetherness are essential. Development cannot be isolated from an individual's craving for anchorage in groups. Here, once again, our traditional socio-cultural model can help us. I find the tribal worldview to be a holistic one. Tribal communities live in smaller communes with shared lifestyles, customs and values. The individual is undoubtedly at the centre, but his relationship with "other" human beings in society, with nature and with the world of ancestors, gods and spirits is integrated into a coherent system which keeps everyone rooted, secure and happy.

I strongly believe that we must look towards the tribal model of civilisation, which has endured for millennia to course correct and find urgent situations to avert catastrophe. I believe that my films, photographs, and this book are a part of this larger project: a project that explores, documents and preserves, in both archival and more living forms, the ways of life that are fast disappearing.

On reflection, it seems incredible to me that most of us do not completely comprehend the impact our environment, place, people, society, culture, and lifestyle have on our personal values and belief systems, which have been ingrained into us all from childhood. I would find myself completely mesmerised in the mystical world of "Dev Bhoomi", experiencing its unique realm of magic and the warmth of genuine human connection. It is easy to become a believer and have faith in a seemingly vibrant and more wholesome culture. Back in Delhi, the urban myth that I had lived in would envelop me swiftly. The contrast to Dev Bhoomi was, and still is, startling. Shuffling between these two worlds constantly over the years and intensely connecting with Dev Bhoomi whilst living in Delhi allowed me to look at both as objectively as possible. These are two different worlds, far removed from each other in lifestyle, cultural values, social connections and personal aspirations.

I feel connected to the mystical mountains of the Kullu Valley, and I spend a couple of months there every year. However, today I feel far removed from the world of Dev Bhoomi, Devtas and Goors. It was as if a veil had been lifted for me by Divine Grace, for a point in time, and I was allowed to experience a different reality. A distinct way of being and relating. Now it seems as if that veil has been dropped back!

However, I am still left with the treasures of experience, memory, learning and growing in awareness. I carry these gifts from Dev Bhoomi in my being, for which I am deeply grateful. My heartfelt appreciation to the Himachali people, whose unique and valuable culture has stood the test of time.

Introduction

"Shamanism in India is a complex and multifaceted spiritual practice that reflects the diverse cultural traditions of the country. Shamans play a crucial role in mediating between the human and spirit worlds, offering healing, divination, and spiritual guidance to their communities."

– Dr R.S. Khare, an Indian Anthropologist

Origins and History of Shamanism

Shamanism is an ancient spiritual tradition found in indigenous cultures worldwide. The journey into modern shamanic studies took a significant turn in 1938 with Mircea Eliade's influential work, *Le chamanisme: techniques archaiques de l'extase*. Eliade, a historian of religion whose work is considered to be a classic on shamanology, highlights the striking parallels found in shamanic cosmologies and beliefs across different cultures. He proposed that the remarkable similarities among shamanic traditions worldwide stem from a shared cosmology that originated with early humans during the Palaeolithic period among early nomadic cultures.

Michael Witzel, Sanskrit scholar and comparative mythologist, proposes that all of the world's mythologies, as well as the concepts and practices of shamans, can be traced to the migrations of two prehistoric populations: the "Gondwana" type (circa 65,000 years ago) and the "Laurasian" type (circa 40,000 years ago). He writes, "Shamanic practices have been assumed for the Paleolithic and for the Neolithic periods, for which good archaeological evidence exists."

There is a broad consensus amongst leading anthropologists that shamanism emerged from the traditions of hunting and gathering cultures that believed in animism—a belief that everything in the world is animated by a distinct spiritual essence that organises the universe.

The practice of shamanism has been documented throughout Asia, Oceania, North and South America, Africa and parts of Europe.

Interestingly, Dr Albert Villoldo, who has studied the shamanic healing practices of the Amazon and the Andes for more than twenty-five years, validates that "The Andean shamans of Peru, with whom I trained for several decades, trace their spiritual origins back to the early peoples that settled at the foothills of the Himalayas nearly 50,000 years ago. Migrants from the Indus Valley in the northwestern regions of South Asia (modern-day Pakistan) were among the first medicine men and women to cross the Bering Strait from Siberia after the last glacial period and were known as the Laika, the Earth keepers of old."

Throughout its history, diverse shamanic traditions emerged worldwide alongside the region's cultural mosaic. Tribal societies developed their unique approaches to shamanism, incorporating elements of ancestor worship, spirit possession, and rituals centred around the natural environment.

However, the spread of major organised religions often sought to suppress or transform shamanic practices, leading to their decline or sometimes outlawed or driven underground.

For instance: the spread of Christianity from around 400 CE led to the systematic destruction of shamanic practices across Europe and beyond, with the church outlawing local rituals and destroying temples. In the Caribbean and America, Catholic priests accompanied Conquistadors, branding indigenous traditions as "devil worship" and executing their practitioners. Similar campaigns against perceived witches occurred in North America, while more recent missionary efforts also targeted shamanic practices, including the defacement of ancient petroglyphs in the Amazon during the 1970s. Despite such threats to local practices, in certain cases, shamanism did not completely disappear but instead merged with the major religions, facilitating its survival through syncretism and cultural adaptation.

Hence, as societies evolved, encounters with other cultures and the rise of organised religions brought both challenges and transformations to shamanism. Some shamanic traditions integrated with dominant religious systems, adopting new forms and syncretic practices. This is the form encountered in India and other parts of South-East Asia.

Definition of Shamanism

Shamanism predates organised religion. The term shamanism comes from the language of the Tungs (Evenki), an indigenous group in Siberia. The Siberian Manchu-Tungus word šamán means "to know in an ecstatic manner"; this expression was applied to all native spiritual healers by Russian settlers. The noun is formed from the verb ša: "to know"; thus, a shaman is literally "one who knows".[1] Interestingly, Mircea Eliade noted that the Sanskrit word śramana, designating a wandering monastic or holy figure, has spread to many Central Asian languages along with Buddhism and could be the ultimate origin of the Tungusic word. He describes shamanism as the "ultimate expression of an innate and timeless human religiosity centred on the ecstatic trance" and views it as the oldest form of religion. He notes that shamanism likely emerged as a response to the challenges and mysteries of the

1 Buženková (2010)

natural world, which were considered to be inhabited and governed by spirits. Shamans served as mediators between humans and the spirit world, and shamanic practices were integral to early human societies, providing healing, guidance, and spiritual insight.

There is a definition offered by Michael Harner, an anthropologist who spent years with tribes in the Amazon, in the 1950s and 1960s (Smoley and Kinney, 2006), and later became a shaman himself. Harner (1982) defines a shaman as "a man or a woman who enters an altered state of consciousness at will to contact and utilise an ordinarily hidden reality to acquire knowledge, power, and to help others".

Shamanism encompasses the premise that shamans are intermediaries or messengers between the human world and the spirit world. Therefore, shamanism might be defined as a family of traditions whose practitioners focus on voluntarily entering altered states of consciousness in which they experience themselves or their spirit(s), travelling to other realms at will and interacting with other entities in order to serve the community.

It is also important to note that while the term "shaman" has gained popularity in many regions, indigenous communities have their own specific terminology for individuals whose practices might be referred to as "shamanic" by ethnologists and anthropologists. The idea of shamanism is dynamic and ever evolving, encompassing a diverse array of concepts that have evolved significantly over time, with its definitions shifting based on personal experiences and cultural contexts.

Belief System of Shamanism

Shamanism manifests in myriad forms, yet it is bound by a tapestry of shared beliefs that resonate with all shamanist communities and unite its diverse expressions. Central to shamanic traditions is the conviction that spirits exist, playing crucial roles in individual lives and human society. Shamans, as mediators, possess the unique ability to communicate with these spiritual realms, navigating the intricate relationships between humans and unseen, non-human entities. Within this realm, spirits can be benevolent or malevolent, leading to the shaman's vital function in healing ailments that arise from harmful entities.[2]

Shamans often take the role of healers in their communities and use rituals, ceremonies, traditional herbal remedies and trance states to cure illness—physical, mental and spiritual. These altered states of consciousness are achieved by harnessing the visceral power of drumming, chanting, dancing, fasting and sometimes psychoactive substances.

Shamans also act as spiritual guides and advisors, helping members of their communities to make decisions about the cornerstones of life, such as farming, marriage, birth, and death. This position is even more significant when you consider that shamans guard, preserve, and transmit cultural heritage through such roles. Besides healing, the shaman can perform other varied forms of divination and sometimes foretell future events. Shamans perform a variety of functions depending upon their respective cultures: healing, leading a sacrifice, preserving traditions by storytelling and songs, fortunetelling, and acting as a psychopomp ("guide of souls").

A single shaman may fulfil several of these functions by communicating directly with the spirits at will or through trance. The latter has two forms: first, trances of possession, in which the body of the shaman is possessed by the spirit, and second, wandering trances, in which his soul departs into the realm of spirits. In the former the possessed gets into an intense mental state and shows superhuman strength and knowledge: he quivers, rages, struggles, and finally falls into a condition similar to unconsciousness. After accepting the spirit, the shaman regains a degree of consciousness and becomes its mouthpiece—"he becomes him who entered him".

---

2 Eliade (1964)

The Making of a Shaman

Anthropologists generally agree that the shaman acquires his profession through inheritance, instruction, or an inner calling, but each of these terms requires some qualification. In this context, "inheritance" means that the soul of a dead shaman, or alternatively the so-called shaman illness, is inherited. The inner "calling", in reality, is not the call of the person but of the spirit who has chosen him and who forces him to accept this vocation.

According to the abundant literature on the subject and the experience of investigators in the field, no one voluntarily ventures into the shaman role, nor does a candidate have time to study the role. He does not become a shaman simply by willing it, for it is not the shaman who summons up the spirits but they, the supernatural beings, who choose him.

The initiation of a novice, which typically starts with a spirit's selection, is often met with reluctance and resistance by the person. This initiation is characterised by a series of challenging and sometimes dangerous trials. The process concludes with a profound transformation, involving a metaphorical death and rebirth.

The initiatory crisis of the future shaman is usually indicated by involuntary shaking induced by the spirits in some form or other. This state is also called the "shamanic illness". The shamanistic initiatory crisis functions as an involuntary rite of passage for the future shaman, and it involves both a more-or-less serious physical illness and/or a psychological crisis. This state is well attested across all shamanic regions by various scholars.

Precepts and Practices of Shamanism

Shamanism is characterised by a set of core precepts and practices that are common across various cultural traditions. Central to shamanic beliefs is the interconnectedness of all living beings with nature and the spiritual world, as well as the existence of multiple realms of reality. Although each culture imparts its own distinct flavour to shamanic practices, certain foundational principles form a common fabric that transcends geographical boundaries and cultural contexts.

Whether it is the Amazon rainforest or the Himalayan foothills, the shamanic worldview reveres Earth as a sacred entity, a living organism pulsating with spiritual energy and entities deserving of respect, gratitude, and protection. It is within this sacred tapestry that shamans traverse the boundaries of the physical and spiritual realms, acting as intermediaries and healers who bridge the gap between the seen and the unseen.

Across the continents, shamans engage in practices that honour and harmonise with the natural world. Rituals involving the elements—earth, water, fire, and air—are conducted to establish a profound connection with these elemental forces. Through ceremonies and sacred offerings, shamans seek to restore balance and maintain the delicate equilibrium of the natural order. They perceive Earth as a sentient being by aligning themselves with the rhythms of nature, shamans tap into the ancient wisdom that flows through the land, awakening their own spiritual potential and fostering a profound sense of belonging.

Let's look at regions across the world that still practise shamanistic traditions.

South American Shamans

In South America, the Shipibo people of the Peruvian Amazon have a long tradition of shamanism, with healers known as "curanderos" using plant medicines and spiritual ceremonies to treat physical and emotional ailments. Unlike their counterparts in other regions, divine possession is not a central aspect of their practice. Instead, they communicate with spirits and entities through rituals, ceremonial offerings, and plant medicine, such as ayahuasca.

Arctic Regions

Among the Inuit, shamans known as "angakkuit" serve as healers and spiritual guides. The angakkuit lead ceremonies to honour the powerful spirits of the sea and sky, ensuring villagers uphold sacred taboos that safeguard their well-being. When disturbances arise—be it illness, dwindling food, or harsh weather—the angakkuit have to navigate a delicate negotiation with the spirits to restore harmony between humanity and nature.

Siberia and Central Asia

Shamanism has deep roots in the indigenous cultures of Siberia and Central Asia. Among the Tuvan people of Siberia, shamans known as "kam" perform rituals and ceremonies to communicate with spirits and ensure the well-being of their community. In Mongolia, the practice of shamanism is known as "buu", and shamans play a vital role in rituals such as the annual Tsam dance.

Africa

In countries like Nigeria and Cameroon, traditional healers known as "juju men" or "witch doctors" use herbs, rituals, and divination to address spiritual and physical ailments. The San people of southern Africa have a rich tradition of shamanism, with healers known as "medicine men" using trance states and rituals to connect with the spirit world.

Australia and Oceania

Among the Aboriginal peoples of Australia, shamans known as "ngangkari", or "clever people", use traditional healing methods and rituals to maintain spiritual balance and harmony within the communities. In the Pacific Islands, shamans known as "kahunas" in Hawaii or "tohunga" in New Zealand perform rituals and ceremonies to communicate with ancestors and nature spirits.

Shamanism in India

Shamanism in India has been shaped by the historical and social contexts surrounding Brahmanical religion and its identification with Aryan origins. The Brahmanical practices, including Vedic deities and rituals, became associated with a dominant Aryan identity, while non-Brahmanical and non-scriptural traditions were redefined and labelled as shamanistic or ecstatic, presenting a notion of spirituality disconnected from institutionalised religion. This framework elevated certain aspects of Indian spirituality while marginalizing others, particularly those outside Brahmanical traditions. Shamanism within India brings to mind the rich traditions of Adivasi and tribal communities, where spiritual practices are deeply rooted in oral traditions, passed over generations and marked by dramatic and performative elements.[3] Rituals often involve trances, communication with spirits, and navigating significant rites of passage and important events.

The religious life of many village folks and indigenous communities, although they coexist with the established traditions of Sanskritic Hinduism, are distinctly their own. These practices include numerous rituals showcasing a rich tapestry of local beliefs. Some of these observances may echo Sanskritic themes, representing localised interpretations, but many are entirely unique. This vibrant religious landscape features practitioners such as shamans, diviners, exorcists, healers, and worshippers dedicated to particular gods. Indian shamanism embodies unique spiritual practices marked by magical rituals and distinctive healing

3 Dandekar (2018)

methods, typically linked to community-oriented societies. This vibrant tradition often unfolds in rural areas, particularly during festivals, where shamans lead ceremonies, participate in music and dance, offer sacrifices and perform other divinations and healing rituals.

One major element of shamanism is the application of traditional healing practices from the past. Beyond modern-day psychiatrists and physicians, India has a rich tradition of addressing psychic distress and physical ailments through various explanatory systems and healing techniques. These traditional healers, such as vaids in Ayurvedic tradition and hakims in Unani tradition, and other practitioners like palmists, astrologers, and shamans draw from a blend of astrology, medicine, and magic, combining it with folk culture and practices. This is also followed by spiritual leaders known as sadhus and swamis, who specialise in the restoration of moral and spiritual well-being.[4]

If we look at Hindu thought, disturbances in the self are linked to the broader concept of karma, influencing the individual's lifecycle. This view is adopted by shamans and folk healers when addressing social disharmony, as they consider not only the living family and community members but also the ancestral spirits, along with other cosmic beings that inhabit the Indian spiritual landscape.

Indian healing practices uniquely intertwine the sacred with the healer-patient relationship, creating a profound bond that transcends mere treatment. Here, the notion of the sacred extends beyond divine entities to include ancestral spirits, forest spirits, and even the haunting spectres of evil spirits. This spiritual dimension unites a diverse array of healers, from gurus addressing spiritual discomfort to shamans confronting ailments caused by malevolent spirits. This presence of sacred elements in the traditional healing culture is highlighted by Sudhir Kakar in his work *Shamans, Mystics*

4 Kakar, S. (1982)

and Doctors, as he writes, "The whole weight of the community's religion, myths and history enters sacred therapy as the therapist proceeds to mobilise strong psychic energies inside and outside the patient which are no longer available in modern society."[5]

In essence, sacred healing lies at the heart of shamanism in India, serving as a powerful conduit for spiritual restoration, cultural continuity, and the deep connection between individuals and the divine, ensuring that the wisdom of ancient practices continues to nurture and transform lives today. It encompasses tribal knowledge, myths, oral traditions, and folklore transmitted through generations binding the community together. While shamanism in India may not be as well-documented or widely recognised, it is a widespread tradition.

Here are a few examples of shamanic practices being observed among tribal groups and others in the country.

The Adivasi Tribes

The Adivasis, or indigenous tribal communities of India, have their own unique shamanic traditions that are deeply rooted in their cultural heritage. Among tribes such as the Santhal, Bhil, Gond, Oraon, shamans known as "bhagats" or "ojhas" play a crucial role in healing, divination, and spiritual guidance. Similarly, the Jadupatuas, a subgroup of the Santhal tribe residing primarily in the regions of West Bengal, Bihar, and Jharkhand, are polytheists who venerate a multitude of deities, spirits, and ghosts associated with the forests, hills, and streams in their environment. They believe that their lives are steered by the wisdom of their ancestral spirits. Let's look at a few other communities that observe shamanic practices in the country.

5 Kakar, S., 1982, p. 5

The Bishnois of Rajasthan

The Bishnois are a community in Rajasthan known for their deep reverence for nature and wildlife conservation. Bishnoi shamans, known as "bhagats", play a role in mediating between humans and nature spirits, performing rituals to protect the environment and ensure the well-being of the community.

The Kuruba Tribe

The Kuruba, also known as the Kuruba Gowda, is an indigenous community found in parts of south India, particularly in Karnataka and Tamil Nadu. Among the Kuruba people, there are shamans known as "Devara Kaduva" or "Kattuva", who serve as spiritual healers and mediators between the human and spirit worlds.

The Toda Tribe

The Toda are an indigenous community living in the Nilgiri Hills of Tamil Nadu, having a rich cultural heritage that includes shamanic practices and rituals. Among the Todas, there are shamans known as "Pujari" or "Kurukkal", who perform ceremonies and rituals to communicate with deities and spirits. These shamans play a significant role in maintaining spiritual balance and harmony within the community.

The Urali Tribe in Kerala

The Uralis, who are great believers of spirits, hill gods, and ancestor worship, often perform shamanic rituals to please their deities and ancestors. Among the Uralis, the shamanic practices are carried out by the tribe's religious head, the Pilathi. This tribal group, much like other traditional shamanistic communities, practises shamanism as both a religious ritual and a sacred form of healing. The Pilathi, similar to the position of a tribal leader, holds the group together, maintains peace and strengthens the community's bond.[6]

The Apatani and Nyishi Tribes in Arunachal Pradesh

They also practise shamanism in order to communicate with the spirit world. Sacred ceremonial rituals and sacrifices are performed by the shamans called Nyub, who conduct sacred healing rituals and solve the problems faced by the people.

Conclusion

Historically, shamans served as intermediaries between the human and spirit realms, playing crucial roles in communal rituals, medicine, and social cohesion. Over the years, shamanism has evolved and adapted to changing circumstances, influencing and being influenced by the cultures it encountered. However, it remains a testament to humanity's enduring quest to understand and connect with the unseen dimensions of existence.

As we witness the resurgence of interest in spiritual healing, self-discovery, and cultural synthesis, neo-shamanism stands at the forefront. Emerging in the latter half of the twentieth century, neo-shamanism blends traditional indigenous shamanic practices, especially from Amazonian, Meso-American, and North American traditions, with modern psychotherapeutic techniques to fit the fabric of Western urban society. Developed as a counter to the materialistic mindset of Western society, it emphasises the need to reconnect with forgotten ancestral wisdom. By exploring altered states of consciousness, practitioners seek to heal and transform themselves, creating innovative paths to personal and spiritual growth that meet today's needs.

6 Menon, I.V. (2015)

Unlike traditional shamanism, where becoming a shaman is a community choice or an inherited role, neo-shamanism empowers individuals to pursue shamanic training on their own terms, democratizing the path to shamanic practice. While the traditional shaman operates within a vibrant community of spirits and teachers, guided by the need to harmonise human and cosmic relationships, neo-shamanism focuses on personal transformation, prioritizing individual growth over communal balance. For example, in Latin America, neo-shamanism finds its most vibrant expression in the Camino Rojo (Red Path), a movement deeply rooted in North American indigenous traditions like those of the Lakota. Here, age-old rituals such as the "vision quest", "sweat lodge", and "sun dance" are creatively adapted into a fresh cosmology. Beyond this, numerous eclectic neo-shamanic paths emerge, weaving together local and North American practices through gatherings like the Eagle and Condor meetings, which reimagine Andean prophecies as a call for spiritual unity. These neo-shamanic circles are woven into broader New Age spiritual networks, where national histories are artfully reinterpreted in pursuit of deeper spiritual connections.

It is imperative to recognise that shamanism itself is a living, evolving tradition that transcends borders and historical confines. The ancient rituals and beliefs that have long defined traditional shamanism are facing unprecedented changes, influenced by modernization and a waning transmission of knowledge to younger generations. Today, there are only a few traditional shamans left. With the encroachment of civilization, the younger generation is more interested in exploring the exciting new options available to them. But spirit works in mysterious ways, and as traditional shamanic cultures dwindle, increasing numbers of world-weary refugees of modern society are finding a path to modern shamanism.

Prologue

It was May 2008, and the four-day Dhungri Mela was in full swing. The villagers gathered around the festival grounds in their colourful attire—men wearing Kullu caps and women wrapped in pattu shawls. A small group of musicians sat in the centre, playing lively traditional music, while locals performed the graceful Kullu natti dance.

At the centre of the courtyard stood a palanquin, adorned with vibrant silks, garlands of flowers, and gleaming metal masks stacked on top. It was held aloft by four bearers who danced to the rhythm of the music. I was told that the palanquin belonged to Hadimba Devi, the patron goddess of Manali.

As I wandered through the grounds, absorbing the atmosphere, the music suddenly stopped, and the palanquin was placed on a cement platform. People approached and bowed reverently. One man stepped forward and stood directly in front of the palanquin, blocking my perfect photo shot. He appeared middle-aged, with a lined face, wispy grey hair, missing teeth, and dusty clothes.

Then, to my astonishment, the man began trembling, shaking violently, and suddenly started jumping up and down, shouting aggressively. The villagers, while giving him space, gathered around him, listening respectfully. He stood before the palanquin, gesturing animatedly as he addressed the crowd. I watched in amazement at this strange scene. His once unremarkable face had transformed—now thunderous, with flashing eyes and exaggerated gestures.

The mood of the festival had shifted. The celebratory crowd was now subdued, listening to this man's increasingly frantic outbursts. Some men engaged with him, even seeming to plead. After about twenty minutes, his tirade ended, and he slumped to the ground. A few moments later, he rose and disappeared into the crowd, and the dancing resumed.

What I didn't realise then was that I had witnessed Tuleram, the shaman of Hadimba Devi, in a divine possession trance, allowing the goddess to speak to her people through him.

This was the first of many encounters I would have with Tuleram and other shamans of the Kullu Valley as I sought to unravel the mysteries surrounding their world. It would be a long, arduous, yet rewarding and enriching journey—one that led me through a landscape of diverse cultures, worldviews, and belief systems. Along the way, I discovered a new self, one capable of bridging the gap between two distinct realities.

*

The word "shaman" is quite familiar to most English-speaking people today. However, the terms "shaman" and "shamanism" were relatively unknown when I filmed my documentary series, *Shamans of the Himalayas*, during 2008–10.

I recollect that most times, people who asked me about my "latest project" would look puzzled when I responded with "Shamans of the Himalayas"!

Inevitably, I would be asked, "But what's a shaman, Anu?"

Unlike these days, fifteen years ago, the word shaman was not so well known. Information or knowledge of shamanism—its existence and history, its precepts and practices, and its role and relevance, in the past and today—was rare. Therefore, before we dive into this book, it is important to have a basic grasp of the above.

Segment 1
Dance of the Divine

"The Goor possesses a virtual monopoly in interpreting the will of the Devta, therefore, [he] is a man of great importance. He has a lot of ritual engagements and no ceremony or undertaking is commenced without first consulting him. He helps in fulfilling the social, cultural, financial, spiritual and religious needs of the people and guides them in all their activities."

– **M.R. Thakur,** ***Myths, Rituals and Beliefs in Himachal Pradesh***

Goor Tuleram and Goor Beliram in the process of ritually invoking divine possession, 2008

Goor Tuleram in a divine possession trance at Hadimba Devi's birthday celebrations, 2008

Goor Tuleram performing Devkhel with the Goor of Devta Shandil Rishi, Shuru village, 2008

Goor Tuleram in a violent divine possession trance, sticking his tongue out; Hadimba Devi is considered to be the incarnation of Goddess Kali, 2008

he rock upon which she is said to have meditated is called g in Kullvi. The shrine to Hadimba, the Dhungri Temple, es its name from this rock upon which it is built. Hordes evotees flock to the temple to receive blessings and ask for a nat, a wish to be fulfilled from the powerful Devi.

Goor Tuleram in a ceremonial procession, leading Devi Hadimba's rath through the village of Old Manali, during Hadimba Devi's birthday celebration, 2008

Guest deities visiting during Hadimba Devi's birthday celebrations, 2008

The Old Manali Village Festival; the rath of Hadimba Devi dances with her people, 2008

The Naggar village festival held near Tripura Sundari's temple. Her rath is dancing with other guest deities, 2008

Anu Malhotra filming Hadimba Devi's birthday celebration, 2008

Anu Malhotra witnessing a pogle (divination session) with Goor Tuleram and his client, 2008

The Myth of Hadimba Devi

Among the many tales that take off from the Mahabharata is th story of Hadimba Devi, which comes to life in the Kullu Valley. During their exile, the Pandavas entered this abode of Hadimba and her brother Hadimb, man-eating rakshasas or demons, while crossing the forests.

Upon sighting the Pandavas, Hadimb insisted that Hadimba appear before them in the form of a beautiful woman to lure them and make a meal out of them. However, Hadimb's plan turned on its head when the mighty Pandava Bheema stood up to him and fatally overpowered him. The powerful Hadimba did not partake in this hostility further. Instead, she married the seemingl indomitable Bheem. As the Pandavas continued to travel onward a pregnant Hadimba stayed back in Kullu. Here, she gave birth a son, Ghatotkacha. At the time of the great war with the Kaur Bheema, heeding the advice of Lord Krishna, summoned h to fight. Ghatotkacha changed the tide of the war.

Meanwhile, Hadimba, seated herself on a rock and intense meditation on Devi Mahishasurmardini, a fie of the Goddess Durga. So powerful were her austeri goddess had no choice but to appear before Hadimb her into her own being, making her one with he the demoness had attained the status of a godde the patron goddess of Manali as well as the royal

Goor Tuleram in a ceremonial procession, leading Devi Hadimba's rath through the village of Old Manali, during Hadimba Devi's birthday celebration, 2008

Guest deities visiting during Hadimba Devi's birthday celebrations, 2008

The Old Manali Village Festival; the rath of Hadimba Devi dances with her people, 2008

The Naggar village festival held near Tripura Sundari's temple. Her rath is dancing with other guest deities, 2008

Anu Malhotra filming Hadimba Devi's birthday celebration, 2008

Anu Malhotra witnessing a pogle (divination session) with Goor Tuleram and his client, 2008

The Myth of Hadimba Devi

Among the many tales that take off from the Mahabharata is the story of Hadimba Devi, which comes to life in the Kullu Valley. During their exile, the Pandavas entered this abode of Hadimba and her brother Hadimb, man-eating rakshasas or demons, while crossing the forests.

Upon sighting the Pandavas, Hadimb insisted that Hadimba appear before them in the form of a beautiful woman to lure them and make a meal out of them. However, Hadimb's plan turned on its head when the mighty Pandava Bheema stood up to him and fatally overpowered him. The powerful Hadimba did not partake in this hostility further. Instead, she married the seemingly indomitable Bheem. As the Pandavas continued to travel onwards, a pregnant Hadimba stayed back in Kullu. Here, she gave birth to a son, Ghatotkacha. At the time of the great war with the Kauravas, Bheema, heeding the advice of Lord Krishna, summoned his son to fight. Ghatotkacha changed the tide of the war.

Meanwhile, Hadimba, seated herself on a rock and began an intense meditation on Devi Mahishasurmardini, a fierce aspect of the Goddess Durga. So powerful were her austerities that the goddess had no choice but to appear before Hadimba and absorb her into her own being, making her one with herself. Hadimba the demoness had attained the status of a goddess. Today, she is the patron goddess of Manali as well as the royal family of Kullu.

The rock upon which she is said to have meditated is called dhung in Kullvi. The shrine to Hadimba, the Dhungri Temple, derives its name from this rock upon which it is built. Hordes of devotees flock to the temple to receive blessings and ask for a mannat, a wish to be fulfilled from the powerful Devi.

1
The Journey Begins

Every journey is a search...
A search to discover the Self.

"Deccan Airways announces that its flight number 321 to Kullu is delayed. Scheduled for 6:00 a.m., flight number 321 will now depart at 7:30 a.m.," a lady's voice drones over the PA system. Oh no, I hope the flight actually leaves today, I think to myself. Flights to Kullu are notorious for being cancelled at the last minute due to poor weather conditions in the valley—and this is the only flight headed there!

Even though I have been up since 3.00 a.m., I am wide awake with excitement. A new adventure beckons, and I am eager to get started. I fetch a cup of coffee, sit down, and make myself comfortable. I close my eyes and reflect on the circumstances that have brought me to the threshold of yet another quest. The paths leading to this journey stretch back two decades. I first visited the Kullu Valley in the 1990s to film my travel programme, *Namaste India*. Even after all this time, I vividly remember how I fell in love with Manali and was instantly attracted to the temple of its patron goddess, Hadimba Devi, set within the enchanting Dhungri Forest. I had never seen such a magnificent pagoda-style

Himachali temple, and even then, I was fascinated by its primal vibe. Over the years, whenever I visited Manali, I always began my filming (or vacation) by paying my respects to Hadimba Devi. The raw beauty of the temple, surrounded by ancient deodar forests and infused with goddess energy, profoundly moved me. I made it a point to meditate in the Dhungri Forest during each visit.

In 2003, after a hectic year of filming and editing, I sought refuge in the mountains, craving solitude without an agenda. It was serendipitous to meet Nitin and Sonia, a young couple from Delhi, living as ghodawallahs in Manali. Ghodawallahs own horses and earn a living taking tourists on treks or using them as pack animals. Nitin and Sonia owned six Himachali ponies and organised a relaxing two-week trek for me to the Deo Tibba Pass in the Himalayas.

On one of our regular walks we came across a procession with a palanquin. As the palanquin drew near, the men carrying it suddenly stopped. To my shock, they rushed towards me, and I froze in place! Just as they were about to collide with me, they abruptly changed direction and dashed away. This chaotic dance continued, with the palanquin bearers stumbling in various directions while the rest of the procession looked on calmly. I was completely dumbfounded. *What in heaven's name is happening?* I wondered. Later, Nitin explained, "Anu, the rath houses a village Devta, or god, and the palanquin bearers are being pulled from side to side by the energy of their Devta."

I was sceptical but intrigued when I learned that this is a common phenomenon. Nitin informed me, "Every village in Kullu and Manali has several Devis or Devtas who are carried on raths." I soon forgot about the incident in the excitement of planning our trek.

It was late afternoon when we set off on our trek from Manali to the outskirts of Prini village. As we walked through the village, we heard the plaintive cry of a trumpet and the beating of drums. We followed the sound to a small field set along the hill face, surrounded by a few village huts, and found a village festival in progress with a group of colourfully dressed men and women dancing the graceful Kullu natti[1] in step with the music. Almost the entire village of about fifty or sixty people were looking on. I was entranced by their shining faces, bright eyes, colourful shawls and Kullu topis.

On one side of the field, a palanquin adorned with silken cloth and flowers lay on the ground. Curious, I crossed over for a closer look and saw that it too was decorated with multiple masks, the central one adorned with sparkling jewellery. When I inquired, a few men seated beside it informed me that it was Fali Naag, the Devta of Prini, and requested me to "please maintain a distance". We left soon after to begin our six-hour climb to Sethan village. It was a full-moon night, and as we walked through the silvery landscape, Nitin explained, "You see, all the villages in the valley have their own Devta. And you know what, Anu? The village shamans, called Goors here, communicate the Devta's wishes to the people."

I was completely enthralled. I kept pestering Nitin to tell me more about the Devtas and shamans. Every starlit evening, while trekking towards the Deo Tibba Pass from Sethan, we would chat by the bonfire, and Nitin would share fascinating stories about the Devtas and shamans of the Kullu Valley. However, his knowledge was limited, as he was originally a Delhi boy and not a local.

Yet, one of his personal experiences stayed with me. Nitin told me that the year before, he had gone high up into the mountains to fetch his horses. It is common practice for all horse owners to leave their horses on the higher slopes for weeks to graze and then fetch them back before the snow sets in. But last year Nitin could not find them. He, along with hired help, had spent a month looking for the horses all over the Hampta Pass slopes, but to no avail. It began snowing heavily and Nitin became despondent, assuming the worst.

---

1 Natti: A group dance native to the Kullu region

At a friend's suggestion he agreed to consult a shaman living in Shuru village, and asked if he could help in locating the horses. Nitin's face had become animated as he recounted what happened. "Anu, the shaman went into a trance and told me that he could see my horses surrounded by snow and told me the exact location where I would find them." The next day, Nitin had taken a bunch of friends and climbed high up above the Jagat Sukh Nalla, waded through thigh-deep snow and found his horses, exactly where the shaman had indicated!

My reverie is interrupted by a hand shaking my shoulder as an airline staff member reprimands me, "Madam, if you're on the Kullu flight, please board now. You are the last passenger." Soon, I am settled into my cramped seat on the tiny fourteen-passenger Dornier aircraft. We take off amidst the excruciating roar of the engines. It's far from the most comfortable flight, especially when we hit turbulence and the aircraft bucks, sways, and shudders. A child begins to cry loudly, the man next to me grips the armrest tightly, and the faces around me grow pale.

To distract myself from my queasy stomach, I close my eyes and force myself to dive once more into my memories. I recall that over the past five years, I've visited Manali twice, and both times I found myself asking deep questions about the valley's fascinating belief system.

Earlier this year, a friend, Kishan Banon, introduced me to Meru: "Anu, here's someone who can tell you a lot about the local culture." Hearing about my interests, Meru took me to a village festival in Sarsai. Situated on the right bank of the Beas, between Manali and Naggar, Sarsai is a small village that stretches from the main road up into the mountains.

The village folk were seated around the festival grounds, wearing their colourful best, the men in Kullu topis and the women wrapped in pattu[2] shawls. A small group of musicians

2 Pattu: Homespun woolen fabric

were sitting on the ground in the centre, playing lively traditional music while locals danced the natti.

In the centre of the courtyard was a palanquin adorned with colourful silks, garlands and flowers with gold-coloured metal masks stacked on top. It was being held by four bearers who were dancing to the beat of the music. Meru informed me that the rath was that of a Devta called Vasuki Naag.

When the music stopped, the rath was placed on a cemented platform. People came up and bowed reverentially before it. One man from the crowd came and stood in front of it. I looked at him, annoyed that he had blocked my perfect shot of the rath.

Suddenly, without warning, the man began to tremble and then shook violently. To my astonishment, he started jumping up and down, shouting in an unfamiliar language. Curiously, instead of being alarmed, the village folk gathered around him and listened to his rant with respect.

I watched in amazement at this peculiar scene. In just a few moments, the man's face transformed completely. From nondescript, he became compelling—his expression a thunderous scowl, his eyes flashing, and his gestures furious and emphatic.

The ambience of the place had undergone a transformation. The villagers, who had earlier been gay, became subdued as they listened to the strange man whose voice and gestures had become insistently louder and more frantic. Some men had begun to converse with him and appeared to be pleading with him. In a matter of twenty minutes his tirade was over, and he slumped and sat down. Thereafter he melted into the crowd and the dancing resumed.

Later, Meru explained that we had witnessed Chunni Lal, the shaman of Vasuki Naag, in a divine possession trance, allowing the Devta to speak to his people through him. I remained extremely sceptical.

However, my curiosity was piqued. What was this religious culture I was witnessing and hearing about? Though it permeated all of Himachal Pradesh, I had never encountered it before, despite having filmed several travel shows here. Who were these Goors? What were their powers? And what exactly was their trance of possession? I had contemplated these questions on my last day in Manali while in the Dhungri Forest. I perched on my favourite rock for a long meditation, and it came to me—I should document this culture and learn more about it.

I was excited and energised about my quest and had discussed my plan with Meru, who was equally enthusiastic. He surprised me by saying, "Anu, if you want to document this, you'll have to act fast. Next month, in May, is Hadimba Devi's birthday, and that's when you should begin filming." The importance of this information wasn't lost on me. Although it would be challenging, with May only two weeks away, I was filled with an inexplicable passion and determined to seize the opportunity.

So here I was, mid-May, ready to film live action after a whirlwind of research, pre-production, and assembling a team.

"Ladies and gentlemen, we are approaching Bhuntar, in Kullu. Please fasten your seatbelts." I snap out of my flashback and look out of the window. It's a brilliant sunny day, and I can feel the aircraft dip lower towards the green mountain slopes. The landing here is always tricky—into the Kullu Valley, cradled by the Pir Panjal Range to the north, the Parvati Range to the east, and the Barabangal Range to the west.

The aircraft swerves right and glides downward between two mountain slopes that seem perilously close. I see the familiar tiny houses dotting the slopes as the plane dips lower towards green fields above a gushing river, finally touching down on a small airstrip, scenically framed by mountains and surrounded by fields of yellow flowers.

My journey to document the shamans of the Himalayas has begun. I am about to step into a new reality, one shaped by the collective consciousness of the people of Kullu and their belief system—a system unique in its cultural context, yet shared across all our histories.

2
Dev Bhoomi

I exit the plane and take a deep breath; the air is cool and invigorating. My gaze travels appreciatively over the mountains that surround Bhuntar's tiny airstrip. A dense green carpet of tall pines and deodar trees covers their slopes, glistening against a cobalt-blue sky. It's good to be back!

Meru is waiting for me with a wide grin. Meru, or Mehar Chand Thakur, is in his mid-thirties and typically wears jeans, a t-shirt, a jacket, and a hipster goatee—giving him the look of a rock musician. He started out as a young trekker and guide, and these days he mostly works with students from foreign universities, helping with research projects on the local environment and culture. Beyond his knowledge of local customs, Meru also speaks the local dialect, Kullvi, making him an invaluable guide. I know his gentle manners, wry sense of humour, and pragmatic approach will be crucial in my mystical exploration. "Welcome back, Anu," he says, greeting me with a warm handshake.

We begin our drive from Bhuntar towards Manali. The Kullu Valley, located in the state of Himachal Pradesh, stretches north until Manali, which is situated at an elevation of 6,730 feet. Beyond Manali lies the Pir Panjal Range where the altitude rises to 14,000 feet at the scenic Rohtang Pass, which further links it to the district of Lahaul and Spiti and then to Ladakh through an ancient trade route.

On our way, we pass shops and stalls selling apples, peaches, plums, and cherries—plump and luscious in the morning light. "It seems that besides tourism, fruit production and trade must be one of the main economic activities here," I remark.

"Correct," replies Meru. "Agriculture is our mainstay, while sheep and cattle herding and handicrafts are also widely practised."

We pass the town of Kullu, the administrative centre of the valley, sprawling across several slopes on the opposite bank of the swift-flowing Beas. Concrete structures have replaced most of the old wooden buildings, leaving the once charming town feeling overcrowded and chaotic. However, outside Kullu and Manali, most inhabitants of the valley reside in picturesque villages that dot these magnificent mountains at varying altitudes. Many of these villages are small, with some having as few as twenty households, while others range from sixty to a hundred.

We discuss the historical origins of the region. I had read that archaeologists identified Palaeolithic and Neolithic artifacts at various sites in Himachal Pradesh, revealing that it was home to some of the earliest humans. According to local folklore that recalls a Puranic legend, this area is considered the cradle of mankind, where life began anew after a great deluge. Meru explains, "It is said that the present world began from Manwalaya, the older name for Manali and the home of the ancient Hindu lawgiver, Manu."

Legend has it that King Shraddha Deva Manu, also referred to as Sage Vaivasvata Manu, was the first man and the progenitor of humans. He is believed to be the first king to rule the earth after saving mankind from the Great Flood. He was warned of the Great Flood by the Matsya Avatar of the Hindu god Vishnu and was advised to construct a gigantic boat. As narrated in the *Matsya Purana*, Lord Vishnu's Matsya Avatar initially appeared as a small carp to King Manu while he was washing his hands in a river. The carp implored King Manu to save him. Honouring the carp's request, King Manu placed him in a jar of water. Soon the carp outgrew the jar, so the King shifted it to a larger bowl. But the carp grew incessantly bigger, and King Manu had to load it from the bowl into a well, then into a river and finally into the ocean. That is when the huge fish transformed into Lord Vishnu and informed King Manu of a catastrophic deluge that would soon flood the entire world. He instructed King Manu to build a boat big enough to house his family, nine varieties of seeds as well as animals and birds to repopulate the earth once the deluge receded.

Another legend tells of the Saptarishi,[1] or "Seven Great Sages", accompanying Manu on the boat. When the entire world was immersed in floodwaters, the boat of Manu was carried towards the Himalayas by Matsya. The boat came to rest at Himavat, the area identified as the present Hamta Mountain Pass near Manali. The Seven Sages meditated there, and soon became Indriyajit, or "victorious over all sensory passions", and were no longer interested in procreation. So, Brahma created Shatarupa, or "she of a hundred beautiful forms", from his left side and gave her to Manu to be his wife. Manu and Shatarupa lived together at Manwalaya and gave birth to many children who repopulated the world once the floods subsided. The story of a great deluge and a mighty ark find resonance with many mythologies across the world.

I had also read that in one of the Puranas,[2] the Kullu Valley is referred to as Kulant Pitha,[3] which roughly translates to "the end of the habitable world". In the times of the ancient Silk Route,

---

1 According to ancient Indian astronomy, the seven stars of the constellation Saptarishi Mandal (part of Ursa Major) are Pulastya, Pulasha, Kratu, Atri, Angiras, Vasishtha and Marichi. The outermost two joined by a straight line and extended northward will meet the pole star (north star / Dhruvatara).

2 Puranas: Purana means 'old, ancient'; the eighteen Puranas, believed to originate around 2000 BCE, are among the oldest set of Hindu literature found. They contain myths, legends and traditional folklore.

3 *Kullu: The End of the Habitable World* by Penelope Chetwode

the Dana Bazaar, now known as the Manali Bazaar, was a major halting station for traders going to and from Central Asia and the Gangetic plains. Local rajas ruled here until the British annexed these lands in the mid-twentieth century. Interestingly the first foreign travellers to visit Manali and Dana Bazaar were the Jesuit missionaries who had been searching for the mythical kingdom of the legendary Christian patriarch and king, Prester John.[4]

During British rule this subdivision became increasingly popular with British officers who would come with their families to escape the blazing summer heat of the plains. Some of them eventually decided to settle here on retirement and form a colony of planters; tea being the first crop with which they experimented, followed by apples, pears, plums and cherries. After Independence the district became a part of the state of Punjab, and it was only in 1966 that it was separated from Punjab first as a Union Territory and then made a full state in 1971.

We drive alongside the gushing Beas, which is the lifeline of the valley. Torrents tumble into the jade river in a series of waterfalls, running over huge boulders, the volume of water increasing day by day with the melting snow from the surrounding peaks as temperatures rise. The Beas originates from the mighty Rohtang Pass as a ground spring. I had visited this area, called Beas Kund, on one of my earlier shoots. There is a shrine dedicated to the great rishi Veda Vyasa, who is said to have classified the Vedas and written the Mahabharata. "Legend has it that he meditated at that spot for twelve years, which then led to the creation of the Beas, so the river is named after him," says Meru, recounting the popular lore.

The glorious river roars beneath us as we cross the truss bridge and drive on the right bank towards the village of Naggar for breakfast. I am enchanted as one always is by the untouched

4 The mythical kingdom of Prester John: Over the course of the Middle Ages, Europeans believed that Prester John was an extremely wealthy African Christian king whose kingdom existed somewhere in Asia.

wilderness: the mountain streams that tumble down among boulders through pristine forests; the *rosa moschata*, the most splendid wild white rose of the western Himalaya that cascades from trees in all its resplendence; and the apple trees, which were laden with cream blossoms on my previous trip, now sprouting tiny apples. In the distance, towards the north, I can see the snow-tipped peaks under which lies Manali.

We round a corner and come across a sight to behold: we are suddenly surrounded by thousands of sheep tended by a couple of gaddis, or nomadic shepherds. "These gaddis have been living like this for centuries," Meru informs me. "They move with their flock to higher pastures in summer, living in temporary dwellings, and return to their villages lower down in winter, trading in wool, milk, and sometimes meat."

"Yes, I know," I respond, recalling the gaddi Nitin, Sonia, and I encountered during our trek to the Del Tibba Pass in 2003. We had set up camp on the Zamir Plateau, where the gaddi also chose to halt with his huge flock of sheep, two guard dogs, and a few horses. It was bitterly cold, and while we huddled around the bonfire, he joined us with an offering of goat's milk. I remember trying to comprehend his nomadic lifestyle, wandering these desolate ranges alone with only animals for company. I attempted to chat with him about it, but our language barrier proved too great—much to Nitin and Sonia's amusement. Nitin told me later, "Anu, you will never truly understand his way of life, intellectually, emotionally, or psychologically. It's an experiential way of living."

I recount this to Meru, who nods in agreement. "I agree, and this holds true for your present project as well. We still consider our lives part of an ancient culture, as these mountains have long protected our people from outside influences. This inaccessibility has allowed us to retain much of our traditional way of life, which is far removed from your cosmopolitan existence. You would need to experience much of our way of life to truly understand it."

I reassure him, "Meru, I have delved into other unique cultures in my previous work, and I understand how different things can be. I always keep an open mind and remain ready for unusual experiences."

The road begins to climb steeply, twisting and swerving upwards to the large village of Naggar. Once the capital of Kullu, Naggar is a small hamlet with a castle as the sole remnant of its blue-blooded history. The splendid views from this quaint village have attracted many artists over the years, the most famous being the Russian artist Nicholas Roerich. Roerich settled here with his wife Helena in the 1950s, leaving Naggar a legacy of a museum and art gallery dedicated to his work.

We alight at the fifteenth-century Naggar Castle, a magnificent structure built in the indigenous timber-bonded style of the western Himalayas, made of alternating courses of dry stone and deodar beams. This architectural style is prevalent throughout the region in both sacred and secular buildings. Constructed in AD 1460 by Raja Sidh Singh, Naggar Castle is said to be earthquake-proof, having withstood the 1905 earthquake. Wooden balconies run along the breadth of the building on two floors, and the entire facade is intricately carved with motifs inspired by local fauna.

We walk through the huge stone courtyard, head to the restaurant on the first floor and settle into a seat by one of the windows. The panoramic overview of the wide valley edged by massive mountains always takes my breath away. Out comes my camera, and I click the spectacular view for the umpteenth time. It always amazes me how the same vista is transformed by the ever-changing light conditions, skies and seasons. Reluctantly I look away and order the aloo puri, which I always have when I visit Naggar Castle.

Meru toasts me with a cup of chai: "Welcome to Dev Bhoomi, Anu!"

"Ah, the land of the gods!" I translate with a smile and proceed to give him a synopsis of my research so far. I begin with the valley's myth of creation.

Folklore suggests that in the mythic past, the great Vedic sage Jamadagini Rishi, known locally as Jamlu Devta, was returning from a pilgrimage to Mount Kailash, carrying eighteen idols of different gods in a kardu, or basket, on his head. As he approached Chandrakhani Peak near Manali, the great demon of Malana, Banasura, sensed the sage's presence in his territory. Jamadagni Rishi was Banasura's sworn enemy. In a bid to thwart him, Banasura unleashed a fierce wind that blew the idols from the kardu, scattering them across the valley. It is believed that wherever these idols fell, they manifested as Devtas. They came to be known as Thara Kardu, or "the eighteen great gods who came out of a basket". Over time, these eighteen gods multiplied, and the Thara Kardu deities became Thara Kror, "the eighteen crore gods" of Himachal Pradesh. It was through this abundance of sacred presence that the land came to be known as Dev Bhoomi.

Meru smiles and says, "Yes, that is indeed our local belief, and it has been passed down by oral tradition for centuries. You see, those initial eighteen gods have grown into so many Devis and Devtas. That is why we have so many temples and shrines in every village."

I had read that the Vedic and Puranic Hindu triumvirate, namely Brahma, Vishnu and Shiva, are worshipped in numerous forms and names all across the valley. The cult of the Devi is also prominent and she is venerated as Shakti in various forms, both violent and benevolent. The great Vedic rishis, Vedic saints and even heroes of the Mahabharata have been deified in the valley. And, Naag Devtas, snake gods, and other nature spirits are also worshipped in Dev Bhoomi.

Meru continues, "But most important for us are our village gods and goddesses. They are numerous and their lore goes back into the hoary past."

"But, what about the shamans, the Goors? How are they part of Dev Bhoomi?" This has been the most mysterious part of this mythical landscape.

"Anu, we have more than a hundred villages in Kullu Valley and each village has one or more Devi or Devta. Most have their own Goor."

I cut in to ask, "But what do these Goors do?"

Meru smiles at my impatience and gesticulates with his hand, motioning me to calm down. He says, "A Goor's primary task is to become a medium for their Devi or Devta in order for them to communicate with our people." Noticing my bewildered expression he explains, "The Goor goes into a trance, which allows the spirit of the Devi or Devta to enter the Goor's body and speak through him."

I can hardly disguise my incredulity. "Really, do you believe that?"

Meru is not surprised by my disbelief, and responds patiently: "Anu, we consider our Devtas to be living gods. They are very important to us and participate in all aspects of our lives, big or small. We don't do anything without asking them, and our Devtas communicate with us through their Goor."

I have lots of questions to ask, but Meru says firmly: "See, you can obviously begin your research about our Goors, but first you have to understand our lifestyle, our culture and our belief systems. Only then will you be able to comprehend what a Goor is. Anyway, you are filming Hadimba Devi's birthday festival the day after. You will begin to have a better understanding once you have personal experiences." I agree and hold all my queries for later.

The drive from Naggar to Manali is such a pretty one, edged with fields and forests and intersected by streams, with slate-tiled roofs of hamlets visible in the distance. We drive past scenes of typical rural mountain life: women working in fields, some carrying large conical wicker baskets, called kiltas, filled with grass or wood; children playing with sticks and stones; and older people sitting in their balconies watching the world go by.

All along the drive Meru keeps calling out the names of the villages and their principal Devta. I listen to Meru absently, more captivated by the scenery, not realizing that in the coming months I would be visiting scores of villages and temples in search of more information on precisely what Meru was telling me about.

The valley gradually narrows as we drive towards Manali. Concrete shops, guest houses and homes hide most of the view, though the pretty homes with blossoming rose bushes and creepers compensate for the absence of the mountain panoramas.

Tourism took off here in the 1990s, and nowadays the Kullu Valley, Manali in particular, is a popular destination for tourists in the summer. It is even frequented during its harsh and unpredictable winters when the snowfall attracts honeymooners by the hordes. This becomes more and more evident as we get closer to Manali and the number of hotels multiply every kilometre, as do the billboards advertising homestays.

We round one particular bend where we see my favourite view of the entire northern ranges spread out in a wide curve. These are massive snow-clad ranges overlooking Manali and other villages like giant sentinels. After spending some time photographing, we drive past Prini village where I had begun my trek five years ago. Back then this village had no modern construction, yet today the place is crowded with brick buildings, housing, shops and guest homes on either side of the road.

We cross another truss bridge over the Beas and reach the central part of the town of Manali. Cars and people multiply, causing the usual traffic jam on the mall road. The mall is lined with shops selling a wide assortment of goods, such as spices, fruits, accessories, clothes and little trinkets, mostly to tourists. The people here are a cosmopolitan mix of locals and other settlers like Punjabi and Kashmiri businessmen along with Tibetan refugees. The rest of Manali is spread over three adjacent hills dominated by the three main villages of Old Manali, Vashisht and Dhungri.

We drive a few kilometres uphill to the Hadimba Devi Temple. Patron goddess of Kullu's royal family, Hadimba Devi is considered to be one of the most powerful goddesses of the valley. Because her temple lies in the protected Dhungri Forest, the heavily wooded magnificent ancient deodars are considered to be the Devi's property, so are assuredly preserved.

A beautiful walk leads us to the temple complex. It stands on a little hill surrounded by a deodar grove in which some of the trees are reputedly over a thousand years old. The temple is built primarily of stone over a cave. It is in the pagoda style with four superimposed wooden pent roofs. The top, at a height of eighty feet, is circular and crowned by a brass ball representing an attribute of the Mother Goddess, and a trident which represents the trishul of Shiva.[5]

This present temple in Dhungri was built in the mid-sixteenth century by Raja Bahadur Singh, the son of Raja Sidh Singh of Kullu, who had built the Naggar Castle. It is locally believed that long before there was already a sacred shrine on the site. We walk up a flight of stairs and step into the stone courtyard in front of the temple.

A covered veranda encircles the building on three sides where various oddities like horns, scrolls and foliage are strung up in corners. The main wooden doorway is decorated with elaborate carvings of gods, goddesses, elephants, makaras[6] and the pot and foliage motifs of the area, all designed in the folk tradition.

I approach the entrance, ring the temple bell and enter through the low wooden doorframe into a large cave illuminated by a dim naked bulb. The main altar of the Devi is tucked beneath a stone slab under which I squeeze and kneel to pay my respects.

I gaze at the mask made in the Devi's likeness placed next to a giant pair of footprints set in stone. These are considered to have been made by the demon goddess herself. I pray to the Devi and ask her to bless my new journey, recalling how this one had begun

---

5 Shiva's trishul: Lord Shiva's trident represents his ability to destroy everything, and thereby pave the way to create anew.

6 Makara: In astrology, the equivalent of the zodiac sign Capricorn

with her. Little do I know how this adventure is about to take me into a completely different dimension of perception.

Our salutations complete, we head to Goshal, Meru's village where his family has invited me for lunch. We drive on a kuccha road past wheat fields dotted with apple trees on one side and a roaring stream on the other. Like most villages in the valley, the village of Goshal is not located on a motorable road, so has to be accessed by foot. We enter from the upper end of the village. Around us is a sea of luscious green wheat fields and trees of apple and other fruits. Further in the distance are cedar forests beyond which lie gigantic snowy mountains. Unsurprisingly I cannot help but pull out my camera to photograph the lovely vista.

Meru scrambles down the steep slope with the agility typical of people here while I step down cautiously, weighing each step for loose rocks. Meru laughs. "You have to find your mountain legs soon," adding ominously, "we have a lot of running to do yet."

We walk down a dirt path past traditional wooden houses with sloping slate roofs standing cheek-by-jowl. Some of these dwellings are over a hundred years old. The ground floor of these buildings usually houses livestock and feed, while the first floor is the living area with balconies extending the frontage. I wave to some elderly women who are looking at us curiously, and I am graced with some toothy smiles.

In front of every house is a courtyard where livestock is reared. "Everyone here has their own source of milk, curd and butter," Meru says. "We use the cow dung to plaster our homes or we use it as fuel." He points to a heap of wood piled up in one corner. "We don't use wood for cooking as gas cylinders are now available. However, we do need to burn wood to warm up our homes during the difficult winters." I notice that the village has access to electricity, many homes have digital TV connections and most residents seem to have mobile phones. These seem to be the few specks of modernity in this otherwise ancient village.

The village wears a deserted look as most of the men are out to work and the women are in the fields or busy with household chores. Meru points out to the wooden looms outside most homes where some women are weaving pattus, or woollen shawls. We pass a courtyard where a couple of women are threshing wheat sheaves whilst an old man sits on the doorstep smoking a beedi. Meru points at another courtyard where two radiant young girls are making a couple of cows walk in circles over sheaves of wheat. "They are getting the kernels out from the sheaf," says Meru. I wave at them, take out my camera and begin photographing at which they giggle and rush to hide behind a wall. It takes much coaxing by Meru for them to return to the courtyard. Meru laughs. "People here are still quite shy, Anu." I am aware of the reservations that villagers usually have with outsiders; that is one of the many challenges I will have to overcome in order to truly understand and appreciate this culture.

Goshal has a deeply peaceful silence, broken by the occasional mooing of cows, birds chirping or wind rustling through trees. Time seems to slow down here. I keep stopping to take pictures of this scenic village until finally I request Meru to take me to the main village temple.

"We have two main Devtas in Goshal," Meru informs me. "Gautam Rishi and Naag Devta. They share a temple, which is unfortunately being reconstructed so is out of bounds." Much later I would learn more about the fascinating Naag Devtas of the valley, but for now I must withhold my curiosity.

We finally reach Meru's home, which is a large three-storeyed wooden building. There is a typical courtyard in front of the house with bundles of logs and sticks lying in places. In one corner are the toilets, which are usually built outside the home.

"Papa, Papa!" I hear high-pitched voices screeching overhead. It's Siya and Shivam, Meru's red-cheeked twin children, leaning half over the balcony. Meru rolls his eyes and laughs, "I am warning you … they are very naughty!"

We enter the ground-floor cowshed through a low wooden door with a carving of Lord Ganesha on the door frame. "The idea of a low entrance door," says Meru, "is to remind us to bow down and surrender our ego before entering our abode."

Inside, we climb a steep, narrow wooden ladder past two low-ceilinged bedrooms on the second floor to the third floor.

Siya and Shivam run up to Meru, shouting out a volley of questions. I greet them and, even though they are curious, they are still too shy. But I have come prepared, and pull out the two gifts I am carrying for them. Soon they are happy to clamber on to my lap and bombard me with questions about Delhi. Meru's wife, Nisha, a pretty young woman with a rosy and glowing complexion, is dressed in a salwar-kameez. She greets me shyly, leading me inside to their cosy living room, which has a stove and chimney at its centre with mattresses spread around it. She introduces me to Meru's mother, who is dressed in the traditional Himachali style with a pattu shawl wrapped over her salwar-kameez, with a woollen scarf covering her hair. I can see that Meru has inherited her kind eyes. She immediately gives me a welcoming hug. I sit cross-legged with Meru and his mother while Nisha serves us piping hot rajma, rice and some local green beans called lingdi, all of which are my favourites.

Meru's mother asks me, "So why are you making a film about our culture, beta?"

"I want to document the Goors and your unique religious belief system."

She responds quite matter-of-factly, "But, for that you will have to get the permission of the Devtas, beta. Otherwise how will you do it?"

I look towards Meru, puzzled.

He responds, "Don't worry, Anu. I will get all the relevant permissions for you from the Devtas."

Later I learnt that every time we would want to film any of the valley's religious activities, we could not do so unless the Devta of the area had given us formal permission. And, exactly how this permission was obtained I would learn before long.

What I also didn't realise at this point was just how deeply the mythical realm of Dev Bhoomi influenced the minds and lives of the local people. I was yet to discover that the village Devtas were not merely objects of worship but an institution governing every aspect of life—social, cultural, moral, economic, religious, and even political. The village Devta or Devi guides all activities, including festivals, marriages, and customs. Under this all-encompassing Devta system, the village functions like a close-knit family, fostering near-perfect unity and harmony.

Meru and I settle down to discuss our schedule for the next day. Meru explains that Hadimba Devi's birthday celebrations, also known as the Dhungri Mela, have been celebrated since the sixteenth century when the temple was first built. The three-day annual fair involves many cultural activities and events. Meru mentions, "So, nine Devtas will be coming for Hadimba Devi's birthday festival…"

I cut in, "There are nine Devtas coming? What does that mean?"

Meru explains, "Between the Devtas of our villages there exist several kinds of bonds and relationships. Some are familial while others are friendships. Thus, the Devtas of the valley are bound by ties of kinship, friendship and social obligation; pretty much like us locals are. They often visit each other at festivals, birthdays and sometimes even on whim."

Having Meru's insights is proving invaluable because he brings to my understanding of the Devta system the fine balance between the subjectivity of experience and the objectivity of the intellect. Meru is at once an insider as well as outsider. His faith is tempered by his contact with people like me and the research students he guides who tend to look at the culture of Kullu through an academic eye. Because he straddles two worlds, he can gently guide me into a deeper, immersive approach that expands my own perceptions.

Meru asks, “Anu, would you like to see how each village gives a send-off to their Devi or Devta?”

“Yes, absolutely!” I reply eagerly.

“But I will take you to only one village so you can observe it for yourself.”

On seeing my disappointed expression, he laughs. “It is okay, Anu. It’s the same in every village. Besides, we only have time to visit one village, then we have to go to the main festival.”

By the time I leave Goshal the shadows have lengthened on the slopes and the skies are streaked with pink and mauve, signalling the advent of twilight. Meru drops me off at my rented cottage in the village of Shanag quite close to Goshal.

I am delighted to see that my stone-and-wood cottage lies in a secluded area and is surrounded by a lovely flower and fruit garden. My first-floor balcony has wonderful views of the valley and the magnificent mountains in the north.

My crew of five—assistant director, cameraperson, camera attendant, sound man, production manager—await me, so we go on to discuss our filming schedule and other production matters. I decided that, while I would personally shoot the celebrations of the village I would be visiting with Meru, the crew would film another village. Later we would meet up and film the main festival together.

Much later, I sit on the first-floor balcony of my cottage and look out at the indigo skies and bright stars, contemplating my eventful day. I realise that I already feel quite distanced from my life in Delhi. My time in Goshal village along with the conversations with Meru and his family bring home to me that we are quite literally living in different worlds. I am now, more than ever, looking forward to unveiling the mysteries that surround their mystical world. I sense that this time it is going to be a long journey wherein I will have to bridge gaps of language, environment, culture and worldview. What I did not anticipate was how this process of enquiry would lead me to discover a new self; one that could traverse the distance between two diverse realities.

3
Hadimba Devi's Birthday Celebrations

A bright light pours over me, warm, overpowering. I must give in to it. I must do what it asks me to do. I open my eyes and see a wooden ceiling, the face of my sunny alarm clock and the glass window lit up with golden light. I stretch languorously in my cosy bed, and gaze appreciatively at my window view of the lush valley surrounded by tall mountains. The leaves of the apricot tree brushing against the window are lit with a luminescent glow, waving in the early morning breeze. I hear the distinct chirp of mynahs amidst a chorus of birdsong and a cow mooing somewhere in the distance. Absolute bliss!

I gaze appreciatively around my guesthouse, and head out to have my morning tea on the wooden balcony overlooking a charming garden dotted with pink hollyhocks, yellow poppies and red geraniums amidst trees laden with tiny apples. A few poplars sway in the fresh breeze and a small brook flows alongside, adding to the sheer melody of the ambience. In the backdrop the Pir Panjal Range soars majestically, sporting snowy crowns that gild to silver when the light plays on them.

"Good morning," a gentle voice breaks my reverie. It's Meru, wearing a traditional Kullu cap and looking quintessentially Himachali. Over a breakfast of fruit, Meru informs me that during spring, around mid-March to mid-May, most of the villages in the valley celebrate their annual village festivals, which are held over a few days. Every village invites a few Devtas from other villages to their celebrations, and each Devta comes with an entourage of scores of village folk. "This is part of an ancient custom. Chalo, we are going to Siyali village. You will understand better when you see things come alive for yourself," says Meru, rushing me out of the cottage.

While we are on our way, Meru informs me that the reigning Devta of the village of Siyali is Lord Shiva who is invited to Hadimba Devi's birthday celebration every year. I am brimming over with questions, but Meru smiles indulgently, saying, "Anu, please observe everything, and then I will answer your queries … to the best of my ability, of course."

Siyali lies close to Manali and is a steep walk uphill. We weave in and out through the village and reach the Shiva temple, but I am surprised to find the place deserted. Meru says, "They must have already gone to the festival grounds. Let's go there!" As we move closer, we hear faint sounds of music and voices, so we abandon our maps and follow the sound through narrow lanes until we come to a large field where it seems the entire village has congregated. At first sight it is picturesque, a riot of colour and sound overwhelming our senses.

A few old kath-kuni[1] homes face the festival grounds at one end, their balconies lined with the shining faces of local women and toddlers dressed in festive attire. They are watching a group of youngsters dancing the Kullu natti in a semicircle. The men are wearing cream-coloured, frock-like, knee-length tunics with a silk sash tied around their torsos; these are matched with cream-

1 Kath-kuni: An indigenous form of architecture native to the Himalayas that considers local climate, availability of resources, seismic conditions, terrains and lifestyles. It uses alternative layers of stonemasonry and thick wooden logs kept in place usually without mortar.

coloured leggings. On their heads are Kullu caps adorned with woollen, flower-like, dangling wreaths in vivid colours. The older women are wearing their traditional pattus with gold jewellery and fresh flowers tucked into their caps while the younger women are dressed in their finest salwar-kameez sets. The folk dancers are swirling large handkerchiefs as they merrily dance in a circle singing a folk song. Inside this circle sits a group of seven musicians, called bajantris, who are playing popular, festive Himachali melodies with their drums and horns. Villagers mill around enjoying the celebration while children of all ages run amok gleefully.

I notice that the Devta's rath has been placed at one end of the grounds. Some locals are paying obeisance to it, making offerings and receiving something from the pujari, or priest, as they leave. I make my way to the rath for a closer look. It is an absolute beauty. Rectangular in shape at the bottom and made of wood, the body is roughly eight feet long and three feet wide. Its sides are covered with multi-coloured silk cloths and shiny dupattas that catch the sunlight and shimmer iridescently. The centre of the rath rises in a slant with each successive layer shorter than the last. On the top is a curved silver lining made of metal with feathers stuck onto it. On one side of the rath the slanted portion holds several silver masks, mukhotas, stacked one atop the other. These are flanked by silver ornaments and staffs on each side creating a rectangular grid. It looks like a tinier version of an opulent royal ride, straight out of the Puranas, a carriage of an all-powerful deity. It is truly a sight to behold!

I head back to Meru, and ask him, "Why is everyone praying to the rath?" Meru explains, "See, once we place the holy cloths and mukhotas on the rath we perform a special puja, or 'ritualistic prayer'. Then the powers of the Devi or Devta are considered to be transferred to the rath. So, technically, after the puja the rath becomes not only the chariot of the Devi or Devta but an embodiment of them. The rath also ensures that Devtas are not just confined to their temples; they move around." I am intrigued by the idea of peripatetic deities.

I ask Meru if all raths are created and designed according to a standard structure that must be followed. Meru answers, "Each Devta instructs the people how they want their rath to be: the shape, style, type of wood to be used, kind of masks to be made … everything is done according to the wishes of the Devta."

Totally confused, I ask Meru, "And how do you discern the wishes of the Devta? How do they communicate these to you?"

Meru responds matter-of-factly, "Through the Goor of course!" Seeing my incredulous expression Meru smiles. "I told you! It would be better to first observe what happens, and then we can get to your questions."

The music changes to an upbeat tempo, and the sound of horns resonates through the festival grounds. A few men come forward and hoist the rath on to the shoulders of four waiting men. The kahars[2] pick up the rath, make their way into the circle where the bajantris are and begin swaying to the beat. There is a loud cheer from the crowd as their Devta joins them in the dance. The rath sways slightly, bobs up and down and moves in various directions.

For a while the men continue to carry the rath so that it appears to be dancing. Once that stops, the village folk line up towards the rath for darshan, paying obeisance with small offerings of money, flowers and sometimes silk cloths.

After the darshan it is time to bid farewell to the Devta. The drummers shift their beats and two others blow the raisinghas, an S-shaped trumpet with an authoritative sound that is often blown when a Devta arrives or departs. At this the chariot bearers begin to move towards the exit. Around thirty men join the procession along with the bajantris and priest to escort their Devta to the village of Old Manali.

2 Kahar is a community known for their role involving the physical task of carrying loads on their shoulders, notably palanquins.

The rath looks significantly heavy with several wooden tiers and layers of silver masks and adornments. I ask Meru, "Don't tell me! Are the bearers going to carry the rath all the way to Old Manali?"

"Yes," says Meru, "but other men in the procession will take turns to carry it. It is considered an honour and a great responsibility in our community to be given the task to carry the Devta's rath."

I start to feel a strong drizzle, and as Meru and I run for cover, I ask, "Will the procession continue in this weather?"

Meru laughs. "Rain or shine our festivals continue. Look!" He points to the receding procession, and I see a man place a protective sheet of plastic over the rath while others don raincoats or umbrellas.

Soon the grounds are deserted. Meru and I make our way towards our car. I have many questions, so we decide to chat over lunch. We cross a truss bridge over the bubbling Beas into a narrow lane leading into the tourist-friendly lane of Old Manali. I cannot help but notice the stark difference. The ambience here is completely different from the one we have just witnessed. Meru and I park our car and begin to walk past various shops. On both sides of the road are small, locally grown stalls selling grungy hippie clothes, bed sheets, curtains, memorabilia, pipes and small trinkets. This is Manali's very own backpacker paradise, crawling with travellers largely from foreign lands looking for a more authentic India or just a quieter, more vibrant place to spend a weekend away from their city lives, resulting in a plethora of quaint cafés, some of them with names inspired by Western music: Moon Dance, Dylan's Café, Lazy Dog and German Bakery. We pass travellers sharing stories over cups of chai or coffee, while trance music thumps in the background.

Meru and I slip into the famous Moon Dance Café. Inside, a couple of European backpackers are having a casual chat with the manager in French. Meru explains that decades of foreign travellers have made many of the locals fluent in languages like German, French and even Hebrew. Our frothy coffees arrive accompanied by freshly baked bagels and cream cheese. As we tuck into our deliciously warm food, I ask Meru about what we had just witnessed.

Meru tells me that every time a Devta leaves their village, the village folk organise a ceremonial send-off and it is mandatory for one male member of every family to accompany the Devta. Meru himself has escorted his own village Devta on such occasions. During festive visits to other villages, Devis and Devtas may stay for a couple of days in the host village along with all the people accompanying them. The villagers host all these guests in their homes and treat them as guests of the divine. The sense of community here can be truly enlightening for a city person like me.

Meru looks at his watch and tells me that we are getting late. We exit the café, and begin walking towards the Manu Rishi Temple, about half a kilometre up the road from Moon Dance, where Hadimba Devi's rath is kept. I feel a strange sense of excitement, and look forward to seeing Tuleram, the Goor of Hadimba Devi, who Meru had described as "a powerful yet colourful character". It has stopped drizzling, but the sky is still grey and I am certain that it is going to pour. I am not wearing my weatherproof jacket and admit to being slightly apprehensive. We pass shops and cafés following a throng of enthusiastic locals who are also heading towards the Manu Temple, which stands on a high platform presiding over the village of Old Manali.

The Manu Temple with its pagoda roof remains true to the local architectural style. It was refashioned with marble floors and vaulted ceilings in 1992. The shrine is dedicated to the legendary sage, Manu, who in Indian mythology was considered to be the first man and the legendary author of the *Manu-Smriti*, "laws of Manu", also called Manava-dharma-shastra.

We reach the courtyard of the Manu Temple where Hadimba Devi's rath has been placed, beautifully decorated with rustling silks and sparkling jewellery. A young man in jeans and t-shirt is fussing about, adjusting the silk cloths on the rath. Meru points him out as Chunni, one of the pujaris or priests, who serves at the Hadimba Devi Temple.

Meru tells me that Hadimba Devi shares her rath with Manu Rishi Devta. While Manu Rishi has only one mask mounted on his rath, most of the silver masks, even the one depicting a man with a moustache, represent the Devi. Mounted towards the front end of the rath is the oldest mask, which is made of ashtadhatu, an alloy of eight mixed metals, depicting the Devi in her feminine avatar as a bride wearing a huge jewelled nathni.[3] Meru informs me, "Hadimba Devi's birthday celebrations are held over three days. Traditionally Hadimba Devi leaves her temple in the Dhungri Forest, and comes in her rath to the Manu Temple on day one. On day two, the village of Old Manali gets together at the festival grounds and felicitates the Devi with song and dance. And today, the third day, after certain rituals are conducted here, Hadimba Devi's rath will travel back to her own temple in a ceremonial procession."

As I begin photographing, I notice several articles have been placed in front of the rath, including two bells and two large metal bowls with long handles used for burning incense, locally called dharj. They have something distinctively aromatic burning in them. Meru informs me that this is the ceremonial dhoop, or incense, burning on hot coals, especially prepared from the leaves of the juniper tree. Locally called bethar, its leaves are only plucked from shrubs growing at high altitudes, ensuring its potency and purity.

By now a crowd of about two hundred has gathered around the courtyard patiently waiting for the ceremony to begin. I, however, am keen to spot Hadimba Devi's Goor, Tuleram, so

---

3 A decorative nose hoop or ring that features a chain connecting it to the ear or hair

we decide to walk around until we finally find him in one corner, dressing himself in a knee-length, cream-coloured robe. It is a frock-like robe, flared below the waist and tied together with a similarly cream-coloured, wide sash. Meru tells me that this is the traditional robe that all shamans wear during most official ceremonies.

I take multiple photographs of Tuleram, who is tall, large-boned and middle-aged. His lined face, wispy grey hair, a few missing teeth and dusty clothes belie the fact that he is a powerful Goor. In a while a few bajantris come and stand around the rath and begin drumming a rhythm. Meru drags me to find a good viewing spot next to the site of action. Soon Tuleram comes and stands facing Hadimba Devi's rath. He is joined by another man, seemingly younger with brilliant blue eyes and wearing a similar robe. "That's Beliram, the Goor of Manu Rishi," Meru informs me. "As I told you, every Devi and Devta has their own Goor."

The Goors stand together, hands joined, eyes lowered in reverence, facing the rath. Right beside them is Chunni, the officiating priest; nine bajantris stand just behind the Goors forming a semicircle, while the village folk stand encircling the ceremonial site. A respectful silence suddenly overtakes the ground as all conversations are cut short in expectation of what is to come. The bajantris begin drumming a slow beat and Chunni begins ringing the sacred bell. Meru tells me that the Goors are now preparing to go into trance and would ritually invoke Hadimba Devi and Manu Rishi Devta to enter their bodies. I can feel a shift in the atmosphere. The rhythmic repetitions have cut down all distractions, even all possibilities of distraction, and have induced a sense of waiting. One can almost sense a trance-like state in the music and the scents.

The Goors begin the invocation by throwing flowers and uncooked rice in all four directions in order to propitiate the cardinal points of the earth. Then they sit down and begin chanting mantras. They wave their right hand over the dharj, directing the smoke emanating from it towards themselves, inhaling deeply. Meru whispers and tells me that this is done to cleanse oneself internally in preparation for the divine visitation. Two bajantris begin blowing a couple of raisinghas, in an ascending tone while the drumming has picked up tempo. Again in a whisper Meru tells me that this rhythmic music is quite critical for inducing a trance. Tuleram picks up a piece of juniper from the incense burner and puts it in his mouth. He then pulls out a strand of hair from his head as an oath to the Devi to pronounce her will correctly. Beliram does the same. I find that I am holding my breath, excited but also a little overwhelmed by the rhythmic music and incantations.

"Is Tuleram really about to go into a trance?" I ask Meru who answers me by putting a finger on his lips and gesturing towards the action.

As I watch intently, shivers begin to pass through Tuleram. In a flash his eyes roll to the back of his head, his head falls back and his cap falls into the hands of a man sitting behind him waiting to catch it. Meru whispers, "The falling of the topi is a sign that Tuleram is now in a trance, or altered state of consciousness, which will allow the spirit of the goddess to enter his body." It is called khel in local parlance. Beliram goes through the same process: his eyes roll back and his cap falls off as his head bends backwards. Both Goors then let their shoulder-length hair loose. Meru explains, "The mark of a Goor is his long hair, which is believed to be an aspect of his power." Tuleram holds the ends of his hair in his hands with eyes closed and begins moving his head from side to side.

The drumming pulsates with a persistent beat and the rath is whooshed off the ground by the palanquin bearers. Both Goors stand up, still facing the rath, and I feel myself holding my breath in anticipation. Tuleram is holding the incense burner in his left hand and ringing the bell emphatically with his right. He is swaying, eyes staring blindly into the distance. He is making strange gulping motions with his mouth and his shoulders shudder with each gulp. The ceremonial horns are blown again and all of a sudden Tuleram begins trembling from head to toe. Soon he is shaking in an uncontrollable frenzy. I am amazed and in awe as I see Tuleram's entire body thrown off gear and out of control. His hair flies about, his face turns red, his eyes protrude from their sockets and the dharj in his hand spews coal all over him—none of which he seems to notice.

Chunni grabs the Devi's bell from him and tries to steady the dharj in his hand. Abruptly, Tuleram stops shaking and stands up straight, imposingly, seeming to grow in stature. Tuleram now looks at everything with a steady, piercing gaze, and I am astonished to see his persona metamorphose right before my very eyes. Meru tells me, "Now the Devi has entered him and will speak through him."

Tuleram begins to speak in an aggressive, guttural tone, moving his head in bursts of energy. The entire congregation listens respectfully with folded hands. Meru tells me later that it was the Devi reciting the history of herself and her people through Tuleram, and translates the gist of Tuleram's passionate speech for me:

Hadimba Devi via Goor Tuleram: "Tusanrabhaaraaasaagey, aasarabhaara Maharaja aagey; Your problems are shared by us (the gods). And our prayers are heard by the Great Lord … I have given Raja's kingdom to him. I have appeared with a hundred different faces, including that of Kali. I have come here to help you. Listen to me, villagers! I have given a lot to all of you and will give you more."

Tuleram's violent shaking subsides although his whole body is still trembling. The gathered devotees address the Devi. Among other matters they raise the chief concern of the day: "Will the rain ruin the festival?" Tuleram holds his hand up in the air, palm facing the sky and begins shaking violently again. He shouts, gazing up into different areas of the sky at intervals.

Hadimba Devi via Goor Tuleram: "I am very powerful! I can turn day into night and night into day! Do you doubt my power?"

A devotee: "Oh, Devi, please ensure that there will be no rain today!"

Devi via Goor: "I can see rainfall in the distance, but I will withhold it. Don't worry, I shall ensure that there is no rain during my festival!"

I look up at the cloudy skies and ask Meru sceptically, "Tuleram just said that he will stop it from raining! What do you think?"

Meru corrects me gently, "Anu, it is not Tuleram speaking. It is the Devi who has declared that it will not rain. Tuleram is just Hadimba Devi's medium, and once her spirit enters him, everything he says are her words."

It is difficult for me to take my eyes off the extraordinary spectacle. Tuleram is awe-inspiring in his transformation as the Devi's medium. A nondescript man has been transfigured into the ferocious avatar of a deity right before my eyes! I look around and observe the faith and veneration that the locals have displayed through the proceedings. They have complete faith that their Devi is speaking to them through Tuleram.

After the speech, Tuleram's shaking subsides. He slumps over, his eyes closed, and lets out a deep sigh. He is perspiring heavily and looks exhausted. A few men support and fan him. Tuleram is no longer in a state of trance though it takes time for him to open his eyes, and when he does they have a slightly lost expression. However, he regains his consciousness soon and continues to participate throughout the entire festival in a normal state. All this time Goor Beliram has been standing aside watching the event. Meru later explains that as Tuleram was Hadimba Devi's Goor, all these ceremonial rituals could only be conducted by him. I notice thereafter that Beliram follows Tuleram's lead, and it is only Tuleram who communicates with the crowd when in trance whereas Beliram only assists in receiving offerings and distributing flowers and juniper to the devotees.

Once he is back to his usual self, Tuleram takes charge of the procession. It is now time to leave as the Devi has to journey back to her own temple. Tuleram leads the procession, followed by Chunni and a few bajantris who continue to play music. The rath is followed by some more bajantris who continue the drumming and about thirty-odd men who follow the entire formal procession. I notice that neither Tuleram nor Beliram are wearing shoes, and am surprised to learn that a Goor is supposed to conduct his duties barefoot; the distance between the Manu Temple and the Hadimba Temple in Dhungri village is a little over two kilometres!

The Devi's procession turns into the narrow lanes of the Old Manali village, which is a sprawl of mostly old-fashioned wooden huts with tiny verandas and stone-flagged courtyards, with adjoining cowsheds under storage rooms that are spilling over with wooden logs and bundles of straw. In the meantime, my crew has had the misfortune of getting stuck behind the procession, so I am glad that Meru had the foresight to ensure that we are ahead of it and I can film everything on my handycam. At various points the rath enters courtyards where women are waiting with plates decorated prettily with offerings of vermillion powder, incense and flowers. They seem delighted to have the Devi's rath in their midst, and joyfully put vermillion on the rath and offer flowers.

As the rath moves through the village, people wait patiently at every turn and in every courtyard to greet their goddess. I notice that some of the older ladies hold actual conversations with the rath, addressing it as Hadimba Mata. Younger children run excitedly towards the rath as well with offerings of flowers. Chunni collects the flowers from these tiny devotees and puts them on the rath. It is an extraordinary experience to witness such loving faith. I am beginning to understand the extraordinary and intimate relationship the locals have with their Devi. She is their mother figure, and they adoringly refer to her as Hadimba Ma.

Tuleram walks on, barefoot, relentlessly ringing the bell, purifying and propitiating certain spaces by waving the dharj or throwing rice and flowers there. He waits patiently as the women and children take their time to greet the goddess. Meru points toward the sky, "Look, Anu, what did I tell you?" I look up to see that, as Tuleram had predicted, the stormy clouds have miraculously abated. The sun is out in its full glory!

Hadimba Devi's procession slowly makes its way through the Old Manali Bazaar where, as before, progress is slow due to the numerous devotees who have lined the streets for a darshan of their Devi. We stay ahead of the rath as it crosses the main bridge, climbs up a slope and arrives within the temple precincts. A huge crowd of devotees await the goddess. Now both Tuleram and Beliram begin to ritually invoke their deities again in a briefer version of the earlier invocation. Both Goors hold their hair, shake their heads and chant mantras while turning in circles. The bajantris blow the ceremonial horns and the drumming picks up tempo. Gradually the trembling begins, and soon Tuleram's body is shaking again, though not as violently as in the previous trance. He does not speak this time but gesticulates with his hands, holding them above his head and then pointing towards his eyes. Meru interprets his gestures for me, "The Devi is reassuring her people that she is present and watching over us."

Tuleram is now walking towards the temple with the rath and the procession following him. Many more devotees are waiting all around the temple, but instead of climbing the steps to the temple Tuleram turns another way, and begins to lead the procession towards a tree. Meru grabs my arm and commands, "Anu, we will have to make a run for it or we will be left behind, and you will miss out on the trance!" Hearing this, something comes over me. I feel a mysterious surge of energy and make a run for the tree, jumping over rocks, reaching there before Tuleram quite easily, to my own surprise.

Then I notice that the tree is not an ordinary one; it is studded with several iron objects like swords, cages and sculptures of birds. A little lamp enclosed in a glass case is kept on a platform in front of it and a bell has been hung next to it. "This tree is the abode of

Ghatotkacha, the son of Hadimba Devi and a great warrior in his own right," says Meru, guiding me to one side of the tree where we watch the approaching procession.

According to myth, Ghatotkacha was born from the marriage of Hadimba and Bheema, after Bheema killed the demon Hadimb, the brother of Hadimba. Ghatotkacha went on to fight the great war on the side of the Pandavas. That he was the son of a demoness endowed him with magical powers, including the ability to fly or to become so small as to become invisible. During the Kurukshetra war he caused serious damage to the Kauravas with his prowess as a half-demon warrior.

Tuleram stops right in front of the tree, and it is then that I realise that he is shivering and shaking again, therefore presumably in a trance. I find myself completely unprepared for what he does next. Tuleram's expression turns demonic; his bloodshot eyes terrify me. Inadvertently I step back startled by the palpable flow of energy that he is emanating. He begins to jump up and down violently, sticking his entire tongue out, so much so that Chunni has to hold on to his waist tightly to prevent him from falling. Meru sees how shocked I am, and reassures me, "Don't be scared. See, Hadimba was a demon before she became a Devi, so she does have an aggressive facet. And, as a manifestation of Goddess Kali, she is just striking Kali's signature pose."

Tuleram continues to address the crowd, which has swelled. His trance lasts about five minutes after which his body stops completely and his face falls to his chest. He is supported by Chunni and Goor Beliram on either side while he catches his breath. Before long he stands up straight and opens his eyes. Once again, I am struck by the extreme transformation of his countenance.

The procession turns around and heads back to Hadimba Devi's temple where a jubilant crowd awaits their Devi. By now I am not only exhausted but also overwhelmed by everything that I have witnessed. Frankly, I need a chai! Meru takes me towards a dhaba, and we walk through all the inexpensive pop-up shops and food stalls that have been set up especially for the festival. We pass hordes of locals buying clothes, costume jewellery, kids' toys and others gorging on jalebis, pakoras and mithai.

I am still thinking obsessively about all that I had seen today. Meru, amused by my silence, teases me, "What happened, Anu? No more questions to ask?"

I let out a chuckle. "Actually, Meru, I have so many questions that I am going to have to note them down and ask them tomorrow; one step after another." I smile at him for steering me so effortlessly through such an eventful day.

"But the grand festival is not over yet," Meru exclaims. "Nine Devtas are coming to the temple. Come on, let's go to the festival grounds and catch the action there."

I forget my exhaustion in an instant and jump up to follow Meru. The festival grounds are quite large, built in the manner of an amphitheatre. Huge cement steps backed by tall deodars line the lengths of the two opposite sides, providing seating for the hundreds who have gathered there.

The locals are dressed in their festive best. The women wear colourful pattus, mostly of checked tweed, edged with bright, colourful, patterned borders. Most of the women's ears are adorned with innumerable gold rings worn on the lobes and around the rims as well. Many wear nose-rings, jewelled neck pieces and their typical colourful headscarves. Everyone is enjoying the dancers who are performing the natti at the centre of the field, accompanied by a large live band of bajantris consisting of a number of dhols, nagaras, dholaks, karnals, raisinghas, shehnais, dhouns (kettledrums), bhanas and thali (percussion). The arena is colourful and the ambience festive, almost euphoric.

Meru points to the raths of a few Devtas placed on a cement platform. "Look, some Devtas have already arrived."

We start making our way towards the raths when there is a huge commotion, and several horns begin to blow. The drums grow excruciatingly loud, and the crowd lets out a huge cheer. Meru, the crew and I scramble up the steps to get a better view of all the action.

As Hadimba Devi's procession enters the grounds after her temple visit, the four raths are picked up by their kahars who rush with their respective raths towards her procession at top speed. One rath is moving really fast with so much force that I am afraid it is going to crash into Hadimba Devi's rath. But, to my surprise and relief, it doesn't. At the very last moment it turns around and the kahars begin to run all over the ground. The other raths seem to be engaged in a complicated dance where they rush towards each other, then tilt and rush their tops against those of the others. Some raths do a wild jig or shake from side to side. I am engrossed yet also bewildered and look pleadingly at Meru for an explanation. Meru gestures for me to look at the other side where processions belonging to another two Devtas are arriving. I am delighted when I recognise one of the raths as that of Lord Shiva's from Siyali.

As soon as these raths enter, a couple of raths from the other end come rushing towards the new arrivals as their kahars run in the same direction. Finally, Meru explains, "See that rath that is running towards Shiv-ji's rath? That is the rath belonging to Kartik Swami, Shiv-ji's son. He is bound to be happy to see his father, is he not? So all the Devis and Devtas are expressing their excitement and joy at meeting others, especially where there is a family connection. These raths are the personifications of the Devis and Devtas themselves, so they are displaying their emotions while moving in this way."

My crew has now entered the arena to film close-ups while Meru and I have taken a seat amidst the onlookers on the steps. I am caught by the enthusiasm of the crowd. Some are pointing out the antics of the raths to each other while others are looking on with shining faces and bright eyes. But, their delight seems to pale in comparison to that of the raths, which are rushing about in wild abandon to greet the last of the guest Devtas. I ask Meru a question that has been troubling me for quite some time: "How do the kahars know which way to go, or rather, which way the Devta would want them to go? How are all of them running in the same direction at the same time?" After all, the kahars holding the front end cannot see or hear the kahars holding the rear end of the rath.

Meru looks at me surprised, and says, "The kahars do not move the raths. Each rath is energised by the power of its Devta, which pulls the kahars in the direction that the Devta wants to go." I stare at him in disbelief. "Okay, don't listen to me. Watch carefully and you will see that there is no way the kahars could be directing any of the action."

The man sitting next to me who happened to hear our conversation pipes in, "Haanji, indeed yes, the raths move as per the Devta's desires. I have held my Devta's rath on many occasions. You can feel the power pulling you in different directions." He pauses to reflect, and then adds insightfully, "In fact, sometimes it becomes difficult to carry and control the rath when it wants to move."

I'm flummoxed by these responses, but decide to keep an open mind and to investigate this aspect later. As I give in to observing the exhilarating action, I realise there is a pattern to the way these raths are moving—some of them very fast, others slower and some at what one could consider a normal speed. When I ask him about it, Meru explains, "This has a lot to do with the personality of the Devta; whether it is aggressive or gentle." He points in the direction of a rath that is moving with an undulating gait and tells me it is the rath of a Naag Devta.

I watch the kahars of different raths carefully and the men who support them from the sides when they rush in one direction or make a turn. I notice the awkward postures the kahars have to make when a rath tilts, turns around or goes backwards. Much later, when I edit this footage and view the close-up footage of the raths in slow motion, I am forced to admit that it does seem as if the raths have a mind of their own! It is as if the driving force of movement emerges from the rath itself, and not the kahars; they are merely dragged along in the direction that the raths take them. Not to forget, the raths are quite heavy, but the kahars seem to carry them with elated reverence nonetheless.

Once the Devtas are done meeting and greeting, the kahars place the raths in a line on a concrete platform at one end of the ground. Lined up in a single row, the raths look breathtaking. The devotees soon mill around to pray, seek blessings and make offerings of flowers, silk cloths or small amounts of money. Meru and I proceed to do likewise, and I am given the chance to closely observe all the different raths and their finery. Up close the raths that looked very similar from afar are actually quite different. Even though most of them are similar in shape with masks mounted on top, they vary in size, cloth, and ornaments. The masks are different too. The one that stands out for me is a circular rath of a visiting Devi that is so tiny that just a single bearer is required to carry it on his head.

I notice that the Goors who have accompanied the nine raths are all wearing their distinctive cream-coloured, knee-length robes, are barefoot and mostly have long hair. They are busy attending to the devotees: accepting their offerings and giving flowers and rice as tokens of their Devta's blessings. I wander through the crowds, taking photographs of the vibrant scenes. Shafts of golden sunlight filter through the tall deodars, making the raths gleam and their glittery cloths sparkle. A mesmeric ambience seems to have enveloped the entire festival ground, touching the crowds with a sacred fervour.

Meru comes and hustles me through the crowd to a vantage point. "So you can film the Devkhel properly," he says. Noting my quizzical expression, he explains that Devkhel means "the dance of the Devtas". "You will see," he adds. I notice a space has been created in front of the raths, and the crowd steps back to accommodate the Goors who stand in front of their respective Devta's rath, dharj in hand. The crowds fall silent. All at once the bajantris begin drumming, forming a semicircle around the Goors. The camera has a nice top-angle view, but I am determined to get a closer look.

I push my way through the people standing who are thankfully in good spirits and allow me to pass and stand right in front. Tuleram begins the Devkhel by performing a peculiar kind of dance with another Goor. The two Goors hold hands and step forward, covering the length of space between them, and backward to the beats of the percussion. At each end they twirl together slowly without releasing their hands. When the dance ends, both hold each other's shoulders at arm's length, shaking their heads towards each other. It is an extraordinary sight in terms of the patience and discipline the dance requires. Tuleram similarly dances with every Goor. Meru tells me that Devkhels are performed strictly by Goors.

While the bajantris play, a huge throng of locals watches quietly and respectfully. The nine Goors take off their upper robes and tie their long sleeves around their waists, becoming naked from the waist up. Each Goor picks up iron objects such as cudgels, kataras, small swords, shangals,[4] chains, and proceeds to dance on his own in a stepping motion. Meru explains, "These are the weapons that the Devta used in the past to subdue demons and evil spirits. We honour them as well as acknowledge the omnipotent power of the Devta."

I watch in awe as an older, frail-looking Goor dances around some weapons with bell and incense burner in each hand. He faces the east, moves three steps and repeats this action for every direction, paying obeisance to the nature spirits for blessing his

4 Shangal: A set of ceremonial iron chains with sharp spear-like ends, attached to an iron ring; it is a traditional weapon used by the Devtas to fight evil

Devta with power and strength. He then puts down the bell and dharj, picks up the shangals, and begins thrashing them onto his back while continuing to dance. I notice that the old Goor is trembling while he does this, and Meru confirms that he is in a trance. Tuleram is next and he dances, taking small steps, jerking a small sword up and down in one hand. He is still shivering, and his persona has again changed into one of sobriety. This dance of the divine continues until late in the evening as all the Goors perform this sacred ritual. No one else can join in. I notice that all through the dance, the crowds watch with reverence, interest and patience; even children of all ages watch with rapt attention and so do I, which is why I am startled when someone holds my hand and pulls me to one side.

It is Shivam, Meru's son, who has come here with Meru's family: Nisha, Siya, Kaushalya, his sister, and mother; they are all here for the festival. The ladies lead me back to the temple courtyard where a large circle of women and young girls have gathered in a circle to sing and dance. Nisha tells me that the songs being sung are in praise of the Devi and the dance is called the Laalhdi, which women perform in her honour. Nisha and Kaushalya join the dancers and try persuading me to do the same, but I am content simply taking in the magical ambience. The pagoda temple and tall cedars are lit up by festive lights, forming a wonderful backdrop to the dancers, who go about their task merrily with glowing faces and joyful smiles. I am beginning to realise that in these people their faith in the goddess and her living presence is absolute, an abiding faith imprinted on their souls.

I am wrenched out of my thoughts by the ceremonial horns blasting in my ear. The ladies part, allowing the rath of Hadimba Devi to enter their circle. There is a huge cheer from the onlookers as this time the ladies receive her with affection. There are glints of tears in their eyes as if they are welcoming back a long-lost child. They propitiate the rath, which is then taken into the cave temple for a final round of pujas.

This is the finale of the day's festivities, and some of the visiting raths leave. Meru says, "Two Devtas are going to stay for another day or so along with the thirty to forty people who came in the procession."

"Where will they stay?" I ask.

"In Old Manali village, with the village folk," he replies, then shushes me and points to a space beside the temple.

Some men including Tuleram have made a bonfire and have sat down to chat and unwind. I look intently at Tuleram, who has changed into normal clothes, and note that his shamanic personality has completely disappeared. He has seamlessly merged into the crowd as an ordinary local man.

I leave the temple reluctantly with Meru and his family, still under the spell of what I have seen and experienced today. And, of course, I have many queries, which Meru promises to address the next day.

4
Enquiries and Investigations

I wake up with a start. The reverberating sound of thunder is making my room shudder. When I look outside the wide window, stormy skies and pouring rain give me reason to snuggle back under my covers. Dreamily I gaze at the misty-blue mountains, revelling in the sound of the rain drumming on the roof of my cottage.

A kaleidoscope of images flashes through my mind as I am reminded of yesterday's experiences. Meru was right! My own experience has given me a glimpse into this culture of which the Goors are an integral part. The lifestyle, belief system and culture of the valley are so very unique and far removed from my urban existence. This is a different reality; one that is sustained by a rich mythic belief system that informs the collective consciousness of the people. My perspective of this unique world is evolving, but I need to know a whole lot more about the Goors.

Tuleram is intrinsic to my quest, I believe. Is he just an ordinary man or does he possess special powers? What was his trance exactly? Was it a divine possession or just a performance? And, what about the raths that seemed to have a life of their own?

When the skies clear, my crew sets off to film the continuing celebrations in Old Manali, which is hosting the two visiting

Devtas and their people. I ask my assistant director to film detailed interviews with as many people as possible.

I make my plans. I want to meet Tuleram first, for at this point all I know about him is that he is the medium of Hadimba Devi. Though I had a glimpse of what he does as a Goor, I have very little knowledge of his role or who he is. Meru is busy until the afternoon, so I decide to do some digging myself and look for Tuleram at the Hadimba Devi Temple.

I take a walk around the temple complex but find no sign of Tuleram. I enter the temple to pay my respects to the Devi only to find Chunni-ji conducting prayers inside. When I introduce myself Chunni-ji nods; he remembers me from the day before. I ask him if Tuleram is around, and he tells me that the Goor usually takes a day off to recoup after the festivities, so he must be resting. I ask Chunni-ji if he has some time to speak with me, and he promises to meet me on his day off.

I meet Meru for lunch at the Lazy Dog, a popular hangout for travellers that has been built on a bank overlooking a thunderous stream. I proceed to bombard him with questions. He laughs and pleads, "Hang on, hang on!" raising his palms in mock defence. "First of all, tell me how you feel about everything that you experienced yesterday?"

I begin sharing my feelings from yesterday. "Frankly, Meru, I was bowled over! I felt as if I had entered another world. You know, I have filmed in Kullu and Manali for three of my travel shows and have been here for a couple of holidays but I had no clue that beneath the tourist circuit lay such a rich and vibrant culture so thoroughly engrained in the everyday lives of its people!"

Meru smiles broadly. "That is why I wanted you to have a glimpse of our culture, our lifestyle and our belief system, but you have only seen the tip of the iceberg, so you need to spend more time to really get it."

He is right, I guess. I go on to ask, "Okay, so yesterday nine Devis and Devtas visited the town with their processions to attend a large-scale festival, right? Who organises all of this?"

"See, all our Devtas have their own managing committee, known as the Devloo, which is responsible for getting all of the Devta's work done. The Devloo includes the kardar (the Devta's manager and accountant), the Goor, the pujari, the bhandari (the manager of the Devi's store), the kathiala (the manager of the Devi's granary), the nishandar (who carries the Devi's staff) and the bajantris, who have learned over generations to play our divine melodies."

I am astounded to learn that such a well-organised system, created in the manner of an official administration, exists to take care of each local Devta's affairs. To think that there are more than three hundred villages in the Kullu Valley,[1] all with Devtas and internal holy administrations of their own!

Meru understands my astonishment and responds, "Anu, you have not seen the extent of the Devta's participation in our daily lives. Let's quickly wrap up lunch. I've made an appointment for you with Hadimba Devi's kardar, so you can ask him everything you want to know."

We dig into our scrumptious lunch of crunchy green salad and grilled trout, which our waiter tells us has been freshly bought from one of the numerous trout farms in the valley. After lunch, Meru and I walk up through the Old Manali village. We walk past the now familiar wooden homes, rustic courtyards, cows chewing on straw, women washing clothes on stone slabs and young kids playing. Soon we reach a smart-looking cottage where a familiar man is sitting on the veranda reading a newspaper. I recognise him easily as he had been at the forefront of all the festivities yesterday. The man I am just about to meet is the administrative backbone of the Devi's affairs, her kardar, Tirath Ram.

Tirath Ram is short and stout with a soft voice that, as I had heard yesterday, becomes quite loud when he wants it to. Tirath-ji has an air of confidence and is clearly competent at handling the

1 There are over twenty thousand villages in Himachal Pradesh where the Devta culture is practised

Devi's responsibilities, something his family has been doing for generations.

Tirath-ji greets us in a rather officious manner, and shouts to order tea for us from someone indoors. "So, Madam, what are you filming and why are you filming us?" he asks politely.

I look at Meru who seems to be just as taken aback as I am. After all, it was through Tirath Ram that our request to film the festival had been put forth to Hadimba Devi, and he had conveyed the Devi's affirmation to Meru just a couple of days ago. Meru begins to answer in his local pahari language, but Tirath-ji interrupts him. He wants to hear me. I outline my project while he looks at me as if trying to gauge my sincerity. Finally he relaxes, reassured that my intentions are sincere, "Okay, I heard that you wanted to ask me some questions. Go ahead."

I ask Tirath-ji what his responsibilities as kardar entail, and am surprised to hear him answer in the manner of a corporate manager: "My job is to manage everything from A to Z. You were at the festival yesterday. It was conducted under my supervision entirely. I take all decisions pertaining to finances, supplies, coordinating with devotees and other practical aspects. I oversee the Devi's sizeable staff and organise everything pertaining to her. Of course, all decisions about the Devi's schedule are first approved by her and then carried out according to her wishes."

From the corner of my eye I see Meru's exasperation when I ask: "And how do you discern her wishes?"

Both Meru and Tirath-ji look at me with the same incredulous expression, and answer in unison: "Through the Goor, of course!"

Hurriedly, I endeavour to cover up my mistake, saying that I had noticed how all the events during the festival seemed to follow one another seamlessly, that everyone seemed to know what to do and when. "Considering the sheer numbers of people, it must be a mammoth task," I add.

Tirath-ji nods in agreement. "We work out the schedule beforehand and explain each person's duties clearly. If the Devi has to leave her temple and travel, one male member from each family has to accompany her."

Out of general curiosity, I ask, "But what if they can't?"

Meru pipes in: "Then we are obligated to pay a fine! However, let me explain that to you later." He gestures towards his watch so I know that my time with Tirath-ji is running out. I jump to my next question about whether the younger generation still respects and follows these norms.

Tirath-ji assures me, "Yes, I agree that some of our young people are moving away from our beliefs, but the majority are still rooted in their Devta. My son accompanies me, assists me and will succeed me. Even the courts recognise this right."

His mention of the court piques my curiosity, but he politely takes my leave, mentioning that he needs to attend to some affairs. I tell Tirath-ji of my wish to interview Tuleram. He promises to put in a positive word for me.

As we walk back I ask Meru, "What was it that Tirath-ji said about the court?"

Meru clarifies, "Our Devtas hold the final verdict on all matters here. They make the rules, and we follow. However, what Tirath-ji is referring to is the court of the Devi and Devtas. As I have already said to you many times, our lives are conducted according to the will of the Devta. We go to them to solve all our problems and guide us."

It would only be in the coming months that I would grasp the immensity of this concept of the all-powerful, all-pervasive Himachali Devtas.

Back in my cottage I mull over the conversations I had with Meru and Tirath Ram. I am completely immersed in the concept of the Devta management system and am curious about the depth and extent of the Devtas' presence in people's lives. I look forward to meeting Chunni-ji the next day hoping I might gain another perspective.

The next morning dawns sunnily, and I am excited to go back to the Hadimba Devi Temple to meet Chunni-ji. While I wait for him, I wander around the courtyard where a long line of devotees waits patiently to enter the sanctum of the magnificent temple. Chunni-ji eventually arrives, dressed in a t-shirt and khaki cargo trousers, topped off by a traditional Kullu cap. I tell him about my quest and am happy to find that he is enthusiastic about it. We stroll in the beautiful forests of the estate while he tells me about himself.

Chunni-ji comes from a long lineage of Brahmin priests who were originally brought in from Kashmir to serve Hadimba Devi. His generation is the sixth in his family to serve the goddess. His father, uncles, some of his cousins and brothers are also serving the Devi as priests, rotating the duties among each family in a precise schedule.

I ask him about his general duties, and he tells me his routine: "When on duty at the temple, my day begins at four in the morning and continues until eight at night. I conduct prayers twice a day, supervise the devotees and give prasad. Whenever the Devi goes to a festival, or makes a visitation upon special invitation from villages or individuals, I go with her as I am responsible for overseeing all the sacred ceremonies and rituals that she is a part of."

I ask a question that has been on my mind: "Do the raths truly move about on their own?"

Chunni-ji throws back his head and laughs. "I knew you would ask me! I am asked that question by outsiders all the time." His turns serious, and says emphatically, "The spirit of the Devta is transferred to the raths through special rituals and mantras, after which the rath moves with the energy of the Devta itself."

It will take more than this to convince me. "But, have you personally lifted the rath and felt this energy that you are talking about? I would love to know your experience."

Chunni-ji says, a mite exasperatedly, "Yes, of course I have carried the rath on many occasions." Looking at me sternly, he continues, "When the energy has entered the rath, you can feel its power while carrying it. It pulls the kahars in whichever direction it wants to go. We could not stop its movement even if we tried! Actually, the weight of the same rath even varies on different occasions. Some days it feels light and some days it becomes so heavy that it's difficult to carry. You need to understand that it is the will of the Devta that moves a rath in a particular direction and that no one can forcefully take a Devta anywhere!"

I ask Chunni-ji to describe some instances where the will of the Devi has overridden the usual course of action. He mentions there are many but decides to relate one incident that left a mark on his memory.

"Many years ago, en route to a village festival, Hadimba Devi's rath went completely off course. This happened despite the kahars' efforts to keep it on track. Everyone was bewildered as we could not understand what was happening. Then the rath stopped at a particular place and, lo and behold, Tuleram went into a trance! Through Tuleram the Devi announced that someone had buried the daggers of Ghatotkacha at that very spot. She asked for those to be dug up and kept safely. Indeed, as they dug at the indicated spot, they came upon the daggers! Thereupon the daggers have been kept safely."

This seems too incredible; however, over time I will document many such incidents from people who spoke to me and my crew. I notice that Chunni-ji is starting to look restless, so I hurriedly ask him about Tuleram and his trance of possession. "I have been seeing Goor-ji since I was a child. He has been chosen by the Devi as her medium, and he is a good one. To get into a trance, he needs to follow certain procedures, chant special mantras and take help from the bajantris who play the right kind of music, the right beat, at the right time." He refuses to tell me what these procedures are but does tell me: "When Goor-ji goes into a trance, I can also feel the vibrations and perceive that a power has entered him. The moment the Devi enters his body can be clearly felt; not just from the falling of his topi … the entire space becomes charged with energy."

The next question I am about to ask must be put as delicately as possible, yet it must be asked. "Does Tuleram always go into a trance, or does he sometimes have to put on a performance? His trance by the tree of Ghatotkacha was quite dramatic…"

Thankfully, Chunni-ji understands my curiosity and answers me candidly. "Goor-ji is the Devi's mouthpiece and that is the sole reason he goes into trance. The Devi observes everything and keeps the sentiments of her people in mind. She knows that her devotees get impressed by a violent trance as it reaffirms their faith in her power." According to Chunni-ji the trance in front of the tree was very real, and he elaborates on how Ghatotkacha is a very strong Devta who draws power from his mother, Hadimba, and father, Bheema, which gives him boundless might.

However, Chunni-ji does make an important admission, which I keep in mind for later. "Sometimes, if Goor-ji's trance is not deep enough and it happens to be an important occasion, he may amplify his performance," he says, "for the benefit of the crowd. But, as I have already told you, we can actually feel it when Goor-ji goes into trance. We know when his trance is a light one. Even so, it is the Devi who puts the words in his mouth."

Chunni-ji asks to be excused, so I ask him a last question: Does he think their system of faith can survive the tests of time and modernisation? He answers confidently, "Definitely. My son is very keen to serve the Devi. Even though he is a child, we see signs of him wanting to serve the holy body of the temple and maybe even become a member of the administration." He pauses to reflect, then adds, "See, there will be members of our family who will not follow the Devi's sacred path and will choose other alternatives. However, there will also always be enough members of our family who will continue this tradition."

I later learn from Meru that the temple kardar collects money from offerings made at the shrine and also from special rituals at the temple or a devotee's home. The collection is disbursed to the Goors, priests, musicians and all those serving the temple.

Devotees also pay money directly into a donation box at the door of the temple, which is used specifically for its upkeep. The allocated percentages vary from temple to temple, but it is clear that the priests receive the lion's share.

After Chunni-ji takes his leave, Meru arrives to take me to meet Chunni-ji's uncle, Pandit Rohit Sharma. En route I relate our conversation. When I express my incredulity about the rath moving "with the energy of the Devta itself", Meru recounts his own experience with a Devta's rath.

"I have grown up steeped in the Devta culture. Even as children, Devtas were part of our play; we would carve small images of our village Devta out of a pumpkin gourd or a piece of wood and perform mock rituals. We would even perform a mock Devkhel and pretend to fall into a trance. As I grew into my teens, I would sometimes be assigned duties related to our village Devta, mostly accompanying the rath during festivals."

I listen closely, for Meru's perspective is extremely important to me. He is the bridge between me and what is in many ways still an alien worldview. He continues, "When I was fifteen to sixteen years old, I was given the opportunity to be a kahar, a palanquin bearer. It is considered an honour and blessing to help carry the rath. And, of course, like you, I was curious to know whether it was true that the rath moved on its own." I lean in closer not wanting to miss a word. "At first I carried it normally, and then distinctly experienced a surge of energy from the rath as it dragged me in a direction that I was not heading into at all. I just had to keep it aloft, but it was moving so fast that at one point I thought I might fall or drop it!"

By now I know that Meru is quite a pragmatic and reticent person, so hearing him attest so strongly to a mysterious energy in the rath gives me something to mull over.

We make our way to Old Manali where Pandit Rohit lives in a small modern cottage. Meru informs me that although the pandit has retired he is considered a fount of knowledge of their belief system, having spent over seventy years in the service of Hadimba Devi as her pujari.

"My father had fabulous aim, even better than an angrez! Mine was quite good as well, although it's not that good now at this age."

A discussion about shooting is not exactly what I had in mind, but here I am learning about the fondness Pandit Rohit has for the sport. We are seated in his tiny living room where a huge altar to Hadimba Devi and other Devtas dominates one end. When I steer the conversation towards the myth of Hadimba Devi, Rohit's face lights up. "I feel extremely fortunate to have been born here in Dev Bhoomi, and that too into a family that has been exclusively chosen to serve the Devi. Serving her is no mean feat. With all that I have experienced, I have come to realise that the Devi chose us because she knew we could do it. Not everyone can do it, you know," he says, his eyes glinting with emotion. "Hadimba Devi is considered to be the most powerful Devi in this area. Because she is an aspect of Kali, animal sacrifices are required to appease her. These are usually sheep."

I ask if sometimes people are uncomfortable with the idea of animal sacrifice. He tells me that many people seeking a solution to their problems are indeed uncomfortable with it, in which case the Devi accepts a coconut sacrifice. However, in the event of a major problem or major festival like Dussehra she specifically asks for an animal sacrifice.

Pandit Rohit goes on to add, "Hadimba was a powerful demon princess who ate humans, continuing to do so even after marrying Bheema until he intervened. The story goes that once she had to break a fast, which she usually did by consuming a human, so she asked her son Ghatotkacha to bring her a human being to eat and, lo and behold, the son brought his father whom he had never before set eyes upon! Bheema had been in the area and had decided to give himself up to save a poor man and more importantly to confront his wife. He made her promise to spare humans, so she decided to devour sheep instead. Over time she became a benevolent goddess who continues to protect the humans in her area."

Pandit Rohit then recounts several episodes of the Devi granting protection and appearing before her devotees in myriad ways: sometimes as a young girl, sometimes as an old woman … I am more interested in the instances of people he has known personally, so he tells of a local man, called Kisnu, a relative of Tuleram. "Kisnu had climbed a very tall tree in a forest, higher up in a mountainous region, to chop wood. It was a tough climb. Once there he became so engrossed in his work that he did not realise time had passed and forgot to pay heed to the worsening weather. It was after sunset that he realised his precarious situation: if he stayed overnight he would surely freeze from the cold winds blowing from the nearby Rohtang Pass; if he tried returning, he could fall and perish while taking the treacherous route in the dark. He felt hopeless knowing that only a miracle could save him, so he prayed to Hadimba Devi and beseeched her to rescue him. To his astonishment, an old lady appeared out of nowhere, took his hand and safely guided him down the mountain without saying a word, and then disappeared. Kisnu was convinced that the mysterious old woman was Devi Hadimba who had answered the call of a troubled devotee."

Another fantastic, movie-like account was of a local woman who had fallen deeply in love with a man visiting from Baltistan. Rohit narrates the story: "She decided to follow him to his home in the mountains of northern Pakistan with a rosy vision of a happy life ever after. However, a rude shock awaited her, for back home her hero already had a well-settled family and children. Not only was the terrain extreme and inhospitable but the family too was menacing and hostile. She began to fear for her life and, though she was pregnant, she fled the place with no idea about the route back home. As it was bound to happen, she was soon lost in the mountains. Starving and alone she was sure she would die in a foreign land. In despair, she called out to her goddess, Hadimba

Devi. Once again the Devi appeared as an old woman and led her all the way home to Manali where she gave birth to a healthy son and lived her days under the care of her family."

I am mesmerised by the magnitude of faith that emanates from these tales of the Himachali Devtas. I was to come across several more such amazing stories over the three years that I would spend researching and documenting the shamans of the Himalayas.

I now ask Pandit-ji to tell me more about Tuleram, at which he gets up and takes out an old photo album, showing me old pictures of the Goor. I grab the few black-and-white photographs eagerly and examine them. Tuleram looks even more formidable in his youth as some faded photographs reveal. While I film these photographs I note that some older scenes from Hadimba Devi's festival three decades ago look much the same as what I had witnessed the day before.

When I mention this to Pandit-ji, he concurs: "Not much has changed in terms of our beliefs, customs and rituals about our Devtas. Our living traditions have been maintained for centuries." He pauses, then adds, "But, I do perceive a wind of change in the youth. They see modern television programmes, and some of them try to emulate a cosmopolitan lifestyle, yet I believe that the faith in their deity remains in their hearts. This is Dev Bhoomi, our Devtas will never allow their power to subside."

Faith in the Devi reaffirmed in its local context, I must now ask a question that I will find myself asking over and over again during my search. "Pandit-ji, I cannot understand this khel, 'the trance that happens to the Goor', nor can I understand the divine possession." I plead with him, "Can you please explain the whole thing to me?" Pandit-ji tries earnestly to find the appropriate language to describe an experiential phenomenon. Later I play back his interview and note the important parts.

The main role of a Goor is to be the medium of the Devta. To allow divine possession to take place, or for their body to be taken over by the Devta, requires them to be in a state of trance, or altered state of consciousness. This could also be described as the attainment of a different level of perception from everyday reality.

Goors work in partnership with the spirit of the Devta that they manifest. In altering their state of consciousness, they can completely efface their personalities, allowing the spirit of the Devta to take over.

Whenever required to enter a trance, the Goor is ritualistically prepared by the priest. The Goor washes his hands and feet, rinses his mouth and occupies his aasan, or consecrated seat, usually a pure woollen blanket. The Goor is then called upon to meditate upon the Devta.

Ceremonial rituals, like reciting mantras, inhaling juniper smoke, the rhythmic beating of the drum and allied instruments, are all vital to achieving a state of trance; all set the tone for divine possession. The community that participates has a collective expectation of the trance performance. Therefore, divine trance of possession is not an individual but a collective, interactive and participatory alteration of a collective consciousness.

Once a trance is over, the Goor remembers nothing of what has transpired. A Goor is chosen by the Devta out of those members of the village who exhibit an ability to go into trance from a very early age. During a festival, where a large number of people are witness, the rath of the Devta expresses its selection by going to the chosen one and knocking off their cap. Sometimes this selection can also happen within a temple complex. Once selected, the person must undergo an initiation and a process of instruction begins. This is a long and arduous affair with wide variations. Generally, the Goor is aided by the former Goor, who very often is an older male relative. The priest of the Devta also helps and offers instructions during the initiation. Instructions entail prayer, meditation, the learning and recitation of mantras, fasting, puja and the ritualistic preparations for the trance of possession. Once they are considered ready, a puja and a havan, a fire ritual ceremony, are conducted. This is the pratishtha, or formal establishment of the deity in the body of their Goor through consecration, when a sacrifice is also offered.

Once we leave I talk to Meru about my discussion with Pandit Rohit. However, I feel there are many more questions I need to ask about a Goor's trance and divine possession. I decide to meet more members of the Devloo, especially the bajantris, while we await Tuleram's acquiescence to interview him.

The following day, while Meru and some of my crew members run around to line up meetings for me, my camera crew and I begin filming interviews with the people to whom I have already spoken. We all meet in the evening, Meru has a smile on his face. "Anu," he says, "I have fixed up a meeting for you with one of Hadimba Devi's bajantris, Mehar Singh. He plays the dhouns, a locally made drum that is one of the main instruments played at every ceremony of the Devtas."

I set off through the lanes of Old Manali with Meru again. The village folk have started recognising me, so whenever I greet someone with a casual "Namaste ji" we are invited with a warm, "Baitho! Chai piyo"; an invitation to their home to drink tea, which is the kind of hospitality one comes to expect in these parts. A few stop us for brief conversations in which Meru is asked about me and my project. Meru patiently answers their questions, all in good humour. I am still adjusting to the unhurried pace of life here along with the gentleness and graciousness of the locals—so wholesome compared to impersonal city life.

As we walk through the village, Meru tells me that in every Devta's procession there are typically ten to twelve bajantris. Their musical instruments include the karnahal, a huge copper trumpet shaped like a flower in bloom that has a loud and strong sound; the raisingha; the dhol, a twin-headed drum; the nagara, a drum with a wide mouth; the dadh, a two-foot-long version of the dhol; and the bhana, a metal plate hung from a thread, which the musician usually dangles from one hand while beating it with a stick with the other to create a clanging sound.

We finally reach an old and modest wooden hut where a man with a small build, wiry hair and stoic demeanour is feeding a calf. Mehar Singh calmly finishes his tasks for the day before joining us in his courtyard. After we exchange pleasantries, he begins telling me about himself. Mehar Singh is from a family of bajantris, having inherited his art from his forefathers. He started by playing the thali as a child and slowly graduated to the dhouns. "In the beginning I used to play the thali on my own, almost obsessively. I learnt how to play by observing my father, and it was only when I had become a decent musician that my father started instructing me in music. Every Devta has its own beat and music, you see, and I had to learn all the proper ragas as well as all the occasions on which they are to be played."

At my request Mehar-ji brings out his dhouns for me to have a look at. "Please do not touch it," he requests just as I am about to. The drum is about a foot in diameter, made from the shell of a bhekhal[2] tree. It is wrapped with sheepskin at one end where the musician hits his daggas, or drumsticks. Mehar-ji tells me, "Once made, the dhouns is unveiled in front of the Devi and then energised by the pujari with some of the Devi's mantras."

Meru adds, "The dhouns has an arresting sound that you can often hear rising above the rest of the instruments, especially when the Goor is about to go into a trance."

Mehar-ji tells me that a religious ritual is performed before the dhouns is used for the first time. "The instrument has to be imbued with the soul of the Devta so that it can act as an instructor to the Goor. The sound of the dhouns tells the Goor what to do, and its power is not limited to just that. The dhouns also commands the other instruments. They have to follow its lead."

I ask Mehar whether the dhouns is played according to the Devta's mood. "We play music according to the occasion,"

2 Bhekhal: Himalayan cherry, or Latin: *prinsepia utilis*

he clarifies. "If the Devta is travelling uphill the music will be different; if they are travelling downhill it will be different; if the Goor is preparing to go into a trance, it will be different; if the Goor is already in a trance, it will be different. We play certain rhythms from certain instruments to help the Goor into a trance, and if those rhythms do not help we play more tunes that assist him. We look at their mood, the ambience, how intense their trance is at that particular time and drum accordingly."

Like Chunni-ji, Mehar-ji tells me that he can also perceive when the divine visitation takes place. "When the Goor goes into a trance," he says, "we bajantris also feel a unique sensation. It only happens at that time."

I ask, "Are the bajantris always able to get the Goor into a trance?"

Mehar-ji has a twinkle in his eyes. "We have a particular manner in which we play to get the Goor into a trance. But, if we realise that he is unable to go into a trance," Mehar-ji says, carefully choosing his words, "we play a special raga and keep repeating it until his trance eventually begins." He tells me that the ragas are strictly handed down to the next generation in the family only when the son is ready to step into his father's shoes.

"So, the bajantris are indispensable to a Goor's trance of possession," I comment.

Mehar-ji corrects me, "No, no! A Goor can go into a trance by themselves in an emergency situation or even to give an individual consultation. In fact any time the Devta wants to communicate with the people, the Goor will go into a trance. Bajantris are required during rituals and ceremonies when things are followed according to the Devta system."

I want to ask many more questions about the rath and Tuleram's trance of possession, for instance, but Mehar-ji asks to be excused. He must now go about the rest of his day. The interview leaves me with a myriad of feelings. This ordinary-looking man is an artist in possession of some great secrets of music; some that could influence a person to go into an altered state of consciousness!

Yet, he had politely refused to let me probe any further. This is a pattern I am coming to notice increasingly: people here are still quite secretive about their religious rituals and practices.

I say this to Meru, who agrees. "See, Anu," he explains it to me as politely as always, "we have kept our belief system under wraps for centuries, and outsiders have never been allowed to even observe our ceremonies. You are actually very lucky to be one of the first persons to have received the Devi's permission to document her system."

I know what Meru says is true as my earlier as well as subsequent research to find authentic documentation of the Devta system yielded poor results. I ask Meru, "Why do you think that I have been allowed to document these secret practices?"

Meru smiles and answers, "Only the Devi knows the reason." He looks down for a while, thinking. "Maybe it is because in this age of Kali Yuga, when our society is going through a rapid phase of transformation in pursuit of modernisation, the Devtas agree with your concept of documenting their system for posterity."

My investigation brings me back to Tuleram. I am keen to meet him as something within me is convinced that he holds the key to my search. As luck would have it, just as we are climbing up to the Hadimba Devi Temple, I see Tuleram standing on the temple veranda. I feel a flutter of excitement in my stomach as I see the distinctive Goor. He is wearing loose, faded trousers, a crumpled, checked short kurta, a sleeveless jersey and a woollen cap, and is busy talking to someone. We walk up to him and I wait, until he finishes his conversation. From up close I notice his eyes are greyish, he has a few teeth missing, his face is deeply lined and his speech is gruff. Surprisingly, as soon as he is done with his conversation and notices us, he turns and walks away. I run after him speaking hurriedly, almost incoherently, "Goor-ji, please, may I have a conversation with you?" Meru repeats my plea as well, but this time in the language of the locals. I see visible discomfort on Tuleram's face. He tells Meru that he is busy and needs to be somewhere else. I plead with him to spare two minutes, but he is not willing to talk to me. He simply utters, "Good morning. Good evening. Goodnight," and departs.

I feel utterly let down. The person I am most interested to know is not even willing to talk to me! After experiencing the willing cooperation from everyone else so far, I am surprised by Tuleram's response and attitude. However, it does not deter me; I am determined to persuade him to do an in-depth televised interview. I know now that it will not be easy.

Noticing my disappointment, Meru says in his usually kind voice, "You are focusing only on Hadimba Devi and Tuleram. They are just parts of a larger, more varied universe." He is keen for me to widen my purview and see other places in the valley too.

I ask him what he has in mind. Meru informs me that the month of May coincides with the flowering season in the valley, and to celebrate it the Shahri Jatra Mela is held in the village of Naggar. "Would you like to go for the Naggar Festival tomorrow? You will get to see other Devtas and Goors there." I brighten, my enthusiasm instantly restored.

We leave for Naggar the next afternoon. What I remember as a sleepy village has been transformed into a vibrant, festive space. There are swarms of people in every lane and excited children run in and out of each other's houses. We move towards the Devi Tripura Sundari Temple, which is a pagoda-style structure with a three-tiered roof similar to that of the Hadimba Devi Temple. Though slightly smaller, it has an impressive entrance and a large covered area in front with a shikhara-styled roof that is used during special ceremonies.

Tripura Sundari is an aspect of Adi Shakti, the primordial feminine energy. She is one of the group of ten goddesses collectively called the Mahavidyas, each representing a form of the Great Goddess Shakti. Though beautiful, Tripura Sundari is fierce and is the destroyer of the demon Bhandasura.

Amidst the festive madness, we somehow manage to meet the man of the hour, the kardar of the Devi, Joginder-ji. Meru introduces me as the director of the film that he had sought permission for. “Ah yes, we checked with the Devi,” he says, then turns around as someone calls him. I feel my heart sink. In a moment Joginder-ji turns back with a smile, and says, “And she has given you her permission to film the proceedings.” I let out my breath in relief, and thank him profusely.

He goes on to inform us that three other Devtas are also attending the festival, and welcomes both me and the crew to have a meal and stay on if we like. I am surprised by this invitation considering the secrecy that has been maintained until now. Joginder-ji is surprised that I find it so strange. He tells me that the people who are accompanying all the other Devtas' processions are also going to be looked after, fed meals and lodged for the night.

Meru chips in, “It is known as khindu.”

I ask Joginder-ji how they make it possible as it means putting up a few dozen people.

“Every household in the host village lodges one, two or more villagers according to their capacity,” he explains. “Considered a part of the visiting Devta's family, all their needs are taken care of, including specially cooked non-vegetarian food as well as alcoholic drinks.”

This is stunning new information! I ask, “Which means that every house in the village hosts guests for a night during festivals?” As a city person, I find the idea quite astonishing.

Seeing my expression, Joginder-ji laughs. “Not for only one night necessarily. Sometimes a Devta may decide to stay for a few days in which case we host all the guests till they decide to leave.”

We hear the familiar music of a Devta's procession making its way towards us. Joginder-ji takes our leave and rushes off to greet a couple of Devtas who are now arriving. Meru and I make our way to the festival ground.

“Meru, your khindu system is incredible! But…” I hesitantly ask Meru what is on my mind, “is everyone happy to host guests from other villages always?”

Meru smiles at me indulgently. "Absolutely, Anu, it is an honour for us to host a Devta's people, for it is like having the Devta visit our home. We go out of our way to take care of them. This is how we maintain our huge network of friendship and goodwill with people from almost every village in the valley."

We reach the circular festival ground that adjoins the temple. It is built as an open arena with huge cement steps carved along the hill face where a huge crowd is seated. There are several stalls with games, snacks and local wares; there is a Ferris wheel at one end and a dance group performing a natti at the other. It is like a smaller version of the Hadimba Devi Festival but just as vibrant, festive and celebratory.

In different parts of the ground, the three palanquins of the visiting Devtas as well as the host Devi, Tripura Sundari, are rushing around for the meet-and-greet ceremony, cheered on excitedly by the crowd. Encircling them, the natti dancers are dancing exuberantly. This goes on for a while until they all line up next to each other and begin dancing together. All sixteen kahars holding the four palanquins are taking small steps to the left, right and forward in perfect unison. It does seem like the dance of the divine! The raths finally make their way to the end of the ground, are turned to face the crowd and set down on the ground.

It is as if the knowledge of what is about to happen has already been perceived by the crowd. Four Goors appear from amidst them, wearing their cream tunics and holding their dharj. They go ahead and sit in front of their respective rath, or rather their Devta. Bajantris form a circle around them and begin drumming in an anticipatory manner. I gently push my way to the front and begin filming while my crew films long shots from the steps.

In order to invoke their Devtas and Devis, all four Goors begin performing the ceremonial rituals that I had seen Goor Tuleram perform earlier. They chant mantras, breathe in the incense from the dharj deeply, pluck a hair from their scalp and slowly lean back. The horns blow, and their caps fall into the waiting hands of their attendants.

The Goors open and loosen their hair, and two of them have hair that almost reaches their waists. The Goors continue to chant mantras while inhaling the incense and shaking their heads. It is like a dance that is choreographed to put one under a spell. A familiar silence engulfs the crowd as it watches intently while I hold my breath and wait for the inevitable to unfold. One by one the Goors begin trembling, shivering and shaking. I can see they have gone into a deep trance as I zoom into close-ups on the Goors' faces. Their expressions begin to distort, and their eyes acquire a glazed look.

The Goor of Tripura Sundari, a short man with a balding pate, wispy hair and moustache, steps forward. He begins to shake violently, then speaks to the crowd that has edged closer to listen. The Goor, as the Devi, repeats the Devi's legend, reminds the people of her powers, questions people's faith in her, threatens to withdraw her protection if their faith is lapsing and promises them her protection and benevolence. The crowd listens respectfully while prominent members of the Devloo converse with her. It cheers when she promises to bestow abundance on them or pacify her when she threatens to forsake them. It was almost exactly as I had seen earlier with Tuleram.

Meru points my attention to the other Goors who have begun dancing the Devkhel. One after the other the Goors pick up the weapons that belong to their own Devta—daggers, spears or shangals—and begin performing the peculiar step dance in circles. Soon they begin dancing with one another, holding hands, stepping in line and twirling at each end, while the bajantris keep drumming.

I look around at the crowd and film the people's shining faces and eyes, spanning their animated expressions, and note their attitude of complete reverence. Once the Devkhel is over, the natti dancers begin singing and dancing again in a huge circle.

The bajantris then come into the centre of the circle and pick up the beat while horns blow occasionally. Lifted by the kahars, the four raths also enter the circle and begin dancing in step with each other. Some exuberant male members of the crowd join the circle of dancers. The dancing together with the lights and sounds make the energy within the arena palpable and exhilarating.

Suddenly one rath breaks the circle and begins running towards one end, tilting frantically to one side. It dashes towards a Goor and, facing him, begins rocking back and forth. Meru explains, "The Devi is expressing her affinity towards her Goor." I edge closer and find the Goor having a conversation with the rath, trying to pacify it.

Devi via Goor: "You must listen to me … and do as I say … I will ease all your burdens…"

Devotees: "Please forgive our mistakes, Devi! We will do as you say."

Devi via Goor: "Stay devoted … I will ensure that all goes well in your festival…"

Devotees: "Praise the Devi!"

All of a sudden there is a roar from the crowd from another part of the festival ground. I swivel around to find the same scenario unfolding with another rath and its Goor. All the while the other two raths keep dancing as do many of the village folk who join in the dance with their Devta. Attending this smaller festival is an incredible experience for me and my crew. It is more intimate, more emotionally vibrant and full of powerful energy. I thank Meru profusely for the gift of this experience. He teases me, "Anu, this is just the beginning. Now that you have really got a feel of our culture, you are ready to delve into our Goor system."

Just as the raths had gravitated towards their Goors, my quest too centres around them. The most important character for me is still Tuleram, and I am determined to learn more about him.

5
Goor Tuleram, the Master Showman

I feel strange because I have never even come close to stalking anyone before, yet here I am intending to follow Tuleram surreptitiously through the Manali Bazaar. This morning, frustrated with my inability to secure a meeting with him, I decided to follow and observe Tuleram while my crew are busy filming interviews with the village folk.

Meru too is busy today, so I wander around by myself in the "hippie lane" of Old Manali keeping an eye out for Tuleram, who, I have been told, usually walks through here en route to the Hadimba Devi Temple. After a few hours I am fed up with waiting and walk into Dylan's to drown my disappointment in a sweet cappuccino. I order and take in the ambience: a couple of young men with blond dreadlocks are smoking weed and playing chess; a group of four tourists are chatting in a relaxed fashion; an Indian couple is looking warmly into each other's eyes. I relax, look outside and suddenly jump up, for there is Tuleram passing in front of Dylan's!

I hurriedly pay and run after him until I spot him crossing the bridge. I stop, panting from the exertion and excitement. I pursue Tuleram from afar for the next couple of hours as he walks through the Manali Bazaar, closely watching his every move.

Tuleram is dressed in his signature checked shirt, brown trousers, sleeveless jersey and grey woollen cap. He carries a worn backpack and walks with a heavy gait. His unhurried pace is slowed even further as people from the area keep stalling him. I notice that many bend to touch his feet and he blesses them with his hands. Some greet him with palms joined in a respectful namaste while others stop for a brief chat. Tuleram seems to be a jovial person, and I see him smile and laugh during many of these interactions. It is a completely different facet of the Goor that I am witnessing.

At Manali Bazaar, Tuleram buys some vegetables and a stainless steel utensil and chats with a few people before heading back to the temple. He is clearly accorded much respect, which I suppose is a great equaliser considering that he belongs to a so-called lower-caste. Despite laws that prohibit caste-based discrimination and affirmative policy actions for the upliftment of backward castes, the inequalities of the caste system are very much a lived reality not just for the majority of the population here in the Kullu Valley but across the country.

I am quite intrigued that the all-important role of being "a vehicle of the divine" is performed by persons of low caste who are imputed to be "untouchable". Meru tells me that Goors and drummers tend to belong to low castes such as the Harijans and Lohars, though sometimes they may belong to a higher caste if it is their family tradition, while the influential pujaris and kardars are always upper caste.

I follow Tuleram to the temple complex where he meets a man he seems to know. Both sit on a bench and start talking. I remain quite afar for fear of being spotted. After a while I see Tuleram take something out of his pocket and hold it in his palm. He stares at it while I desperately try to see what it is—to no avail, for he is too far away. Tuleram then throws away whatever was in his hand and chats a bit more, gesturing with his forefinger as if explaining something. They stand up and walk into the temple. I cannot resist: I go to the spot to look for what Tuleram had thrown. At first I cannot see anything, so I crouch down and discern what looks like a few black sesame seeds. Could this be what Tuleram had held in his hand?

I look at my watch and see that I am very late for my appointment with Meru. I rush to meet him, looking forward to telling him about my observations, hoping that he will not disapprove of my sleuthing. Today Meru and I are meeting at the outdoor coffee shop of Banon's Hotel. This is where we had met the first time when Kishan Banon, the great-grandson of the famous apple planter Lieutenant Banon, had introduced us.

Meru has a hearty laugh when he hears what I have been up to. "So," he asks, "what did you find out by following Tuleram?"

I am not happy to admit, "Not a lot, but I did infer that Tuleram is highly respected."

Meru agrees with me. "All Goors are respected as such…" he says, with a kind of reverence. "After all, they are the mediums of our Devtas who perform this most essential function for us."

"Tell me," I ask Meru, "is it possible that Tuleram had been looking at sesame seeds in his palm?"

Meru nods. "Yes, he must have been answering someone's query. It's one of the techniques a Goor uses to perform a divination." Before I can ask him about methods of divination, Meru says, "By the way I came to give you some good news," his eyes twinkling with cheer. "Tuleram has agreed to give time for you to visit him tomorrow … at his home!" Seeing my face light up, his grin grows wider.

That night I think about the questions I want to put to Tuleram. I am particularly interested in learning about his divine possession and his experience of trance.

The next day Meru and I once again traverse the labyrinth of narrow lanes in Dhungri village that run past several kath-kuni houses, cowsheds and piles of logs. We cross courtyards piled with sheaves of jowar, balconies lined with washed clothes, children playing kabaddi, old people looking out through windows and women weaving on their home looms, until we finally arrive at a long flight of steep, tiring steps. The exhausting climb leads up to wonderful views overlooking Dhungri village, the Manu temple and the surrounding mountains. We walk to the highest row of houses, which are small and decidedly humble.

Meru stops in front of a tiny two-storey wooden house painted bright green. I can see stacks of wood poking out from the lower floor so presume that is the storage area. The living area is on the floor above from where a woman wearing a pattu and headscarf is peeking out. Meru whispers, "This is Tuleram's wife," and greets her with some formal pleasantries and enquiries about the Goor. She tells us to come up as he is expecting us. We climb up a narrow ladder and squeeze through a hatch in the upper floor onto a tiny veranda. Tuleram's wife greets us shyly though warmly and asks us to sit. A fresh-faced boy comes out and greets us in an equally coy manner. This is Devi Chand, Tuleram's twelve-year-old school-going son.

While Meru exchanges pleasantries, I have a look around. The narrow veranda has a small trunk in one corner over which hangs a clothesline piled with lots of garments. Alongside the veranda are three doors that lead to three closet-sized rooms, a bedroom, a mandir and a kitchen. When I see the state of the house with its meagre possessions, I realise that Tuleram's status as a powerful Goor does not translate into economic gains. Despite this, both his wife and son seem content, even proud, to have a Goor in the family.

The man that I have been desperately wanting to meet all week enters the room. "Good morning, good evening," Tuleram says jovially, his smile shining through his overbite as he comes towards us and sits with us on the floor. Meru speaks in Kullvi, explaining to Tuleram why I wanted to meet him. Once again I observe Tuleram closely as he speaks to Meru. He has an expressive face, dynamic gestures, a quick wit. His persona fascinates me. He tells Meru that they are just about to start their evening aarti and invites us to join them.

We squeeze in with them into the mandir they have built inside the house. The shrine is a tiny room with low ceiling and pictures of deities in one corner where Hadimba Devi's picture has pride of place. A multi-camera shoot cannot work here given the space, so we film everything that follows in the house through a single camera. To my surprise it is not Tuleram but his son Devi Chand who leads the prayers. I watch Devi Chand pronounce the verses, ringing the bell continuously with one hand and waving the juniper incense across the pictures of the deities with the other, as if he has been doing this for a long time. He is absolutely lost in this ritual of reverence. Tuleram and his wife are also intensely focused on the puja; their devotion too seems absolute and unshakeable.

Once the puja is over, Tuleram leads us into their living room, which can also be converted into a bedroom. It's the largest space in the house and is quite bare. Tuleram's wife brings tea and biscuits as we sit on the floor and make ourselves comfortable. So far only Meru has been conversing with Tuleram, so to break the ice I ask him, "Goor-ji, why have you been refusing to talk to me so far?"

Tuleram is slightly apologetic. "You see, Madam-ji," he says hesitantly, "Tirath Ram-ji told me yesterday only that it would be okay to speak to you." He shrugs, turning to Meru to add, "In matters pertaining to the Devi, we have to take permission from her, you know." Then turning to me, he asks, "What do you want to know? Feel free to ask anything. But, first you need to tell me what your understanding of who a Goor is."

I am caught off guard. "Um, it is someone who acts as the medium of a Devta, who goes into a trance, invokes the Devta to possess them, and allows the Devta to speak through them," I mumble, carefully choosing my words.

Tuleram seems pleased with my answer and almost cackles, "Very good, very good!"

Encouraged, I ask, "How did you become a Goor, Tuleram-ji?"

Tuleram adjusts his position to reply. "See, Madam-ji," he says, waving his hands expressively, "no one chooses to become a Goor. Why would they? It's a tough job to be a Goor. It's a hard life. Every Devta chooses his own medium, after which we dedicate our life to the Devta and follow whatever he wants of us."

I interject, "But, how does a Devta choose his Goor?"

Tuleram explains, "To become a Goor of any Devta, a person has to experience two peculiar, very specific things. One is that he needs to be able to go naturally into trance, then he will rush to his Devta's temple and begin speaking for the Devta. The second critical criterion is that while the person is in a trance, their topi needs to be thrown off by the rath of their Devta, or any visiting Devta for that matter."

I am delighted to find Tuleram so amenable and communicative. It is entirely unlike the impression I had formed of him at the festival. However, I find that he is not very fluent in Hindi so I have to depend on Meru to explain many of my questions as well as translate whenever Tuleram answers in Kullvi. This is how his story goes:

Tuleram succeeded his father as the Goor of Hadimba Devi. Although there are several instances of sons becoming Goors after their fathers pass away, "a Goor is chosen by the Devta," Tuleram underlines. "I used to get into minor trances even when my father was alive, but I just ignored them." He takes out his family album and begins to show me photographs, pointing proudly to his parents. "My father was a very capable and knowledgeable man and a very powerful Goor. I am not even half as powerful as he was. If he predicted something, there was no doubt it would happen."

Before his father's death, Tuleram had been busy looking after the household and had little knowledge or understanding of what it was that his father did exactly. Then he began to experience minor trances. Tuleram recollects, "My father would just wave them off and give me something to eat, assuring me that I would be fine."

Tuleram's circumstances changed when one day Hadimba Devi and her entourage were visiting the Kullu Raja, the erstwhile King of Kullu. The then pujari of Hadimba Devi, Pandit Rohit, noticed that the Devi's jewelled nose ring on her mask mounted on the rath was broken. As the news circulated, Tuleram took notice. The occurrence was a sign of misfortune. It was only that he did not expect the loss to be so personal. "The Devi mourns any loss of her Goor just like his family does," Tuleram tells me, "as it is customary here that women often forsake some of their jewellery when a family member dies."

Tuleram's father knew that his time was up, so he asked Tuleram, one of his five sons, to stay by his side. He died two days after this incident. In those two days he had tried to pass on as much knowledge to Tuleram as he could. Though Tuleram tried to focus, it was all in vain. "Watching my father take his last breaths was not the time that I could be the most diligent student," he says in a lowered voice, "and I soon forgot most of what he told me."

After his father's death, Tuleram went on to lead his usual life and took up odd jobs to make ends meet. Nine years later, while he was working in a guest house, he recalls, "I suddenly felt a huge surge of energy running through me. I went into a trance so intense that I lost all consciousness. I don't remember but was told by others that I ran barefoot all the way to the Hadimba Devi Temple."

It was the day of the festival of Hadimba Devi's birthday and as was the practice several other Devtas had gathered at the festival ground. Tuleram reached the grounds in a state of extraordinary trance, headed straight to Hadimba Devi's rath and was about to prostrate himself before it. "Suddenly the visiting Shankh Narayan's rath approached me and my topi was thrown off by its handle." The throwing off of the cap by a Devta's rath is considered a stamp of approval from the gods as well as an indication of their selection, and Tuleram was declared the Goor of Hadimba Devi.

Meru adds, "It is not just a matter of an individual having the ability to go into trance, though that is an essential quality of a medium. Being chosen by a Devta in a public forum is something that can change everything." This is an important distinction to draw. I ask Meru if all the Goors in the valley get chosen this way. He answers in the affirmative. Tuleram adds, "This divine selection is like a gust of wind. Nobody knows whom it will end up engulfing."

Tuleram tells me that there were other tests that he had to succeed in before he was accepted as a Goor, but he is reluctant to reveal these. "We have to keep certain rituals secret," he explains. "This knowledge is only for the Devta's selected few." It would not be okay for him to tell me about them. Nevertheless, I remember Rohit Pandit telling me about one where the Goor is required to go high up into the mountains, led by the Devta, to pluck the leaves of the bethar, or juniper, from a tree specified by their Devta.

When I ask about this, Tuleram still refuses to divulge any details. In fact, in several instances the veil of secrecy is raised again and again, and my queries are met with a firm refusal: "No, I cannot tell you!"

By donning the Devi's sacred mantle, life changed almost instantly for Tuleram who now had the huge responsibility of being an important Devi's Goor. He had to learn the rituals, mantras and ceremonial duties of his Devi. I am curious and ask him, "Who taught you these, Goor-ji?" Tuleram admits to having learned all the ceremonial rituals from a mentor, another elder Goor in the village. "But, in everything else I am guided by the Devi," he remarks.

"How does she do that, Goor-ji?" I ask, a tad impatiently.

Tuleram responds nonchalantly, "Arre, madam, she tells me in my head. The directions come to me automatically. How else!"

Tuleram tells me about his duties and responsibilities as a Goor. Along with the change in status come the traditions that have to be observed by every Goor. They cannot go into homes where there has been a birth or death, for a specified period, as those homes are considered to be jooth, or unclean. If a Goor has to travel with his Devta, he can have only one meal a day … and many other such proscriptions and taboos. He is no longer part of the usual village social life. These norms and rituals have to be observed on a daily basis and so place him on the fringe of the village's community activities.

Now that I know a little about Tuleram's background and initiation into shamanism, I gear up to question him about the most mystifying aspect of his life: going into a divine possession trance. My first question is simple: "How do you get into a trance?"

Tuleram says, "It just happens on its own." Seeing my confused expression, he adds, "You see, we focus our minds, recite certain mantras, then inhale the smoke from the dharj. Most importantly, the bajantris help us by playing certain kinds of music. Do you understand?"

I don't understand to be honest. Nevertheless, I ask, "How does it feel when you are in trance?"

"It's like a bolt of current running through my body, and then I don't know what happens or what I say."

I repeat what he has said rhetorically: "You don't know what happens, or what you say?"

"I have no idea what is happening. Actually I am not aware of anything or anyone around me while I am in trance."

It is difficult for me to settle for this, so I continue to prod him by asking the same question in different ways, hoping that he will articulate his experience with more clarity, but the answer is always the same. Tuleram adds, "It is only later when it's over that I realise something has happened. It is then that the pujari tells me all that has taken place and all that I had said while I was in trance." I look at Meru in disbelief, and he nods his head affirming Tuleram's claim.

"How do you feel after a trance experience?" I ask.

Tuleram says, "I only feel tired and a little intoxicated as if I have had a couple of pegs of alcohol."

I ask him the reason for his intense trance at the tree of Ghatotkacha, and he says, "The Devi came to me strongly at that moment to impress the devotees and show the world her power." He goes on to clarify again that trance is something that happens on its own. The intensity of his trance that I had witnessed was of the Devi's doing. She is a living goddess who, reading the mood of her devotees, may decide to display her power and reiterate her supremacy. "And the faith her devotees have in her is because of this very power that reveals itself in our everyday lives," Tuleram concludes.

I shift my attention to someone who has been listening to our conversation intently all this time. Tuleram's young son, Devi Chand, has not moved at all since we began. During the aarti I noticed that the boy seemed quite comfortable to be conducting the ritual. I ask him, "Tell me, do you eventually want to become a Goor?"

To my surprise, he says, "No, no. I want to become a doctor. A Goor's life is very difficult, but if the Devi chooses me, of course I won't have a choice but to go along with her wishes."

Despite his immense faith in their Devi, and the pride that he holds for his father, Devi Chand has a pragmatic outlook: "I have seen my father's experience first-hand; walking barefoot with the Devi's rath over long distances, even through snow; eating very little while on duty; being on call all day and night; he has to prioritise the Devi's work over and above everything else, including his family."

Tuleram agrees. "I don't want my son to become a Goor," he says soberly. "I want him to become a doctor and have an easier life than mine."

Tuleram is getting visibly fidgety and impatient. "See, these questions are only relevant if the Devi eventually chooses Devi Chand as her Goor," he says a trifle irritably.

I insist, "But, he wants to become a doctor."

Tuleram responds firmly, "You could be a doctor, you could be a businessman, you could have a lot of family responsibilities, but if you are chosen by the Devi, you have to leave all that behind and serve her, even if it is tough, physically and financially."

When I enquire about his financial situation, Tuleram informs me that he receives a small percentage from temple collections and other consultations, which tend to be quite meagre. He inherited this tiny house from his father as it is part of the Devi's property. He adds with dignity, "I may be the Goor of a powerful Devi, but I am a poor man!"

I ask whether Tuleram finds his role as a Goor a burden. His eyes become twice their size in sincere surprise. "No, no, it is a great privilege!" he says vehemently. "To be chosen by the Devi is such a tremendous honour! I get a lot of respect from the people here."

Tuleram stands up and stretches. "It's time for my dinner. Please join us in our humble meal."

I politely refuse. Tuleram walks Meru and me out while I thank him profusely for his time and hospitality. He responds amusingly, stringing together his entire English vocabulary: "Hello, welcome, good morning, good evening, goodnight!"

It's almost dusk when we walk out, and the mountains are crowned with peach-coloured, fluffy clouds. The sound of children playing makes me smile. As we start to leave, something unexpected happens. In front of us a man in a kurta is climbing the steps to Tuleram's compound. As he nears Tuleram, his face breaks out in a huge smile and he does something strange. He spreads out his arms and begins to dance as if mimicking a bird. Tuleram's eyes start to dance, he lets out a squeal of delight and begins aping the man. They begin to move around each other slowly and deliberately, waving their arms about. This strange dance continues for a few minutes until they come closer to each other and embrace like long-lost friends. Tuleram shouts, "Ishi, my friend!"

The moment is spontaneous and magical. I realise that even though Tuleram is quite inarticulate on the intricacies of being a shaman, he is a master showman and in this lies his brilliance.

Meru and I make our way to the famous Johnson's Cafe for dinner. Renowned for its excellent food and ambience, I often frequent this trendy restaurant set in a beautiful flower garden. After a splendid repast of wood-fired baked trout, I bring our conversation back to Tuleram. I lament that despite my unrelenting questioning Tuleram had been unable to give me more than a slight glimpse into his world. Meru acknowledges my point, "See, Tuleram is a simple man. He is not literate, nor articulate, and therefore lacks the language for communicating his experiences properly." I am no closer to understanding Tuleram's divine possession trance. I only have an inkling of how he goes into it. I realise that perhaps I am hankering for an intellectual understanding where none is possible. What transpires here is in the realm of faith, imagination and experience.

I tell Meru that I would like to meet as many Goors as possible and also attend all the important local practices relating to their Devtas. Meru grins broadly. "That means you will have to observe our entire lifestyle."

I correct him, "No, only the customs in which your Devtas are involved."

Meru laughs. "That's what I'm telling you," he says. "There is no part of our lives that is untouched by the Devta's will. We won't do anything important without consulting them, and they participate in every aspect of our lives; that's why we call them living gods."

Nevertheless, he agrees that I will have a better idea when I meet other Goors, some of whom will hopefully be more eloquent than Tuleram.

Over the next week, my crew and I scramble all over the valley seeking opportunities to film interviews with Goors, pandits, kardars and other members of the Devloos of different Devtas. Meru's presence is critical in all of this as he convinces the otherwise reticent villagers to talk to me. Then I explain my project and plead with them to allow us to film them.

I meet several Goors and manage to film interviews with quite a few. A few Goors refuse to allow us to film them, citing their Devta's refusal as the reason, while others avoid answering certain questions saying they "cannot divulge that information". Some Goors are fairly eloquent while others cannot find adequate words to express themselves. I find that most kardars are better informed and good communicators, "which is why they are the Devta's managers". Meru smiles at my observation.

Meru also takes me to talk to some of the Devloos of the nine villages that had attended Hadimba Devi's birthday celebrations. Gradually, with each interaction and by watching the footage of all the additional interviews that my crew has documented, I begin to discern a hazy image of a Himachali Goor.

I have learned a few things about the Goors of Himachal. Firstly, despite caste being a significant factor in hill society, a Goor may come from any caste, including the lowest. Secondly, though a Goor commands great respect as a bridge between the people and their Devta, this does not necessarily translate into economic benefit.

I have learned that the job of a Goor is not one that most people aspire to, for despite the prestige it is a life of hardship, the duties onerous and he has to observe several taboos. For instance, he cannot wear shoes of leather, cut his hair, smoke, eat eggs or chickens, nor can he take meals in a house whenever a lady has her period. Yet, once the Devta has chosen, their will cannot be denied. Many are the stories of reluctant Goors who have eventually had to submit to an insistent Devta. An ability to go into a spontaneous trance is central to being chosen as a Goor. Yet, even that is not enough, for a person cannot proclaim himself as a Goor. It is the Devta who chooses his medium, and he must do so by knocking off the prospective Goor's cap publicly.

Once the Goor is selected, he does not automatically enter a "Goorship"; he is still a bathar, or novice. To be a real Goor, he has to undergo several rituals and trials. Every Devta has their own tests to find out whether the bathar is competent. For example, in the case of Jamlu Devta of Malana, the bathar has to go through two ordeals to prove his worthiness for the exalted post. First, "a trench is dug and the Goor-elect is made to lie in it. A wooden plank is laid over the trench, earth is shovelled over it and seeds are strewn over the earth. After half an hour, the earth and plank are removed. If the Goor-elect is still alive, he is declared to have passed the first test. He must then go to Girwa Kothi, a mountain cliff at an altitude of 16,000 feet, which is no easy task."[1]

The bathar then has to learn a large number of mantras relating not only to the ceremonies and rituals of the Devta but also the ill health, worries, problems and troubles of the individual and the community. A complete mantra of a particular subject is known as a mala, and a perfect Goor is supposed to know more than five hundred malas. However, there are no written records of these malas as they are all learnt by heart from the previous senior Goor.

Armed thus, with the authority of the Devta and knowledge of mantras, the Goor is a man of great importance and influence. His many ceremonial and ritual engagements help in fulfilling the social, cultural, financial, spiritual and religious needs of the people by guiding them in their activities. Though I have gathered considerable information, I am now acutely aware that what I have learned thus far is the tip of the proverbial iceberg. Every conversation I have had with Goors and members of the Devloo have hinted at deeper, uncharted depths, which I look forward to exploring.

1 *Myths, Rituals and Beliefs in Himachal Pradesh* by M.R. Thakur

6

The State of Trance

The capital city of Delhi sprawls beneath me, shrouded in a familiar brown smog. The aircraft swoops down from the clear blue skies into the brown haze, landing me back into the city that has been my home since I was a child, but which now seems alien to me at so many levels. My time in Dev Bhoomi has altered me more than I know.

Driving through dusty roads and traffic snarls, I look at the passing concrete jungle in dismay. Has the population and number of vehicles on the road increased while I was away? The city seems even more polluted and frantic than a month ago.

The stark contrast of the environment and energies between Kullu Valley and Delhi are always such a shock to my system! Already I miss the mountains, the green vistas and tall trees, the clarified air and the chirping of birds, the quiet and the peace.

It takes us days to settle down. Revisiting my experiences of the past month by watching all that we had filmed is refreshing. I am once again struck by the unique culture of Dev Bhoomi.

What had perplexed me the most was Tuleram's khel, his "trance". When I watch the footage of Tuleram going into a trance at the Manu temple and the Ghatotkacha tree, I am still astonished by the strangeness of the events.

My editor, a couple of members of my crew and I slow the footage to closely examine Tuleram's body movements. We observe how his feet begin trembling slightly and then see the tremors taking over his body until he is shaking uncontrollably. Tuleram's changing expressions and voice, the glazed look in his eyes seem completely genuine.

"There is no way that he could be faking this!" an assistant director, Avantika, emphatically declares, and everyone tends to agree with her.

In an attempt to understand this mysterious phenomenon, I take a deep dive into research. Over the next couple of months I scour bookshops, physical and virtual libraries and the internet to put my hands on authentic and peer-reviewed material. Hours of reading and studying unfamiliar worlds is a fascinating albeit intense experience. To put it briefly, what I discover is that shamanism and the phenomena of trance are not uncommon at all!

Anthropological evidence reveals that shamanic traditions are a universal form of cultural practice around the globe. They represent humanity's earliest spiritual practices going back about 30,000 to 60,000 years. Shamanism thus predates all known organised religions.

There are several broad domains of shamanic practices that include African, Siberian, Mongolian, Native South and North American, Asian-Pacific and Australian. Broadly, each region of the world that had a shamanic belief system practised trance possession. Many regions in India continue to practise shamanism today.

The word shaman has its etymological roots in the language of the Sym Evenki peoples of the Tungus region of southwestern Siberia where the word šamán means "one who knows".

The Oxford English Dictionary defines a shaman as "someone who has access to and influence in the world of benevolent and malevolent spirits; a shaman typically enters into a state of trance during a ritual, and practises divination and healing."

Mircea Eliade, Romanian professor at the University of Chicago (1907–86) and a historian of religions and religious phenomenon, described shamanism as "a cultural practice that has no fixed religion or dogma". Shamans and the belief system of their communities are linked to their particular, and peculiar, mythologies. This is why, for instance, shamanism practised in South America presents itself quite differently from shamanic practices in other parts of the world.

However, wherever shamanism has been practised, there has been belief in the existence of other realities: worlds or dimensions other than the one that we experience in our everyday lives. It is strongly connected to nature and affirms that a universal web of life, power or energy connects and supports all life. And, since all life forms—humans, animals, trees, mountains, wind, oceans, et al—are interconnected, a mutually supportive balance and harmony amongst them is essential for human well-being.

While shamanic practices are diverse, one common pathway involves the phenomenon of intentional induction of a trance, or "altered state of consciousness". This phrase was first used by Dr Charles Tart, American psychologist and parapsychologist, to describe those mental states in which people feel that the quality of how they experience the world is different from ordinary awareness. Our normal, waking consciousness, or ordinary state of consciousness, is but one specific type of consciousness. Trance is an altered state of consciousness that is transitory.

Who goes into trance? Everyone. Everyone experiences some altered states spontaneously, as the ability to shift from one level of consciousness to another is wired into the human brain. Altered states of consciousness include a wide variety of experiences, such as the limitation of consciousness, powerful focus and the liberation of the unconscious.

On any given day people experience these trance states. For instance, the limitation of consciousness, through focus on reading, working on a computer, watching an engrossing film or sport, requires a mental focus so complete that we lose awareness of ourselves and our body.

Dreaming is another altered state that we all experience spontaneously. We perceive these altered states as being ordinary because everyone engages in them. These altered states of consciousness are considered beneficial for the human psyche. However, states of trance can be deliberately induced by using a variety of techniques that include prayer, religious rituals, meditation, pranayama, music, dancing, drumming, fasting or the consumption of psychotropic drugs. It is interesting that throughout history techniques for invoking shamanic trance have been extensively cultivated and revered.

Shamanic trance is a volitional, self-induced state of altered consciousness. I found an extensive documented history of shamanic trance, as evidenced by case studies of anthropologists, ethnologists and experts from associated disciplines.

Nishimura (1987) described three types of shamanic trance, although they are not always distinct:

1. Ecstatic trance, in which the shaman's spirit purportedly leaves the body and communicates with animal or other spirits in their domains;
2. Possession trance, in which animal or other spirits enter the shaman's body, sometimes to the exclusion of the self;
3. Dreamlike trance, in which the shaman remains in possession of the self and meets animal or other spirits in a shared domain.

Essentially, a shaman goes into trance to access a larger field of consciousness, known by many names: the sacred realm, the mythic realm, the collective unconscious, God, the great mystery, etc. Shamans in trance gain access to this field of consciousness, beyond three-dimensional space, where they are connected with a collective experience and a store of wisdom that spans time. "His or her trance consciousness enables communion with the spirit energy of the universe."

Shamanic trance occurs in a cultural context. The community's belief systems give meaning to the shamanic rituals and ceremonies that precede and accompany a shamanic trance, the most important being music.

Throughout the world shamans have used music to invoke trance. The function of music is to provide atmosphere, to evoke identification processes in groups and to induce a trance. Anthropologists and other researchers have documented the similarity of shamanistic auditory rituals among different cultures. The usage of repetitive rhythms to induce trance states is an ancient phenomenon. What research has revealed is that the body rhythms of the listeners entrain with the rhythms embedded in shamanic music.

This is why rhythmic drumming remains at the core of shamanic music. The knowledge that our brainwave patterns are influenced by rhythm is something humans understand instinctively, I guess. I wonder about this at length. Entrainment is the synchronisation of our body's rhythmic cycles, such as breathing, heartbeat and, more importantly, our brainwave activity to a particular pattern.

There are four principal brainwave states—beta (15–40 cycles a second), alpha (9–14 cycles a second), theta (5–8 cycles a second) and delta (1.5–4 cycles a second)—common to all humans. Research shows that when our brain is actively engaged in mental activities, it generates beta waves. The alpha frequency happens when our mind slows in rest or meditation. Delta frequencies denote sleep, and dreamless sleep generates a theta frequency. Interestingly, the theta frequency of brainwaves also denotes daydreaming or deep meditation, which are other altered states of consciousness.

Drumming at the rate of four to seven beats per second will tend to slow down brainwaves to a theta rhythm—a corresponding four to seven cycles per second—thus putting the listeners into an altered state of consciousness that's characteristic of many meditative disciplines.

What fascinates me about this knowledge is the realisation of the importance of music and rhythm in entraining our brains to a theta frequency. This is the frequency where all the magic happens!

I am reminded of an incident that had taken place a few days earlier. While editing a sequence, my editor abruptly walked out of the studio holding his head. When asked what the matter was, he responded, "While I was editing Tuleram's trance sequence and laying down the audio track, I suddenly felt hypnotised ... like I too was going into a trance!"

I realise now that what had happened was brainwave entrainment. By continuously listening to the music and drumming that the bajantris played while Tuleram was invoking a divine possession, the editor's brain had entrained to those rhythms that induce an altered state of consciousness. Subsequently this was my personal experience too. My editing stints without taking breaks became much shorter!

On further reflection I realise why rave parties and trance music are so popular in cosmopolitan cultures. The music usually played at such events have rhythmic drumming that entrains brainwaves into trance states, which can be enjoyable and provide some outlet to pent-up psychic energies.

Scientific advancement and new technologies, like computerised EEG, regional cerebral blood flow, and nuclear magnetic resonance imaging, have documented similar neuro physiological markers in diverse trance states, including yoga and shamanic practices, Zen Buddhist and transcendental meditation, psychedelic experiences associated with hallucinogenic drugs, mediumship/psychography, hypnosis and shamanic states.

A glimmer of intellectual understanding dawns. I realise why the ability to enter a state of trance (or altered consciousness, or theta brainwaves) is so important to becoming a shaman; which is why the ability to enter some form of trance is universal in shamans worldwide.

The world over, shamans have played pivotal roles in their communities as healers, oracles, medicine men and even psychotherapists for healing their community, gaining knowledge, dialoguing with spirits and mythic beings, and living in greater harmony with the earth. The noted Indian psychoanalyst Dr Sudhir Kakar, in his study of religious psychology, writes, "The Shaman is a religious specialist who connects his community with everything that is sacred and gives meaning to life. He is the mediator between the supernatural and the community who makes the desires of one known to the other."

Therefore shamans—whom we in the supposedly civilised world have called "medicine men" and "witch doctors"—are vital members of their communities.

Shamans have for centuries revered and practised the tribal techniques encoded in the compilation of rituals, mantras, laws and genealogy. Their compilations take on a life of their own, a self-replicating power that compels its people, for their welfare and protection, to keep repeating its prescribed words and acts.

I am amazed at the sophistication of the idea of preserving techniques by embedding them into religious practices and rituals. What is even more amazing is to realise that our ancient forebears had scientific knowledge of the human brain that modern science is only just beginning to learn. It is humbling to realise how much instinctual wisdom we have lost in our industrialised, cosmopolitan worlds. In most shamanic communities worldwide, this wisdom has been passed down through generations by being embedded in shamanic practices.

The dismissal of shamanism as primitive mysticism is a glaring example of colonial anthropology. Shamanism has not just been scientifically disparaged, it has also been politically oppressed, suppressed and forbidden by hierarchical systems throughout the world and in every known period.

Unfortunately, that is why most of us with mainstream education are ill-informed about our own cultural ethnology and traditional culture. For most of us cultural outsiders, an intellectual understanding is perhaps all we may experience, and without the lived experience of a particular culture, can we really appreciate it? Shamanic culture is a form of consciousness that may at first seem strange and foreign. Yet, it is nonetheless oddly familiar, stirring memories of a time when we all understood without reflection whatever our senses encountered; the rocks, trees, animals, wind, rain, sun, moon, all of which were alive with their own intelligent spirits and guardian deities to protect them.

After this research and acquiring something of an understanding, albeit an intellectual one, I am keen to explore Dev Bhoomi once again. Armed with new awareness and knowledge, I hope to be able to see it with different eyes. What I am about to discover will push my "intellectual understanding" of the Goors; another veil will lift, allowing me to enter a deeper world.

Segment 2
Cosmic Conversations

"Trance mediums work in partnership with the spirit of the god they represent and completely efface their own individual personalities. The medium personally alters his or her state of consciousness and allows the spirit of the god to take over. They do not remember what they experience while in trance, as they speak in the voice of the god."

– **Uma Singh, *Between Worlds***

Goor Tuli, medium of Devi Navdurga, in a violent divine possession trance, 2008

Goor Tuli channelling and speaking as Devi Navdurga to her devotees, 2008

Goor Tuli channelling and speaking as Devi Navdurga to her devotees, 2008

Goor Tuli channelling and speaking as Devi Navdurga to Anu Malhotra and Mehar Chand, 2008

al is said to have slithered out by breaking the upper
of the bhaandal, and even today this part of a bhaandal
ed on his rath during processions, a symbol of his escape.
e eighteen serpents are said to have scattered across various
s of Kullu, where they are worshipped in Naag temples. It is
id that the bhaandal kept at the deity's temple in Goshal is
me one that the serpents broke out of.

Goor Hardayal and the Goor of Shandil Rishi conduct a ritual propitiation for their deities at a festival at Shuru village, 2008

Goor Hardayal conducting a poochh (divination session) for devotees, 2008

Goor Hardayal performing a Devkhel with the Goor of Devta Shandil Rishi, 2008

Anu Malhotra filming a private poochh (divination session) with Goor Tej Singh, a medium of the Naag Devta of Halan village, who is in a divine possession trance, 2008

The Myth of Naag Devta

According to myth, Naag Devtas, or divine serpents, underworld (paatal). Their kingdom is said to stretch fro to Kashmir, passing through the district of Mandi, th and into Lahaul and Jammu. In the Kullu region eightee deities are worshipped across various towns and villages.

According to one legend, the powerful Naag Devt Naag, came to rest near the village of Goshal after an inter where he defeated Jadyali Rakshas at Jadyali Nalah. He st village home where the young daughter of the family, Sul fell in love with him. Basuki Naag decided to marry her a to the rituals of a Gandharva marriage. He declared that mother eighteen Naag sons; and exactly as he foreto months, the girl gave birth to eighteen male serpent housed them in a large clay vessel, known as bhaan dialect. She then began worshipping them, devote milk every day.

One day, Sulakshana went out for some erra entered the room where the bhaandal was ke no knowledge of Sulakshana's offspring and the bhaandal. Startled upon seeing the sna burning coals she was carrying into the ve to extinguish the flames by pouring milk serpents, fearing for their lives, broke o

Goor Hardayal and the Goor of Shandil Rishi conduct a ritual propitiation for their deities at a festival at Shuru village, 2008

Goor Hardayal conducting a poochh (divination session) for devotees, 2008

Goor Hardayal performing a Devkhel with the Goor of Devta Shandil Rishi, 2008

Anu Malhotra filming a private poochh (divination session) with Goor Tej Singh, a medium of the Naag Devta of Halan village, who is in a divine possession trance, 2008

The Myth of Naag Devtas

According to myth, Naag Devtas, or divine serpents, ruled the underworld (paatal). Their kingdom is said to stretch from Shimla to Kashmir, passing through the district of Mandi, then Kullu and into Lahaul and Jammu. In the Kullu region eighteen serpent deities are worshipped across various towns and villages.

According to one legend, the powerful Naag Devta, Basuki Naag, came to rest near the village of Goshal after an intense battle where he defeated Jadyali Rakshas at Jadyali Nalah. He stayed in a village home where the young daughter of the family, Sulakshana, fell in love with him. Basuki Naag decided to marry her according to the rituals of a Gandharva marriage. He declared that she would mother eighteen Naag sons; and exactly as he foretold, after ten months, the girl gave birth to eighteen male serpents. Sulakshana housed them in a large clay vessel, known as bhaandal in the local dialect. She then began worshipping them, devotedly giving them milk every day.

One day, Sulakshana went out for some errands and her mother entered the room where the bhaandal was kept. Her mother had no knowledge of Sulakshana's offspring and happened to open the bhaandal. Startled upon seeing the snakes, she dropped the burning coals she was carrying into the vessel. Even as she tried to extinguish the flames by pouring milk into the bhaandal, the serpents, fearing for their lives, broke out of the vessel. Naag

Dhumbal is said to have slithered out by breaking the upper portion of the bhaandal, and even today this part of a bhaandal is carried on his rath during processions, a symbol of his escape.

The eighteen serpents are said to have scattered across various villages of Kullu, where they are worshipped in Naag temples. It is also said that the bhaandal kept at the deity's temple in Goshal is the same one that the serpents broke out of.

7

Goor Hardayal, Oracular Shaman

Two months later, in July, I am back in Manali. Weeks of research and editing footage have allowed me to grasp nuances and details that I had missed while filming. I realise that what I have captured is rare and valuable material that has remained hidden in plain sight of travellers to Himachal.

The monsoons are in full swing, and each night brings a torrential downpour that thunders on the sloped roof of my cottage. Thankfully, it usually clears up by morning, unveiling treetops swathed in drifting mists and clouds settling low in the valleys. When I step out, the humus squelches beneath my keds and every leaf is dripping. Village children in bright gumboots splash their way through puddles.

Meanwhile, Meru too has been busy making arrangements for me to pursue my quest of meeting other Goors. "In Shuru village there is a powerful Devi and her Goor is also very strong. It is not far from here, so we can go there tomorrow," he says. We set off the next day for Shuru, just five kilometres from the Manali Bazaar. As we drive up a steep mountain road, Meru fills me in on Sharvari Devi, the goddess after whom Shuru is named: "She is a manifestation of the Goddess Parvati, the consort of Lord Shiva. She is an extremely powerful goddess known for her immense healing powers and benevolence. And Hardayal is her Goor."

I gather that Hardayal is a popular oracle and adept at magico-religious practices. Meru says, "People go for their healings … like, whatever problems they have, they go and do the poochh there."

"What's the poochh?" I ask.

"A poochh is when you ask a question of the Devi. The questions are answered through the Goor."

"So, does he go into a trance then?"

Meru nods. We pass orchards brimming with fruit-laden apple, pear, peach, and plum trees; we pass one- and two-storey small brick-and-cement houses and typical village chai shops and arrive at where we have to disembark.

We ascend a flight of stairs at the top of which is an arch embedded with figures of Lord Shiva and Goddess Parvati. Meru rings the bronze bell suspended from a long chain before we walk into a smallish compound with cemented stepped seating leading to a large, tiled courtyard in front of the temple.

Shuru Temple is the charming double-storeyed abode of Devi Sharvari, traditionally built of wood and stone. The gabled roof and veranda are completely wooden. The veranda's pillars have elaborate wooden carvings of deities and decorative flower patterns. On the gable, the carvings depict Devis Parvati and Sharvari, the benevolent aspects of Shakti. The temple is fronted by a large, cemented compound edged by a railing that overlooks the valley. Colourful temple flags mounted on tall poles flutter merrily, and the view from here is magnificent.

As we look out at the verdant valley and tall mountains across, a middle-aged man wearing a kurta, dhoti and Kullu cap walks towards us and greets us warmly. He has an odd wrinkle, a few missing teeth, a headful of grey hair and a pleasant manner.

Meru introduces me to Pandit Tikaram, the temple priest. We exchange a few pleasantries before he escorts us inside the complex for the Devi's darshan. I ring the bell and walk onto the veranda where an idol of Goddess Kali sits ensconced in her own little wooden temple. We pay obeisance to her before stepping inside. A resplendently dressed metal idol of Devi Sharvari is placed in a tiny sanctum at the far edge. Meru and I sit outside while Tikaram takes my offerings—comprising a coconut, flowers, sweets and a red chunni—enters the shrine and touches them to the idol's feet. He brings out some agarbattis for us to light, puts a tikka on our foreheads and offers us prasad to eat.

I notice that Sharvari Devi's idol has a very sweet face, looking every bit the benevolent goddess she is known to be. I bow my head in respect, close my eyes and open my heart to try and commune with her. I feel a peaceful energy emanating from this sacred space and lose track of time. When I look up I find Tikaram smiling at me. He says in a kind tone, "Madam-ji, our Devi is very kind. If you ask for anything with a pure heart, she usually gives it to you."

Tikaram points to a squat metal container that is almost entirely full of ash, "This is the Devi's havankund, where all our havans take place. You know," he says, opening his eyes wide, "this is the source of Sharvari Devi's power. This ash has never been removed after a havan for hundreds of years, and yet there is never an overflow of ash; it disappears on its own! Isn't it a miracle?"

We step down into the courtyard, and Tikaram takes us to a corner where an ancient stone idol of Mahishasurmardini stands draped with puja paraphernalia. "This Devi is a form of Kali, so all animal sacrifices are made to her. Sharvari Devi is a sagun, benevolent, goddess and does not accept any blood sacrifice."

Meru picks up that I am about to ask Tikaram a torrent of questions about animal sacrifice and hurriedly changes the subject. He tells Pandit-ji about my documentary and my desire to see and film the poochh session at Shuru. At the mention of filming, Tikaram's amiable manner changes abruptly. He refuses point-blank. "No, no, that is not possible, madam. You are welcome to watch our poochh, but you cannot film it." He speaks to Meru now, a tone of accusation heavy in his voice, "You know this, Meru. No outsider has ever been allowed to film our Devi's rituals!"

I invite Tikaram to have tea with us at the chai shop where I plan to continue my pleading. He agrees. However, Tikaram remains adamant about the documentation. Finally, Meru speaks to him in Kullvi, telling him why it is important for us to document their culture, how I have good intentions and, above all, how even Hadimba Devi had granted permission to film her entire birthday celebrations.

I pipe in, "Pandit-ji, why don't you just ask Devi whether she will give us permission?"

Meru reiterates my request, and after an hour of intense discussion Tikaram agrees to ask the Devi. He tells us that he will let us know the verdict this evening.

I am restless all evening, but there's no news from Tikaram. I prepare myself for a negative response. However, the next morning Meru calls to inform me that he has been called to Shuru in order to ask the Devi's permission for filming. I am elated and exclaim, "How wonderful, Meru! What time do we have to be there?"

Meru chuckles at my enthusiasm. "Not you, Anu," he says, to my disappointment, "only I have to go for the pogley."

I ask him, "What is a pogley?"

But Meru is in a hurry. "Later," he says, "I will explain later. For now, you just sit and pray that we get the Devi's permission."

I am excited and anxious, fervently hoping that we get to film the poochh. I make a prayer to Sharvari Devi asking for her grace. I also pause to reflect how, though I am approaching and viewing the phenomenon of divine possession trance through a psycho-scientific lens, I am constantly crossing the mental line between scepticism and belief. I do realise, though, that perhaps it is not possible to arrive at any meaningful understanding of such a subtle field of experience without a personal degree of subjectivity. As I wait for Meru's call, I sift through some research that Avantika has put together from talking to Sharvari Devi's kardar.

It turns out that Sharvari Devi and Hadimba Devi have an interesting connection. Folklore has it that Hadimba had won her Devi status by praying devoutly to both Sharvari Devi and Kali Ma for twelve years before the goddesses were impressed and elevated her to divinity. The kardar had told Avantika an interesting tale. Since Hadimba was a devotee of Sharvari Devi, even today whenever Hadimba Devi enters Shuru village, her rath is lowered so that the hanging cloth at the back gives an impression of sweeping the floor of the area belonging to her Devi, a symbolic gesture harking back to when Hadimba as a disciple would sweep the area before conducting her prayers to Sharvari Devi. However, Hadimba Devi can never come face-to-face with Sharvari Devi, for then she would be reduced to a mere disciple.

I mull over the strange and wonderful mythology of Dev Bhoomi, increasingly enjoying its romantic appeal. My mobile rings; it's Meru. "Sorry, Anu," he begins.

"Oh no!" I exclaim, ready to begin lamenting when he laughs merrily and repeats: "Yes, sorry, Anu that you don't have time to prepare. We have permission to film tomorrow morning's poochh. So, get your act together!"

I do an imaginary jig in my head and thank the Devi for her graciousness. I am excited to go and discover another aspect of Kullu shamanism and of the living gods who communicate so readily with their people.

The next morning Meru, my crew and I are back in Sharvari Devi's temple in Shuru. Meru promises to explain the pogley later and instructs me to watch carefully for now.

It's a sunny day. The only people out in the temple courtyard are Tikaram and a couple of devotees. Meru tells me that people from Shuru can consult the Goor of Sharvari Devi, Hardayal, individually on any day. Special poochh sessions, however, are held on two days, Tuesdays and Sundays, when those from elsewhere are also allowed to attend.

Tikaram greets me warmly. His eyes are twinkling. "I told you na, Madam-ji?" he boasts, though in a reassuring manner. "Our Devi is so kind that she's granted your request, though this is a first!"

I thank him, and he takes us to pay our respects to the Devi inside the temple. As we wait for Goor Hardayal to arrive, I notice that more locals have started to trickle into the temple compound.

Soon, a stocky middle-aged man with a thick black moustache and pleasant face strides in. He has a prominent overbite that makes him look stern, but when he smiles, he looks quite jovial. Hardayal is wearing a spotless, cream Goor's robe and his hair is tidily tucked into his Kullu topi. A couple rush towards him and respectfully touch his feet. Hardayal greets them cheerfully, frequently flashing his buck-toothed smile and laughing. Eager to meet him, I urge Tikaram to make an introduction.

"Not now, the poochh is about to begin. You may meet him afterwards," Tikaram says.

I observe Hardayal from one end of the compound, noting his easy and nonchalant manner. He seems so different from Tuleram; he does not have the intense aura one would expect of a figure of authority. His manner is relaxed and casual.

Soon, Hardayal goes to the stone idol of Mahishasurmardini and rests his head at its feet for several minutes. He then moves towards a wide cemented platform close to the bottom of the temple steps and sits down cross-legged. At least thirty or so people have gathered in a circle around him. Tikaram emerges from the temple with a bell and smoking dharj, and hands both to Hardayal, placing a mound of rice on a piece of paper before him.

Meru urges me forward with my handycam, whispering, "The poochh is about to begin."

I feel a frisson of excitement as I note Hardayal's intense expression when he shuts his eyes and becomes very still. The entire crowd is silent in expectation.

Hardayal opens his eyes, picks up some flowers and throws them in all four directions. He then begins to ring the bell loudly whilst deeply inhaling the juniper incense from the dharj. He puts the bell down and begins chanting some mantras under his breath. Tikaram sits in front of him, ringing the bell stridently in measured beats. The atmosphere of anticipation is palpable.

Hardayal plucks a hair from his forehead uttering, "Praise the Devi!" He then puts a piece of juniper in his mouth, his head bends downwards then backwards, his topi falls off and someone catches it before it touches the ground. Hardayal's hair is let loose, and I'm surprised to see how thick, long and wavy his mane is. Hardayal's eyes are still closed, and his expression is of complete self-absorption as he caresses his hair, moving his head from side to side. Tikaram stops ringing the bell and stares at Hardayal. I am holding my breath wondering: Is he going into a trance now?

I watch Hardayal intently and notice a tremor growing in his hands. Soon his hands and eventually his arms begin shaking uncontrollably. Suddenly he shrieks a long-drawn "Eeeaaaaakkk!" His eyes shoot open, his hair flies across his face and his body leaps about three feet upwards ... still seated cross-legged! I stumble backwards in shock, startled by the energy, intensity and spontaneity of that moment. Meru steadies me and picks up my handycam which I had dropped in panic.

Goor Hardayal's whole body is shaking uncontrollably, his eyes protrude, and his expression has become fierce. He is unmistakably in a state of trance, and I am once again astounded by the complete change in persona of the man. Tikaram and everyone else present greet their Devi reverently.

Hardayal blows on the incense burner and begins to speak in a loud and high-pitched tone, recollecting the Devi's history. Meru keeps whispering his interpretation of all that is being said. I would by and by learn that most divine possession trances begin with the recitation of the God's history and mythology.

Sharvari Devi via Goor Hardayal: "I come from Shuru village. I am omnipresent. I exist in all four directions. I am present in

Gautam Rishi, Manu Rishi, Vyas Rishi, Shandil Rishi and Shringa Rishi. I am with all eighteen Naag Devtas. I am present in Malana, Chandragani, Shirgan, inside Faah, the Jayadhara waterfall, Doga, Chand Choraha, the Soyil waterfall, Hamta, Sukh Soha, Red Bhadke, Mangodi, Indrakile, Jalodijot, Indrasoh, the Athara Kardu, inside the house, in water, inside a girl, inside a Brahmin's house—wherever I am, I have now come out. I speak the truth no matter the circumstances."

Almost immediately a couple sitting in front of me begin talking to Hardayal, or rather to their Devi:

Woman: "Devi, we have been suffering for a long time."

Man: "We are both sick all the time. The doctors say there is no illness, but we are in bad shape."

Woman: "Devi, please tell us what to do. Please speak!"

Devi via Goor: "I have come from afar. I have always blessed you. Whoever comes asking, I fulfil all their wishes."

Hardayal becomes silent but continues blowing on the dharj, smoking up the smouldering juniper, while rocking his body and head from side to side, eyes closed. The couple persist with their pleading.

Man: "Devi, you will have to tell us what to do."

Woman: "If you don't tell us, we will keep sitting here."

Man: "Devi, please speak! If we have committed any mistake, please tell us!"

Woman: "Please, Mother, talk to us!"

It seems like a conversation between two errant children and their irritated mother who is not willing to hear them out.

Devi via Goor: "You have made mistakes."

Woman: "Devi, we are sorry for our mistakes."

Suddenly the bell that Hardayal has picked up begins to clang loudly as his shaking hands tremble violently. He opens his eyes, which are bloodshot and ablaze with anger. Devi Sharvari is clearly angry and screams at the couple who are talking to her.

Devi via Goor: "You have lost faith in me, and you have even stopped praying to me! I have always blessed you and your people and fulfilled all your wishes. You, however, have not done what I told you to do!"

Man: "We make mistakes! We are human after all. We beg your forgiveness."

Woman: "Yes, we faltered in carrying out your suggestions, Mother, but we will do as you ask now. Please forgive and bless us!"

The couple request the forgiveness of their Devi with joined hands, bowing their heads in penitence, but the Devi is unrelenting.

Devi via Goor: "I always give you more than you desire; I protect your household and will continue to fulfil your wishes. If I fail, do not revere me."

Man: "No, no! You are our mother. To whom else can we turn but you?"

Woman: "Mata, please, we ask you to help us. We have no peace at home."

Devi via Goor: "Yes, you are my children. I will always take care of you. So, let me tell you the cause of all the unexplained illness and misfortune in your home: it is an oprah."

Black magic!

Man: "Devi, what shall we do?"

Woman: "Mata, please remove it!"

Devi via Goor: "Someone wishes bad times upon you."

Woman: "If these are bad wishes, who has done this to us? Mata, please tell us."

Devi via Goor: "Some near and dear ones that you also know of, and I also know of."

Woman: "Mata, if they are near ones then only you can do something. We are helpless."

Devi via Goor: "I will try to bring everything in front of you. I will take away all your problems and throw them far away from you."

Hardayal takes three flowers and forms a triangle on the ground with them, then picks up one flower, waves it over their heads and throws it behind them. The man puts a few grains of rice in Hardayal's hand, which the Goor studies intently.

"This is a form of divination," Meru whispers in my ear.

Devi via Goor: "Visit me again and I will tell you what to do. In the meantime, observe the taboos I have told you about."

Man and woman: "Thank you, Mother! Praise be to the Devi!"

The couple stand and walk to the back of the crowd. Later I will see them discussing their interaction with Tikaram, as Hardayal will not remember what had transpired.

It is now the turn of the only man in the crowd dressed in Western clothing to speak to the Devi. His branded t-shirt and fashionable jeans are anomalies here, and I am curious to hear what he wants to say.

Man: "Mata, you know that my business is in the doldrums. You had asked me to come back, and I have. Please help me now."

Devi via Goor: "I will keep you protected. All I need is your devotion."

The man joins his hands, bows his head to the ground and grovels in devotion.

Man: "You have always done that, Mata. Please help me! Please revive my business!"

Devi via Goor: "I am very powerful. I can even make a lame person walk on two feet, I can straighten a hunchback if I want to and my power remains unchanged. I will crush all the malignant spirits under my feet."

Man: "You asked me to come again. Please tell me what to do, Mata."

Devi via Goor: "I take great care of you and fulfil every wish you make. You make your wishes in the evening and by morning they come true."

Man: "Devi, you are still as powerful, and I am devoted to you, but what did I do wrong? Please tell me."

Once again Hardayal's face contorts. He flings back his hair and his body jerks violently as he begins screaming in seething anger.

Devi via Goor: "I asked you to give up excessive drinking. Did you do that? I asked you to maintain peace and harmony at home. Did you do that?"

Hardayal's voice thunders, and the man looks crestfallen. It is obvious to everyone present that the man had certainly not done as the Devi had commanded.

Devi via Goor: "Devotion! You promise me devotion, yet you do not listen to me! You do not obey my commands."

Man: "Devi, believe me, I adore you! I will do as you say, Mata."

Devi via Goor: "Come back when you have done my bidding, then I will help you."

The Devi dismisses him, and another man moves forward and sits in front of the Goor.

As the Devi chastises him, I am amazed that people do not seem to mind being called out for their bad behaviour in front of so many others! This openness in discussing personal problems in the presence of the community is commonplace in the valley. Bonds of togetherness ensure easy familiarity and comfort among the hill folk, I believe. I wonder how much of that has to do with these rather public poochh sessions.

Hardayal picks up some rice from the sheet of paper in front of him and places it in the man's hand. Meru tells me later that reading rice grains blessed by the Devi is also a way of prophesying; odd and even numbers of grains signify positive or negative results respectively. The grains that Hardayal has placed in the man's hand are an odd number, so Tikaram tells him that the Devi felt that his problem would be over soon if he does as the Devi has instructed. The man reverently praises the Devi.

The other local people who had been sitting patiently through the first interactions begin addressing the Devi with their individual issues. The range of problems put forth to the goddess vary from serious issues like illnesses, accidents, bankruptcy, to simpler ones like setting dates for weddings, approvals for potential marriage partners, disharmony at home or even interpersonal issues.

The Devi's devotees have come to their mother with full faith, with problems that range from physical and mental health, financial, and career-related, to familial and community-related issues. The Devi's suggestions and solutions can range from herbal cures, behavioural changes and pujas to animal sacrifices and even exorcisms.

The Devi answers each petition to the individual supplicant's satisfaction by giving them diagnoses and suggestions. Although the format of pleading with their Devi remains the same, I do observe that there seems to be an ease in their conversations, a certain intimacy as if they were really speaking to a loved one and not a figure of authority. There seems to be very little distance between the mortal and the divine.

I notice that the Devi does not provide any solution right away. In fact, people who are visiting for the first time are almost always asked to take another appointment. Meru explains later that continued visits are often ordered by the Devi to both test and ensure the faith of her devotees.

What I have witnessed today is truly akin to conversations with a goddess! It is extraordinary. The locals have a hotline to an intimate deity from whom they seek advice as they would from a family elder. I watched the Devi and her Goor play the roles of doctor, psychiatrist, counsellor, astrologer, life coach and spiritual guide.

I ponder intently on the poochh until Meru shakes me out of my reverie. "Anu, the poochh is over, but you should interview the last lady who spoke to the Devi. She knows Hindi well, so you will understand what she has to say, and I think you will find it interesting."

Meru's last remark intrigues me, and I walk across to where my crew has already set up cameras for the interview. Meru introduces me to Kala, a youngish pretty woman dressed in a salwar-kameez, who has come here from a nearby village. I remember her being the last person at the poochh, but since she was speaking in Kullvi, I just stepped aside to take photographs.

I invite Kala for a glass of chai over which I ask why she has come for the poochh. She tells me that her family is facing a lot of problems. Most of them are falling sick. Her younger sisters feel they are often being gripped by an unseen force even though there is no one around. The family also hears sounds of footsteps and doors being slammed when there is no one walking. They have been turned into nervous wrecks with these mysterious incidents, which they feel are a result of a ghost haunting their home. Kala seems quite terrified. "I am afraid that if things get any worse, the ghost will finish off our entire family!"

Although I don't know what to make of Kala's story, I am concerned because she sounds so distressed. I ask, "What did the Goor, I mean Devi, say to you?"

Kala replies, "The Devi deduced that my home is being haunted by a ghost called Narsingh and that an exorcism is necessary."

I am curious. "But, if you have so many problems at home why don't you all consult the Devi of your own village?"

"I came here for the poochh because there is no Goor in my village. Our Devta has not chosen anyone to be his Goor for seven years, so even though our Devta knows our problems, he cannot speak to us. If only we had a Goor, we could talk to our own Devta," murmurs Kala tearfully. She adds, "Coming to Shuru and speaking to the Devi has given me great comfort."

The people of Dev Bhoomi want to speak often to their Devtas through the Goors. This frequent access to the divine realm gives meaning and context to their everyday lives and addresses their fears, sorrows and concerns. Kala's story is certainly an unusual one, and I have lots of questions for Meru. We thank Tikaram and enquire about Hardayal but are told that he has left. I tell Tikaram that I am keen on interviewing the Goor, and to my delight he assures me that he will fix a meeting with Hardayal soon.

We leave Shuru village and drive to Meru's home for a late lunch. The poochh session has greatly fascinated my crew as well who are deep in discussion about Hardayal's uncanny leap in the air and the issues that had cropped up in the poochh, particularly Kala's ghost story.

After lunch we go over the footage of the poochh and are again stunned at Hardayal's spectacular jump. We all sit down together and ask Meru to encapsulate the events of the poochh and explain certain things.

Meru reiterates that everything in the lives of the devotees depends upon their village Devta. He stands and beckons us, "Okay, come with me. Let me show you something." We follow Meru out of his family home and walk through the village to a site where his new home is being constructed. Meru points to the works. "The foundation is being laid, but before beginning the work we invited our Devta to bless it. The next invitation to him will be before the roof is laid. Every step of building this house will be blessed by our Devta."

As we walk back, Meru explains that even the making of the shrine that the house will contain and the consecration of the Kul Devta, or clan deity, would be overseen by the Devta so that it is done following his guidelines. Lastly the Devta will be consulted when the stove is being installed as the kitchen is considered central to a Kullu home. The family will move in after an opening ceremony is held. All these steps will ensure that the house has good energy, and that the Devta is looking out for the family.

Meru concludes, "Consulting our deities in all aspects of our lives is very much part of our traditional culture here in the Kullu Valley and has been since time immemorial. We conduct our lives according to the guidelines laid down by the Devta. That is why our Goors are so important as it is through them that we can speak directly to our Devtas."

Avantika pipes in, "So, every time you want to ask your Devta something, the Goor has to conduct a poochh and go into trance?"

Meru replies, "No, no, the Goors know several methods of divination. We also have other forms of prophecy."

I remember the pogley (divination ceremony) that had informed Tikaram of Sharvari Devi's acquiescence to our filming and ask about it. Meru seems lost in thought, but finally says, "See, you all come from a completely different culture. I'm sure it's difficult for you to understand ours, so I suggest that we attend more poochhes and interview more Goors. Then you may be better able to understand and appreciate our way of life."

Wise words, I think, as I continue to mull over the day's events. There is so much I want to ask Meru, particularly about the oprah, or black magic, and the Narsingh ghost. I am also intrigued by Hardayal whom I hope to meet soon to know his story and prowess as a Goor.

I have become aware of a subtle shift within my mind, a shift beyond a mere intellectual understanding of the Devta system of these hill communities. Meru's advice was indeed sage: Knowledge can only be truly transmitted through the experiential.

8
Poochh Sessions and Divinations

Goor Hardayal starts to ring the Devi's bell. He comes closer, holding the bell right in front of my face, ringing it stridently. Locks of his thick, black hair writhe and twist like live snakes, his eyes stare deeply into mine and his intense expression is frightening. I jump back … and wake up! My mobile is ringing incessantly. I am still groggy as it is only 6 a.m.

"Good morning!" chirps Meru cheerfully over the phone. "Good news … Hardayal has given us time for an interview this morning. I'm coming to pick you up in an hour!"

My grogginess vanishes instantly, and I race to get ready. Soon, we are driving back to Shuru village and as usual Meru uses the time to brief me about the subject of the day.

Hardayal has been a Goor for over twenty years, is married and has three grown-up children. Unlike a majority of Goors in the valley, he does not come from a lineage of Goors. He was chosen quite out of the blue.

Meru and I begin our climb up the long, cemented stairway to the temple. "I can see that you are developing your mountain legs, Anu," Meru jokes, noticing my increasing ease and stamina. I know that Meru is right. I am indeed not just developing my mountain legs but also my mountain eyes, ears and instinct!

We reach the temple precincts where there are several women busy cleaning: polishing the metal idol, scrubbing the floors and sterilising the interiors by applying a layer of cow-dung on the floor. Here too as in more mainstream shrines, seva, or service, is seen as a form of worship.

A short way from the temple, Hardayal's house is a fairly large, two-storey construction made of brick and cement with a spacious courtyard in front. It is clear that Hardayal, unlike Tuleram, is no struggling shaman.

Hardayal's wife and son greet us warmly in the courtyard and rush inside to inform Hardayal as well as to fetch tea and snacks, with typical pahari hospitality. Hardayal walks out with his huge signature smile and easy charming manner, sits down with us on his veranda and begins chatting with seeming candour. We set up to film the interview. After some casual conversation, I ask, "So, Hardayal-ji, please tell me, how and when did you become a Goor?"

"One day I had gone to Shaleen village with a bunch of village folk escorting our Devi, who had then been visiting her brother, Shandil Rishi, after a span of nineteen years. You know, Sharvari Devi originally manifested in Shaleen before she walked and came to Shuru. Anyway, while in Shaleen, I suddenly got into an intense trance. It was a strange experience, but after that incident I did not experience any trance so dismissed it as an aberration. After about a year, during the birthday celebrations of our Devi when several Devtas were visiting, I again got into an intense trance in my house. My parents were alarmed and locked the door from outside, but somehow, I got out and ran, still in a state of trance, straight to the temple. I went and sat next to the Devi's rath. I don't remember this, but I'm told that I was in a heavy trance for a long time after which the Naag Devta from Prini threw off my cap with the handle of his rath, and all the Devtas present accepted me as Sharvari Devi's Goor."

Hardayal is fluent in Hindi and much more lucid than Tuleram. Thus, I am able to converse with him with greater ease, requiring minimum interpretation from Meru. Hardayal declares that he did not have any senior Goor to mentor him; most of the rituals were taught to him directly by the Devi. "The Devi taught me the rituals." This is exactly what Tuleram had said.

I interrupt Hardayal. "Sorry to interrupt, Goor-ji, but how did the Devi teach you the rituals?"

Hardayal seems unfazed by my rude interjection and responds spontaneously, "Madam-ji, the Devi talks to me according to my need, sometimes during meditation and sometimes by instructing me as I perform a ritual."

Hardayal confesses that his family was just as shocked as he was upon his being declared a Goor. His parents and wife were upset as serving the Devi involves immense hardships and strict taboos. They also knew that Hardayal's priorities would change completely. He could no longer just be a regular householder and farmer; he would be at the Devi's beck and call around the clock.

I am curious about something else Hardayal mentioned: "What taboos do you have to observe as a Goor?"

Hardayal answers, "Well, we have to maintain a high degree of cleanliness in our lifestyle and diet, especially as Sharvari Devi has particularly lofty standards. When my wife was about to give birth, I had to leave the house and stay away for fifteen days. And, when my parents passed away, I had to leave home again and could not perform their last rites."

Meru turns to me and explains the concept of shuddhi, or purity, and jooth, or impurity.

Notions of shuddhi and jooth are found all across Indian society and religions and are often the basis of social hierarchies. For the Goor who is an extension, or limb, of the divine, the taboos are even stricter. Broadly, death, sex, menstruation and childbirth are considered impure. All contact with bodily fluids such as blood, semen, excrement and sweat are polluting and require ritual purification. Apart from these there is a range of dietary taboos and fasts that a Goor must observe to be effective in his temple duties and to be a fit receptacle of the Devta. Failure to comply with these taboos can result in dire consequences for the Goor, his family and the community. Certainly, for a householder like Hardayal these restrictions would be difficult to observe.

"How did that make you feel?" I ask sympathetically.

Hardayal smiles. "I felt a lot of confusion and discomfort in those days, but as time passed, I became used to it."

"Do you feel that a Goor's life is a difficult one?"

Hardayal promptly dismisses the idea. "No, no, it is not like that. For us the Devi and her requirements have the highest priority in our lives." He adds with a chuckle, "The only things I find difficult are walking barefoot through snow, as I feel cold, and eating only once a day when I perform her duties. The rest is my fate, which I accept and enjoy."

Hardayal's financial situation seems quite good. His home is well-furnished, and I can see a cable TV connection jutting out from the roof. His four children, two sons and two daughters, are educated and well-dressed, each sporting a cell phone. I ask him candidly, "So, do you make your living off the earnings of the temple?"

He is just as frank in his response. "No, I don't get money from temple offerings. I get half the money that is offered by people when I do my poochh, the other half goes to the pandit. People who consult me individually also give what they can. I also have earnings from the apple orchard given to me by the Devi. So, by Devi Mata's grace, I have enough to lead a comfortable life."

Meru explains that most village Devtas own land, which they hold legally in their name. The village Devtas have special jurisdiction over their har, or their "territory of influence" within a village. In the seventeenth century, Raja Jagat Singh, a predecessor of the current royal family, gave large pieces of land in every village to the local Devtas who presided over their respective hars. Some of this land was used for cultivation and a tax was paid for it to Lord Raghunath, the ruling deity of Kullu and its erstwhile royal dynasty. This system continued under the British rule until 1972 when Prime Minister Indira Gandhi's government brought in the Himachal Pradesh Tenancy and Land Reforms Act, which allowed cultivators to own the land they worked. As a result, most Devtas were left with only small pieces of uncultivable land. With the success of apple cultivation, these hitherto barren tracts turned productive and became a means of income for those who serve the temple.

All the members of the Devloo have been given pieces of the Devta's land to allow them to sustain themselves as the duties and responsibilities of the temple keep them too busy to earn a regular income. Hardayal was granted an apple orchard, which he maintains with the help of his wife and children. However, having the orchard is a privilege that comes with the status of being part of the Devloo and the Devi's Goor. The lands granted to the Devloo will not stay with their current custodians forever; they will be passed on to whoever will be chosen for the next Devloo. How incredible, I think, and ask Hardayal how he perceives his vocation.

Hardayal joins his palms and lifts them to the sky, saying, "I have received so much respect that I feel quite fulfilled. My aim in life is to serve the Devi and in turn our people."

I now turn our conversation towards the poochh that we had attended yesterday hoping to get some clarity on several issues. I begin by asking how he feels during trance and divine possession.

"I first feel tremors going up my spine and then my body begins to shake."

"And then…?" I prompt him enthusiastically.

"And then I don't remember anything!"

"So, do you not remember what you had said about the oprah and Narsingh?"

"No. I have to ask Pandit-ji about what the Devi said!"

I am disappointed even though I know about a Goor's temporary amnesia during trance. "Okay, please tell me about your various methods of divination; that would help greatly."

Hardayal laughs. "That's a long conversation. I have to go now, but you're welcome to come back and talk with me again." Turning to Meru, he says, "Now that the Devi has given madam permission to film our rituals, I trust there's a good reason she wants it done. I'm happy to oblige."

Speaking with Hardayal makes me realise that it is not the privileges and benefits that come with the position that drive these men to do what they do. Goors receive respect and benefits, but their lives are bound by rules and regulations. They can no longer call their life their own. All decisions are taken by the Devi who controls even the Goor's closest relationships to some extent. Hardayal did not merely accept the Devi's will, he surrendered completely and is content to serve her and her devotees. His work as a Goor is a social service. He has submitted himself to the greater good of the community by speaking or divining the will of his Devi.

Over lunch I question Meru closely about other methods of divination, for as I have learned all methods do not involve trance.

Meru explains, "The Goors of Kullu Valley employ various methods of divination to decipher their Devta's will without having to go into trance. Divine possession trance is something that comes to them mostly at festivals or special occasions when the Devta is out and about on their palanquin or at special pooches, pujas or ceremonies where there is a gathering of people. The everyday methods of divination conducted for individuals or families are of many kinds."

The one that interests me the most is the famed pogley that Meru had spoken about, so I keep pestering him until one day he finds out that Goor Tuleram is scheduled to do a pogley for a woman from Old Manali. "And to ease your anxiety, Anu," he pauses deliberately, smiling at my expectant expression, "I have permission from both the woman and from Tuleram for you to film the divination session."

On the assigned afternoon, I set off excitedly with Meru up the path to the Devi Hadimba Mandir where the pogley is to be conducted. The dappled sunlight through the tall deodars never fails to lift my spirits, and I stop for a while to breathe in the delightful vision.

We find Tuleram sitting in the temple courtyard, chatting animatedly with a local lady sitting across from him. I greet them both, exchange a few pleasantries and sit down beside them. I am meeting Tuleram after a few months, and he turns to me saying exuberantly, "Oho! Are you still filming us? Now you want to film the pogley also. No problem. I will show you how it's done." He gets up and walks away to fetch something.

Several objects are lying on the ground in front of us. There are three plates—one with flowers, the second with rice and the third with ash—and a smallish copper pot filled with water.

I turn to the woman and ask her what it is she wants to know from the Devi. Unfortunately for me she does not speak Hindi, so Meru translates.

The lady's main concern has to do with her daughter's marriage. An attractive girl, she has been receiving numerous marriage proposals from "good" families, with several of them from eligible young men. Despite this, none of the proposals has worked out. The families meet, agree to the match and everything seems fine but something always ends up going wrong. Recently the girl received another suitable marriage proposal. The lady wants to consult the Devi to know whether it will work out this time.

Tuleram comes back carrying some cow-dung in his hand. He proceeds to mix the ash and cow-dung and rolls three small balls. "The balls are called pogley," Meru whispers.

The Goor looks up and addresses me dramatically, "Now see what I'm going to do!" He stuffs one ball with rice, the second with flowers and the third he leaves empty. He points to each pogley ball and explains, "The flower is for a favourable outcome, the rice for a negative outcome and the last empty one means there are obstacles that need to be overcome with the Devi's help."

Tuleram closes his eyes and begins muttering something. I look enquiringly at Meru who whispers that Tuleram is praying to the Devi for an accurate prediction. He explains that the Goor will keep the lady's question in mind while immersing the three pogleys in the water-filled copper pot. One or more of the pogleys will rise to the surface. Tuleram will pick up the floating pogley, open it and check its contents, which will indicate the Devi's answer.

I ask the woman if she has faith in what the ball will reveal. She tells me confidently that a pogley is a very accurate way to receive a prediction from the Devtas. She adds, "We have been using this pogley for generations, so we know from experience just how successful it is." I can sense in her tone her discomfort at being asked this question. After all, her faith in her Devi is absolute.

I focus on Tuleram who is still chanting. Suspense fills the air as he becomes silent, picks up the three pogleys in one hand and drops them simultaneously into the water. All eyes are on the copper pot as the balls sink. One pogley bobs up. The lady's face is anxious as Tuleram takes out the pogley. I find that I am holding my breath while he breaks it open with his fingers. We peer at Tuleram's hand and see that it's the pogley filled with flowers.

There are smiles all round. Tuleram is jubilant. "See, Madam, see! This pogley has flowers, which means that this lady's problem will get sorted out and her daughter will get married. Praise be to the Devi!" The lady smiles as she hands Tuleram some money, touches his feet and proclaims, "Jai, Mata-ji!" Her earlier tense countenance has transformed as she cheerfully waves us goodbye, saying, "I'm rushing to give my family the good news. Do come for the wedding if you are still here."

I ask Tuleram about other methods of divination that he uses besides a pogley or checking grains of rice and black sesame seeds. Tuleram is amused by my avid curiosity and lets out a laugh. "Madam-ji, you want to know everything! Not planning on becoming a Goor, I hope?" He laughs riotously, but reaches into his pocket and takes out a small, narrow, rectangular piece of metal with a few dots etched onto it like a dice. He places it in the palm of his hand and shows it to me. "I also use this to predict or cross-check answers received by other methods."

I reach out to touch it, but Tuleram closes his palm admonishing me, "No, madam, this is only for me to touch and use." Then holding it up between his fingers, he says, "I chant my mantras and ask a question while rolling this around in my hand. Then I open my hand and see which facet faces me. By noting the symbols on the facet facing me and those on the other facets, I can make a fairly accurate prediction." Tuleram collects his things and saunters off, singing his usual "Good morning, good evening".

Quite fortuitously, albeit accidentally, we learn that we can film another instance of a person communicating directly with her Devta and receiving guidance.

This manifests when Meru takes me to Nashala village to meet the Goor of Chamunda Devi, whom we had seen at the Naggar festival some months earlier. Chamunda Devi is one of the fiercer aspects of Shakti and her temple is a beautiful old wooden structure built on a stone platform and surrounded by ancient cedar trees.

As we walk onto the large ground, we hear the familiar music for the Devtas. We find the bajantris drumming a rhythm and the Devi's palanquin being lifted by the kahars. Meru makes enquiries and is told that the Devi is preparing to leave on an unscheduled journey to visit her sister, Bairwali Mata, in Devi Kothi village.

We spot the Goor standing right in front of the rath, having a chat with the pujari. An old lady, wearing a colourful pattu and headscarf and adorned with several gold earrings and a couple of nose pins, comes and stands directly in front of the rath.

To my astonishment she begins directly addressing her Devi's rath in all earnestness: "Devi Mata, the people in my family are not getting along with each other. There are constant fights, and the general atmosphere is very tense. I am quite aggrieved, dear Devi." The lady bursts into tears. "Please help me, Mata!"

As she speaks the rath begins to move towards the Goor who pushes back the handles of the rath with his hands. The rath moves back but rushes back towards the Goor again with greater velocity. This happens over and over again as the lady stands with joined hands pleading with her Devi, "Please help me, Mata! Tell me what to do!"

The rath moves towards the Goor with greater force. He begins to shake as he goes into a trance. He turns his face to the lady, stares piercingly at her and speaking loudly and quickly pronounces the Devi's words: "I will come to your house and cure your problems myself."

Almost instantly the trance is over. The lady bows reverently to the Devi's rath, which has started moving out of the temple compound, accompanied by all the members of the Devloo and the intense music of the bajantris.

The event is so unexpected and swift that I am a bit lost for words. Meru reminds me that when the Devi travels, she inhabits her rath, so in effect the rath is itself the Devi. Therefore, often the rath is consulted for problems in a common practice known as khadi poochh. He adds, "Just before a Devta's rath leaves their temple, a devotee can go up to the Devta to ask a question, which the Devta can choose to answer right there."

I am beginning to understand the pervasiveness of divine guidance in the lives of the Kullu people. So far I have only seen this work at an individual level, but Meru has informed me that the Devtas also address common village issues related to community constructions, installation of modern infrastructure and other public works. When I express my keenness to witness such a session, Meru is doubtful whether I will be allowed to film it but promises to find out.

Finally, after a week, Meru drives me to the village of Nasogi where a community poochh is about to take place with the Devtas of the two villages of Nasogi and Kulang. En route, Meru reveals that this permission came through with great difficulty and only after the pandit of Devta Siyali Mahadev of Nasogi agreed to do a pogley. "And we got lucky again … the Devta agreed! Anu, the gods of Dev Bhoomi clearly want us to document their ways. This is probably the first time our Devta culture is being filmed so thoroughly."

We park at the foot of the village and begin climbing uphill through its meandering ways. I ask Meru, "What is the problem that the villagers are trying to resolve?"

Meru explains, "Some people belonging to both villages are upset with each other. I think it has something to do with the people of Nasogi who, when they visited Kulang with their Devta during a festival, felt that they were not taken care of as well as they should have been. A lot of bad blood has been brewing between them ever since. The two Devtas have come here to resolve the matter once and for all."

We arrive at Nasogi and walk expectantly through the deserted village until we reach the temple where a huge crowd of people from both villages has gathered. Devta Siyali Mahadev's temple is a recent wooden structure covered with carvings.

On a wide platform in front of the temple sit the raths of Devta Siyali Mahadev and his guest Devta Parashar Rishi from Kulang. The bajantris are playing their instruments but the ambience is solemn. The crowd seems tense, hardly interacting as they usually do at fairs, festivals or social gatherings. We stand quietly in a corner trying to be as unobtrusive as possible.

Soon, Mannat Ram, the eighty-one-year-old Goor of the resident Devta, walks in with a young man, both wearing their Goor cloaks. Meru whispers that the young man is Inderchand, the Goor of Devta Parashar Rishi, and is only in his mid-twenties. He is the youngest Goor I have come across. When I mention this to Meru, he points out that although there may be differences in the age and experience of Goors all are considered equal as mediums of their respective deities.

The two Goors begin ritually propitiating their Devtas in the time-honoured method that has become familiar to me; the bajantris beat a staccato rhythm, the pandits ring the Devta's bells, the Goors inhale from the two smoking dharjs whose smouldering fragrance wafts over the crowd. They mutter their mantras, pluck a hair each from their foreheads, untie their hair and lean back until their topis drop from their heads. Both Goors are trembling as their trance sets in.

While Mannat Ram's body moves with tremors, Inderchand's body shakes violently. The crowd recognises the divine visitation and collectively bows, greeting their Devtas with cries of "Praise the Devta!"

Then the pandits begin conversing with their Devtas:

Pandit: "Salutations, dear Devtas, we have come to you to help us solve this problem that has been driving us apart."

Devta Siyali Mahadev via Goor Mannat Ram: "I am omnipresent; I am in the clouds, the thunder, the wind and the water. I will do all I can to safeguard all humans on earth. Devotees, I will resolve your problems today. If I make any mistake, kindly forgive me!"

Pandit: "Oh, please Lord, do not speak to us so! We are merely your subjects and you are our master. You do not make any mistakes."

Devta Siyali Mahadev via Goor Mannat Ram: "Then let go of your differences. Make peace with your brethren. If you value my words, you will not face any problems in resolving your problems. You have my blessings."

Goor Mannat Ram turns his face downwards and I am unsure whether he has come out of his trance, but Devta Siyali Mahadev speaks no more. It is now the turn of Inderchand. He has a cherubic face with a moustache and lush long hair. It is difficult to imagine him commanding this large gathering, but when he finally speaks, he does. The Devta is very angry and begins shouting.

Devta Parashar Rishi via Goor Inderchand: "This is Kali Yuga, but I am still powerful in this age. I am looking for my space in

Satya Yuga, the pure age. I want to go back to my original dwelling space because you people of today do not value a hermit."

Pandit: "Dear Devta, this is not true. Forgive us if we have made any mistakes. We are your children; we carry you in our hearts and we depend on you."

Devta Parashar Rishi via Goor Inderchand: "Don't worry, I create reasons for celebrations where none exists. I will examine what is causing the problem. Whatever it is, I will find and rectify it. You must stop fighting. I am with you and for you; I am omnipresent. I am an ascetic, I am Rishi Parashar. I am fire and I can burn everything away. I will solve your problems. Make peace."

After similar kinds of conversation as well as discussions between the pandits and other members of both Devloos, the matter is finally resolved to the satisfaction of both villages. Members of the two Devloos hug each other. Immediately the mood changes to one of celebration, visible in the many faces around that have broken into smiles. Meru relates that the people of both villages have resolved to spar no more and respect the dictates of their Devtas.

The bajantris begin playing merrier music, and to ritually symbolise the resumed friendship between the villagers of Nasogi and Kulang the two Goors perform the Devkhel. As the two Goors dance the peculiar steps, holding each other's hands, I see some people becoming emotional. Such is the power of faith, I think, marvelling at what I have just witnessed.

9

Tuli, the Intriguing Female Shaman

After witnessing the peace-brokering role of the Devtas in the dispute between the villages of Nasogi and Kulang, I begin to understand how the overarching authority of the Devta system frequently challenges the established mores of village society. I have already observed how the Devta culture did not differentiate between caste or class in the selection of a Goor, and I now begin to wonder if it also transcends gender, for Kullu society despite its gentleness is strongly patriarchal.

I request Meru and Avantika to research and find a female Goor, and a few days later my wish becomes a reality. Avantika has heard about a practising female Goor, who is based close to the Manali Bazaar.

A week later we are granted permission to meet her. Squinting against the sun, Meru and I gaze up at an unimposing cement structure with a pyramid roof. It is a stiff climb up the hillside from the main road where the Beas flows.

The temple is one of those generic concrete shrines that dot both urban and rural landscapes in northern India. The entire complex could probably fit no more than fifty people. At the entrance is the likeness of the Devi's feet and I bow down to pay my respects.

At one end of the courtyard is a small stone Shivling, the symbol of Lord Shiva, and a pit in the ground for conducting a havan. At the other end is the temple sanctorum within which is a small round stone structure, the Devi's pindi.[1] Beside the pindi is a framed poster of the nine forms of the goddess Navdurga, whom Tuli Devi serves as a Cheli, a "female shaman". She is the only woman shaman of Sarahan, Manali.

Tuli Devi lives within the temple precincts and has no hesitation in allowing herself to be interviewed. She lives in an adjoining room with her three children, two school-going daughters and a son Sunil who assists her in the temple and does a few odd jobs. Tuli Devi is a short, stocky, middle-aged woman. She is voluble and forthcoming.

"I began to experience trance when I was just twelve years of age. I would lose myself for periods of time. It was others who would later recount what I did during those spells. All I knew was that I would feel an intense shiver and would completely lose control. At that time my mother was very ill. Though she had been taken to doctors and to Goors, and in fact my own father was the Goor of Khodu Devta, she continued to be sick. Then one day I went into a deep trance. Later I was told that I had run my hand over my mother, diagnosed her illness and cured her instantly," she recounts.

I absorb all this. Perhaps because Tuli is too accessible, unlike the Goors I had met so far who had sought their Devta's consent before speaking to me, I sense a certain wariness within myself. But, I am determined to keep an open mind.

Tuli reveals that when she was twenty-one years old, she went into a deep trance and announced that she was the medium of Navdurga Ma, a composite Devi representing the nine forms of Devi Durga that are worshipped separately during the nine days of

---

1 Pindi*:* In northern India a pindi is a rounded rock outcrop believed to be a manifestation of the mother goddess

Navratri, a festival celebrated across north India.[2] The nine goddesses are Shailaputri, Brahmacharini, Chandraghanta, Kusumanda, Katyayani, Kalaratri, Siddhidatri, Skandamata and Mahagauri. Tuli was married by then, and soon after this incident she along with her husband built a small shrine where the temple stands today.

Tuli claims to have discovered the pindi in the temple complex while in a trance. Beside the pindi in the sanctum itself is the Devi's rath, fully decorated and surmounted by nine masks. Unlike the palanquins of other deities, which are only decorated if the Devta wants to venture out of the temple for festivals or special occasions, the rath of this Devi is always decorated. A devotee can only pay their respects from outside while only Tuli and her son can enter the temple sanctum.

Once she was formally recognised as a Cheli, the Devi barred the couple from running a business. Her husband gave up work and dedicated himself to serving the temple. When he died unexpectedly a few years later, the Devi indicated that Tuli's son Sunil had been chosen to step into his father's shoes.

"But how did she indicate this?" I interject.

"My boy became mysteriously paralysed despite being otherwise healthy. He had no fever or any other symptom, but his knees swelled up and he was unable to sit or stand," says Tuli. "We were worried sick, and no medicine worked until one day I went into a trance and the Devi speaking through me said that Sunil was paralysed because Mata did not want him to go to school; she wanted him in her service."

---

2 Navratri: "Nava" (nine) and "ratri" (nights) is a major Hindu festival celebrated for nine nights and ten days. It begins on the first day of Devi Paksha (the fortnight of Devi Durga, the bring fortnight of the month of Ashwin, usually September-October) and ends with the celebration of Dussehra festival. This festival intertwines religious devotion, fasting, and joyous festivities, celebrating the divine feminine through dance, offerings, and the unique ritual of Kumari Puja, where young girls embody the aspects of Goddess Durga.

Tuli tells us that despite her faith she resisted. She told the Devi that she would only accede to this if the Devi demonstrated her power by healing the boy instantly. And miraculously that was exactly what happened: the next day Sunil was cured.

Nonetheless, it was a heart-breaking decision for both mother and son, but there was no going against the Devi's wishes. Tuli assured the Devi that Sunil would not attend school but devote himself to her service.

It is a disturbing story, yet it is one with which I am now familiar. When the call comes, it brooks no argument.

Tuli continues, "You see, my husband died, and Devi needed another man to serve her. As a woman I am hampered during those five days of menstruation. I cannot enter the temple at such times; I shift to the rooms below. Also, as a woman I am not permitted to conduct occult rituals, especially those that require interventions in the funeral grounds."

A few years later when Sunil was seventeen, he accompanied the Devi's rath to Manikaran where she had gone to take a bath in the sacred lake. At Manikaran the rath of another visiting Devta knocked off his cap and he was pronounced the Goor of Bhoothnath, an aspect of Lord Shiva. Clearly this was a family of shamans; after his father and mother, Sunil was the third fully ordained shaman.

Tuli articulates the difference between a male and female shaman. For instance, she has never dropped her cap or followed the occult initiation rituals I had heard about, but she does keep her head covered and hair tied under a scarf. Sunil, now twenty-two, a lanky and cheerful young man dressed in a sky-blue windbreaker over a dhoti, has made peace with his chequered destiny. Mother and son serve the temple and make ends meet doing small jobs. Tuli works from home as a seamstress making alterations to clothes and Sunil is a jeweller's assistant, but this is only in between temple duties, their primary calling.

Tuli invites me to attend her poochh session the following day. She informs me that she conducts regular poochh sessions every

Tuesday and Sunday and that these are very popular, especially with women. I do not need to be asked twice, and the next day Meru and I arrive early with my camera team. Something tells me that we are in for an interesting experience.

As people begin to gather in the temple courtyard, Sunil and his sisters begin to sing hymns in praise of the Devi. There are no bajantris here. Tuli's brother and a devotee pick up the Devi's rath and begin to move amongst the devotees. The pattern here is quite different from the more orthodox poochh I had attended at Shuru. I note that when the rath stops in front of men, they shoulder the poles of the palanquin and begin to move among the crowd; when it stops before women, they stand and begin to dance to the music. It is a fascinating tableau.

As Tuli makes an entrance, the rath rushes to hover around her. She is dressed in a flaming red cloak with golden trimmings and a matching scarf. As a medium of the Devi, she is not bound by the convention that restricts a widow to wearing white or light colours. Her outfit instantly adds drama and vibrancy to the moment. Unlike the male Goors I had encountered, it is clear that the Cheli (and her Devi) script the format of their own shows. Even some of her methods of divination are unlike those I have encountered so far. Tuli is something of a new-age shaman, more urban in her choice of clothes, music and format.

A woman, Gelmu, stands up and walks to Tuli. She begins to discuss her marital woes; she had a failed first marriage and is worried that this second time also things are not looking harmonious. There are constant squabbles between the husband and wife, too many for Gelmu to just brush aside. It is a sensitive topic, but I note the intimacy with which the woman speaks to Tuli. It is a truism that a woman has more insight and empathy towards the problems of other women. I notice that the number of women devotees far outnumber the men present. Clearly Tuli is filling a void by playing the role of a much-needed spiritual guide and relationship counsellor.

Gelmu's fears are assuaged by the Devi in a way I have not seen before. Tuli holds up a chart with the Hindi alphabet in front of the rath. The rath points to specific letters, and Tuli combines them to interpret the Devi's answer, much like an Ouija board. The Devi advises the woman to keep faith in her marriage and assures her that peace will soon follow. I remain sceptical, but Gelmu seems completely satisfied with the Devi's reassurance.

Tuli and her Devi employ other methods of divination that are equally unconventional. The Devi answers questions in the affirmative or negative through the rocking of her palanquin. If the palanquin moves to one side it is a "yes", if it swings both sides it is a "no".

Other women come forward to consult Tuli, some on their own and some are brought by the rath, which is still moving around seeking out petitioners from among the devotees. A woman says she is having trouble making her children study, and the Devi requests a repeat visit for a solution. As women bring their domestic problems to Tuli, I begin to peg her as more of a guidance counsellor, but I could not have been more wrong. The woman who began her journey as a shamanic healer soon assumes that avatar in as powerful a performance as any I have witnessed.

The rath stops in front of a man seated in the crowd. I had not noticed him earlier but now see his face contort in pain as he tries to stand up. He sits down again but the rath does not move away. It remains in front of him as if insisting. The man raises himself to his feet painfully and manages to drag himself to the middle of the compound where the rath has now positioned itself. The man sits down in front of the rath, which then bends forward pressing into the man's shoulders even as he writhes in pain. The rath through its movements instructs the man to lie down on the ground. A woman next to me whispers in my ear that his name is Deepak and that he has been sick for a long time.

The rath then rushes to the temple sanctorum where the Devi's shangal is kept. Tuli's brother picks up the iron chains and places them on the palanquin. The rath returns to where the man is lying and bends close to him, moving the shangal over his body. Through it all Tuli is simply watching the proceedings from one end of the courtyard. The rath then leaves the shangal on the man's body and rushes headlong towards Tuli who pushes it back by its poles. This happens two or three times until Tuli begins to shake violently. The scarf on her head comes loose and Sunil rushes to catch it. Tuli is now throwing her head forward and back in head-banger fashion. In one hand she holds an iron trident, her dark hair flowing around her face. The image is not very far from that of a rock star. She continues to jerk her head energetically as she stands in the same place, blowing air out of her mouth forcefully. Tuli is now in a trance. Shaking her head and sometimes grinding her teeth, she appears to be in some sort of pain herself.

Finally, she charges towards Deepak brandishing the trident. Deepak lies very still. She places the trident on his chest lightly and then returns to the place where she stood earlier. Sunil takes the trident from his mother's hand and hands her a sword in its place. Immediately Tuli begins to shake even more violently. Gripping the sword tightly, flailing her arms, she rushes as if to attack Deepak as he lies helplessly on the ground. In her red cloak she is a fearsome sight, evoking an image of Goddess Durga slaying a demon. Yet, Deepak is unafraid, lying motionless as Tuli rears above him like a tigress about to pounce. Tuli places the tip of the sword on the ground and outlines the man's body. She returns to the temple and Sunil hands her a fistful of holy ash. She comes back and blows it all over Deepak. She has stopped shaking and appears to have come out of the trance. She seems tired and worn out.

Meanwhile, the rath continues to circle Deepak until he sits up. The poles of the rath are placed on his shoulders again. After the rath moves away, I am amazed yet strangely unsurprised to see him stand up and walk away with ease. I have been so gripped by the spectacle I have just witnessed that it would have been anti-climactic if a miracle had not occurred. As Deepak walks out of the temple, I rush to speak to him. He tells me he belongs to a nearby village and comes to the temple whenever he encounters a problem he finds difficult. He had first come here with his sick child and the Devi had cured him. That had been the beginning of his relationship with the Devi.

Today he is here because months of medical treatment have failed to address the pain in his legs. I note their faith in the gods does not prevent villagers from seeking medical help for their health problems. As most Himachalis are generally well-educated, it is usually only when medicine fails that they turn to their Devta. Deepak tells me that the Devi's intervention has certainly made a difference: he had come to the temple assisted by people and is returning unaided and on his two feet. He admits that he still feels a little pain in his legs, but from the time the rath first came to him, he is now feeling much lighter.

"I felt a burden lift off once the rath came onto my shoulders. The Devi told me that someone had put a spell on me by giving me something vile to eat. Did you not see her battle with the evil spirit with the trident and sword? I am confident that I will now be fully cured soon," Deepak tells me earnestly. The rath had returned to Deepak's shoulders to infuse him with divine, positive energy.

It is mandatory in such cases where black magic has been used to afflict a person that the victim once cured must leave the premises immediately for fear that the expelled dark spirit might re-enter the host. So Deepak hastily takes my leave.

When I discuss my thoughts with Meru that Tuli Devi's poochh has been very different from the divinations I have seen so far, I find him somewhat sceptical. He does not fully accept Tuli as an ordained Goor: firstly, she has not been selected by her Devi in the traditional way; secondly, he is uncomfortable with her unorthodox methods. Therefore, he tends to suspect her as an imposter.

"But, she has a substantial following, Meru," I persist, "and people seem to believe in her."

Meru points out that most of the people we had seen at the poochh are not locals. They tend to be poor immigrants from

Punjab, Bihar and other places who come to the mountains as labourers. Many belong to lower castes with little recourse other than the comforts that Tuli offers. Tuli's faith in her Devi, and moreover herself, has blossomed into her thriving shamanic practice as a service to her community. Post her poochh session, Tuli begins counselling women who openly discuss intimate problems with her. They come seeking her guidance for issues about husbands, in-laws, children or neighbours. For the local women Tuli offers a forum to express their female concerns that they may not have with a male shaman. She is also iconic for them as an empowered woman who followed her heart, and albeit the struggles has forged a unique niche for herself in this conservative patriarchal society.

I am also grappling with the idea of evil spirits. Deepak had spoken of being afflicted by an evil spirit, and Kala in Shuru had also claimed that she was a victim of an oprah, an "evil spell". It is one thing for me to accept the well-documented state of trance and altered states of consciousness but quite another to wrap my head around the idea of invisible entities, especially those that could be harnessed to afflict unsuspecting humans. Yet, the people of Kullu are very matter-of-fact about the existence of evil spirits.

What are these evil spells and spirits? I decided to discuss this with my crew for another perspective. They too are reluctant to accept these beliefs, nor had they hitherto encountered any such forces. Avantika says that she had only heard of nazar, or "the evil eye", and jokes that she had a cousin who used it as an excuse for poor grades in school. But, as someone making a serious study of the shamanic practices of the people of Kullu it is no laughing matter. It is possible that I will encounter more such ontological problems and will need to be prepared to investigate, despite my conditioned resistance to such alien notions. When we study the non-physical, we are in uncharted territory without a compass, and the spiritual landscape of Kullu is littered with challenges to our certitudes.

10

The Cosmopolitan Paharis

I realise how much my experiences over the last few months have begun seeping into my subconscious, colouring my dreams, my imagination and my waking mind. For the people of Kullu, communicating with their gods through their Goors is a part of their everyday landscape. Divine healings are as normal as a trip to the doctor. They view reality through the prism of their mythologies.

Tribal and ancient cultures have always had an innate understanding of the importance of myth and storytelling. It is not mere entertainment but a conduit to pass along and preserve the knowledge that is necessary for the tribe's health and survival.

Myths are powerful modes of communication that establish a relationship between the macrocosm (universe), mesocosm (society) and microcosm (humans). This communication is established through narratives, symbols and rituals.

If myth is an idea, mythology is the vehicle of it. Mythology constitutes stories, symbols and rituals that make a myth tangible. Mythology is "an intricate set of interlocking stories, rituals, rites and customs that inform and give the pivotal sense of meaning and direction to a person, family, community or culture".[1]

---

1 Devdutt Pattanaik (2008)

Every culture has its own set of sacred narratives, ceremonies and rituals that condition the minds of its people to make them look at the world in a particular way. Therefore, myths are essentially cultural constructs that transmit a traditional culture-specific understanding of the world that binds communities together.

From myth comes belief, from mythology customs. Myth conditions thoughts and feelings; mythology influences behaviour and communication. Myth and mythology thus have a profound influence on culture. For any communication to be an expression of myth, it must be viewed as sacred by the communicators and their audience. The sacred belongs to the realm of faith, not reason, to "mythos" not "logos". Myth transmits a traditional culture-specific understanding of the world. Myth needs faith, not proof.

An expression of myth becomes sacred when it is of anonymous origin; that is, a revelation or communication from a non-human source. For example, no one knows who first composed the story of Brahma. The epics of the Ramayana and the Mahabharata are traditionally considered itihasa, or "history". However, both Rama and Krishna acquire mythical power only because they are incarnations of Vishnu who walk among humans to restore and maintain order in every world cycle. Thus, history becomes sacred when placed within a divine plot.

Mythology tends to be hyperbolic and fantastic to drive home a myth. The unrealistic content draws attention to the idea behind the communication. The mythic imagination connects the conscious mind with the subconscious. It facilitates communication between the sacred and ordinary realms, providing a bridge in which the inexhaustible energies of the cosmos and spiritual potentialities may pour forth into our awareness. Thus, myth and mythic imagination are nothing less than living roots informing the fact of being human.

It is not only traditional cultures that are shaped by myths but also modern ones, for myths persist in the subconscious for generations long after the mythologies are forgotten. For instance, in the Western world even though the Biblical myth of creation has long been outgrown, still the core idea that man is God's most superior creation made in God's image, distinct and above nature, persists.

Yes, city dwellers are no less shaped by modern myths. Western materialism and capitalism are myths that have pervaded almost all urban cultures around the world. These myths make us believe that happiness is found in success and wealth and that consumerism is the key to personal fulfilment. These narratives shape and influence our lives and cultures from birth to death.

Our aesthetics, ethos and worldviews are shaped in childhood and throughout life by our verbal and non-verbal environments. Everyone, rich or poor, educated or illiterate, carries within themselves a large non-literate subculture as part of their mythic imagination. We are as shaped by myth as the people of Dev Bhoomi.

I decide to seek a point of view that I have not yet explored: that of the cosmopolitan paharis. Like Meru, others living in the valley are as connected to the cosmopolitan world beyond Kullu as they are to the traditional world within it. So, what is their perception and experience of local culture?

I decide to visit my friend Kishan Banon. After all, he is the one who introduced me to Meru and has been badgering me for an update on the filming. The Banons are descendants of a Captain A.T. Banon of the Royal Munster Fusiliers who settled in Manali in the 1870s. A pioneer of apple cultivation in the region, Captain Banon married a local girl from Old Manali and had a son, Kishan's father.

I drive to Kishan's hotel, Banon Resorts, which lies in the heart of Manali about a kilometre from the Devi Hadimba Temple. Kishan was educated at the Bishop Cotton School, Shimla, and spends half the year in Delhi. Straddling as he does the realities of both cosmopolitan and local worlds makes him an intriguing subject to research. I join Kishan in his blossoming flower garden for high tea where he regales me with his usual jokes. In his mid-fifties, good-looking, fair-skinned and cheerful, he is the quintessential Anglo-Indian, a community that is fast disappearing. Kishan is quite interested in my filming and asks me to relate some of my experiences.

When I tell him about the Hadimba Devi festival, Kishan informs me that Hadimba Devi is his family's patron deity. He says that he is a complete believer and that for him it is not just a matter of faith in what has been passed down through generations, but he has personally experienced the powers of the Devtas and Goors several times. I am delighted when he offers to share some anecdotes.

"Our family is very close to Hadimba Devi," Kishan says. "Whenever she leaves her temple to go to a particular place her rath has a fixed route it traverses."

"Yes, I've been told that," I acknowledge.

Kishan continues, "During Hadimba Devi's festival you filmed the Devi's rath returning to her temple in Dhungri from the Manu temple."

I nod.

"Did you see the Devi's rath stopping at a few homes in Old Manali?"

I nod again.

"Well, one of those homes is my mother's maiden home. The Devi always stops for the ladies of our extended family to greet and give good wishes."

I do remember those scenes well; they had been quite touching.

Kishan continues, "Some years ago the Devi's rath skipped passing our family home because the young generation of kahars took a shortcut. My grandmother had been waiting for the Devi at our family home, flowers in hand." He sits up animatedly. "What happened was that at the end of the shortcut the rath went haywire and began moving from side to side but not forward! The kahars tried their best but the rath forcibly made them turn around and go back to our family home. Once she received the flowers from my grandmother, the Devi resumed her journey peacefully."

I am stunned.

"Yes," Kishan says emphatically, "there were many witnesses to this event including the kahars themselves. I know this is hard to believe, Anu, but I myself have had a similar experience. Once, I had the opportunity to carry Devta Vasishtha's rath when he was to visit our home. The Devta indicated that I lift his rath, which I did. I had expected the rath to be heavy, what with all the solid wood, masks and ornamentation, but it felt surprisingly light. I could feel a force directing me to go wherever the Devta wanted to go. At one point the rath wanted to go around the village and made us run all over the place! I tried to resist the force but just couldn't. It was too powerful. It was an amazing experience; totally nerve-wracking and exhausting though."

Our discussion moves towards Goors and my experiences with Goors Tuleram and Hardayal. I am interested to know how Kishan perceives the shamans of the valley.

"Anu, I think our Goors are mediums who can venture into the psychic realms and access available energies when in trance." He describes an encounter: "This one time my mother fell violently ill and no doctor was able to diagnose her problem. A Goor from another village was called. He read mustard seeds and diagnosed her problem. You know, Anu, he gave her some sacred ash and within half an hour she was totally fine!"

I am still absorbing this information when Kishan talks about another instance. "I remember a cousin of mine was unable to conceive for several years. When she consulted her village Goor, he told her the exact date that she would give birth to a son and that she would have to name him after Lord Shiva. The Goor's prediction turned out to be absolutely correct."

For Kishan it is a matter of faith. "This Devta culture has been engrained into our psyche since we were infants. As children we would play games of Devta make-believe where we would pretend that it was festival time, make tiny toy raths, carry them and take turns pretending to be a Goor in trance!" he says, laughing at the memory.

I hear a familiar voice behind me. "What are you laughing about?" It's Meru belatedly joining us. We bring him up-to-date on our conversation. Meru turns to Kishan, saying, "Talking about cosmopolitan people, I think Anu should meet Chris, don't you think?"

Kishan snaps his fingers, exclaiming, "That's right! What a good idea, Meru!"

They tell me about Christopher Oldmeadow, a British gentleman living in the village of Halan. Chris had come to the valley nearly thirty-five years ago and had never left. He had married locally and is a father to six children. A keen angler, he runs a company that organises angling trips. Despite being born Catholic, he has embraced the local culture and its beliefs.

"And, his wife's brother is a Goor!" states Meru, which makes me all excited. I insist that Meru fix an appointment for me to meet him. Kishan suggests that we go to Halan to meet Chris as we might be able to meet his brother-in-law as well. He offers to organise the visit for me.

A few days later, Meru and I are walking up a steep mountainside to reach Chris's home in Halan village.

"How long will it take us?" I ask Meru, daunted by the task of climbing literally to the top of a mountain.

"Depends on how fast your mountain legs can carry you," Meru responds cheekily.

The sun is shining brightly, and thankfully there's a lovely breeze as we plod up the zig-zag path. Soon we are walking through apple orchards and maize fields edged with huge sunflowers. Meru tells me that the Devta of Halan is a snake god, Naag Dhumbal. Actually, Chris's brother-in-law is both priest and shaman of the Naag Devta. I am intrigued by these Naag Devtas, who form the most mysterious and impenetrable cults in the valley.

We reach a tiny bridge that is submerged in a few inches of water from a nearby waterfall. Meru attributes this overflow to the fact that we are close to the territory of a Naag Devta. He explains, "Our Naag Devtas are considered to be water gods. They control the rains, floods and droughts. It is to them we pray if we need rain."

We reach flatter ground after a couple of hours. A signpost says: *Salutations to Dhumbal Devta. Wearing leather shoes or carrying leather in any form is prohibited in this village. Those found guilty will be fined INR 1000.*

This ban is in keeping with the Devta's dictates, which Meru had warned me about earlier. Failure to comply would not only warrant a fine but also social disapproval as the village community would regard it as an insult to the Devta. Meru tells me that such bans are common and are simply part of the rules laid down by the Devta or Devi of the village. For instance, Naag Dhumbal has disallowed activities like the use of horses and building a road to the village. Meru surmises, "The locals accept and appreciate such orders as they know that the Devta has only their best interests at heart."

We are now approaching Halan, and I see that it's a tiny village. Being cut off from the road has ensured that it remains almost like a village lost in time. Most of the homes are small ramshackle wooden huts with slate roofs, attached cowsheds and stacks of firewood and hay piled up outside. The huts are set within fields and fruit orchards; agriculture along with rearing animals seem to be the primary occupations. There are hardly any modern interventions except for mobile phones. Many homes have looms where a few women are busy weaving. A few young boys pass us carrying heavily laden apple baskets on their backs while younger children play in the fields.

While I am photographing the village, an old and distinctive woman approaches me and looks me up and down curiously. She is fascinated by my outfit of t-shirt and trousers and the camera in my hand. The old lady questions Meru sharply after which they enter a long conversation with much finger-pointing towards me.

In the meantime, I am soaking in all the little details of her appearance; her flashing light eyes, the deep creases on her face, six tiny earrings on each ear, huge gold pins on either side of her nose, a colourful scarf over her head like a bandana that many women sport. She is wearing the traditional pattu over a salwar-kameez over which she wears a pearl necklace and some silver chains to hold her pattu in place.

Meru chuckles and says, “She is asking which part of the world you are from, and to ensure that you are not wearing leather.”

The lady allows me to take a few photographs of her after which we make our way to the temple. The Naag Dhumbal Temple is a towering, three-tiered wooden building, mounted on a high stone platform. Meru points to the stones that have been intricately assembled without any bonding medium, which is an ancient architectural technique of Himachal.

The main entrance of this magnificent temple has remarkable carvings of heads, which Meru informs me are exactly like the masks on Devta Naag Dhumbal’s rath. I would have liked to explore this fascinating structure, but the “No Outsiders Allowed” sign deters me. I wonder, if this Naag Devta is not open to outsiders, how did he accept Chris into his fold?

We reach Chris’s two-storey blue house with attached cowshed. Despite my mountain legs, I’m exhausted and throw myself into a chair on the veranda as soon as we arrive. I am admiring the view when Chris walks out with a cheerful, “Hello there!” I turn and shake hands with a middle-aged man with ruddy complexion, blond hair turning grey and startlingly blue twinkling eyes. “Welcome to my jhopri (hut),” Chris greets me. His easy manner and quick wit are endearing. I take to him immediately.

He calls out to his wife to bring some water in a charming colloquial way: “*Ouu Shanta, paanilaaona*!”

Meru grins and informs me, “Chris speaks fluent Hindi as well as Kullvi.”

Shanta walks out carrying glasses of water. She is a stocky woman with a robust complexion and kind eyes and is dressed in traditional attire. Shanta greets me warmly. Although more comfortable speaking Pahari, Shanta speaks passable Hindi. She hands Chris a plate of rice grains to sort and excuses herself to finish preparing our lunch.

"Now you know who the boss is," Chris says affectionately. I sit down with him on the veranda as he sifts through the rice, weeding out tiny stones.

Chris tells me about his life back in England where he was a police officer. He was newly married when his wife eloped with his best friend. He decided to go on a travelling spree to mend his broken heart, boarded a plane to Bangkok and took a stop in Mumbai en route. He met some compatriots there and joined them in a sprint across the country from Goa to Dharamshala to Kullu. Chris bid goodbye to his friends and decided to stay on for a while in the valley as he saw ample opportunity to indulge in his passion of angling. "So, on day two I decided that this valley was paradise: huge trout, amazing flora, superb weather, nice people. I decided to stop for a couple of months and stayed thirty-five years," he recalls. "I know now that it was all destined. I was always meant to be here and have a life with Shanta."

It was a feeling Shanta eventually shared. First, they became friends, and then they married. Of course, she had no idea this would happen when they first met. Shanta's parents had invited Chris over for tea as a neighbourly gesture. Chris was smitten with Shanta at first sight, but Shanta later tells me she "didn't take much notice". Chris's visits became regular, and a few months later, he asked her father for permission to marry her. When her parents asked her about it, she was hesitant. "How could I marry a foreigner and leave my land?" she wondered. But when her father told her that Chris planned to settle here, she agreed. Now, after more than thirty years of marriage, it's clear they have a happy and strong relationship.

I am curious about how the obviously conservative villagers of Halan had accepted Chris into their fold. We are interrupted by Shanta who asks Chris to fetch some milk to make us tea and disappears back into the house. As he milks their cow, Chris tells me that the villagers had initially ostracised the couple. "A gora, or foreigner, was a curiosity, but I was shunned as a cow-eater."

When Shanta suffered a miscarriage, the village was rife with gossip that she had been punished for marrying a foreigner with a beef-eating past. Shanta sought the Devta's counsel. "In the poochh, fortunately the Devta rubbished the gossip and pinned the miscarriage on circumstances." Chris sighs in remembrance. "The Devta had told Shanta that he would visit our home with his Devloo. Subsequently the Devta's visit changed everything. All the people who had been turning their nose up at us were made to eat humble pie as no one could have disputed the Devta's acceptance of us." The boycott was lifted, and Chris was made to undergo a purification ceremony.

I ask about the ceremony and Chris says a tad seriously, "You know, Anu, the puja had the whole village in attendance. A ram was sacrificed and offered to the Devta and its head was handed to me! I had to drink blood from its head. I was accepted because I didn't die on the spot." The drinking of the ram's blood was a test of Chris's worthiness.

We now move into their large traditional kitchen and I watch them put the finishing touches to the meal in a shared choreography: Shanta cuts the homegrown beans while Chris chops the onions; she adds oil to a wok and he stirs the chickpea curry; Shanta makes balls of dough, which Chris flattens with his hands; she rolls out the puris and he fries them.

While we are eating the delicious lunch, I ask Chris about his familial links to shamans. Chris tells me that many of his in-laws are shamans and that his father-in-law was the first shaman he had encountered.

"I saw my father-in-law trancing out, talking in tongues, going into the fire … It was mind-boggling given my background," Chris recalls. "My brother-in-law, Tej Singh, the Goor of Naag Dhumbal, has often gone into the fire raving and ranting in trance, fire flying everywhere, and it does not even singe the hair on his legs! I am always totally amazed. Unfortunately, I've never had a camera to hand."

I explain my project to Chris and beg him to introduce me to Tej Singh. So far, we have not had permission to film any of the Naag Devta temples or even to interview the Goors or pandits of the elusive Naag Devtas, so I am particularly anxious. The couple keeps looking at each other while listening to my pleas. They quietly exchange a look and Shanta nods.

Chris announces, "One of our daughters has been keeping unwell for months. The doctors haven't been able to find a cause, so we have requested Tej Singh to do a poochh to ask the Devta next week." They promise they will try to swing it.

The sun is setting in a burst of ochre and pink as Meru and I walk back discussing Chris's incredible life story. I ask Meru how it was that Shanta's father despite being a Goor only sought the Devta's approval after they were married. "I think it was possibly because Shanta had been previously married, and her family was keen on seeing her settled again. It would have been difficult to find her a local boy," Meru informs me. As we pass the Naag Dhumbal Temple I stop and enter its open courtyard to send a sincere prayer to the Naag Devta for a positive response.

11

Goor Tej Singh, Shaman of a Snake God

A week later I am back with my crew, staring ruefully once more at the steep climb up to Halan village. I am on tenterhooks as we hope to be filming Tej Singh's poochh at Chris and Shanta's home that afternoon. Meru and I had spent the past week trying to convince the couple to allow us to film it. Chris had asked Tej Singh who had conveyed to us that filming the poochh would only be possible if the Devta agreed on the day itself.

We are waiting for Hari Narayan, or Harry, Chris's youngest, who is supposed to receive us. Shortly we spot a rosy-cheeked, cute, nine-year-old boy running down the slope. He greets us with a huge smile, speaking in English, "Sorry, I hope you haven't been waiting too long?" Harry leads us up the mountain and is full of boundless energy and endless stories. He takes us on shortcuts through orchards, fields of corn and sunflower beds, pointing out some lovely sights on the way.

Harry asks me, "Did you know that it's my Dad's birthday today?"

"Yes," I reply, "your mom told me."

He goes on to describe the preparations going on in his home for the birthday party. I am disarmed by his friendly chatter and exuberance.

We reach a large building made of brick, mud and wood, which Harry says is the mandhar, or Naag Dhumbal's "store". Meru tells me that every Devta has one of these; a sacred space where the Devta's rath is stored.

We are greeted affectionately by Chris and Shanta in front of their lovely cottage. They introduce me to Tej Singh, a slim man with pleasant face, greenish eyes and an impressive moustache. Dressed in the typical woolen short kurta and pyjama worn with a short woolen sleeveless jacket, Tej Singh is the pandit as well as the Goor of Naag Dhumbal. He smiles, joining palms and greeting me with a "Namaste, Ji," in a soft voice. I am anxious to know our fate and ask with bated breath, "Goor-ji, has the Devta allowed us to film the poochh?"

Tej Singh laughs at my eagerness, saying, "Let's see. I will certainly ask."

Apparently, the poochh is going to be conducted in the cottage attic where there is a small prayer room, which is the abode of the family's Kul Devta. And it is the Kul Devta whose consent is required for our filming today as the poochh is being held privately at home.

While Shanta and Tej Singh go up to the attic to begin the puja, we walk into the kitchen where Chris and Shanta's five daughters are busy with the birthday lunch preparations. All the girls are absolute beauties with light eyes and sharp features complemented by rosy cheeks and beautiful hair. The two elder sisters are married, the middle two are in college and the youngest is still in school. They have come specifically for the poochh and, like Harry, are extremely friendly. They banter playfully with Chris and Meru and make me feel welcome. Chris points to Leela, his third-born, for whom the poochh is being conducted.

I go across to have a chat with her. Attired in jeans and shirt, Leela confesses that she has been experiencing strangeness for quite some time. "I feel much pain in my body; sometimes it's in my hands, sometimes feet or somewhere else. I feel tired all the time. I know something is not right even though all my tests are fine, and the doctors say I'm okay."

I look at my watch and realise that half an hour has gone by and there is still no confirmation from Tej Singh. My heart sinks and I fear the worst. I look at Chris enquiringly, but he just shrugs. Simultaneously I send another prayer to the Devta just as Shanta enters the room looking serious. She ushers her family up the stairs and beckons me and my cameraman. I am elated and take the second camera to operate myself.

The wooden attic is as large as the house and has windows along one length filling the space with natural light, which is perfect for a film shoot. Shanta cautions us to position ourselves at the far corners of the attic and to be quiet and unobtrusive. I have never seen a poochh in such an intimate setting before, and I send a prayer of gratitude to the Devta. Shanta hands everyone a few flowers to offer to the Devta. Tej Singh prays, dharj in hand, to idols and photographs of a few Devtas in the corner of the tiny temple room. We hand the flowers to Tej Singh who offers them to the Devtas. Shanta and Chris sit by the windows while the children sit across from them. I position myself in the front corner from where I have a good view of everyone, particularly Tej Singh. My assistant director and cameraman take up position in the back of the room. Shanta puts a tikka on everyone's forehead as Tej Singh begins to propitiate both the Kul Devta and the other Devtas. He soon emerges from the temple room with the dharj and inhales the smoke deeply. I notice that he is still wearing his cap although his hair has now been let loose, cascading down his back.

Tej Singh stands facing everyone with closed eyes and a solemn expression. There is pin-drop silence and the atmosphere in the attic has suddenly turned intense. After a while Shanta stands up and begins to address Tej Singh respectfully with hands joined.

Shanta: "Devta, are you here? We have called you to help us."

There is no response from Tej Singh who just stands there completely still, eyes closed.

Shanta: "Devta, please come to our assistance. We plead with you, Devta!"

Tej Singh remains standing still and silent, and I see the tense expression on everyone's face.

Shanta: "Devta! Devta, we seek your guidance. Please help us, please!"

Shanta keeps pleading at length, and just when I think, Oh God, nothing is happening, I notice Tej Singh's toe twitching.

Shanta: "Devta, there seems to be some problem afflicting my daughter. She has been suffering from severe body pain. Devta, please come and guide us."

Suddenly Tej Singh's foot begins to tremble, then both legs begin to shake. He opens his eyes and begins breathing heavily. The mood in the room turns electric, and I am barely breathing.

Shanta: "Devta, please help us, your children! Devta…"

Tej Singh begins shaking uncontrollably. I zoom in with my camera and observe every bit of his body trembling and shaking to an unimaginable extent. His eyes are blazing, his face contorts and his persona transforms from sober to aggressive. Tej Singh has entered a state of trance. He raises his voice to a very high pitch and begins roaring.

Devta Naag Dhumbal via Tej Singh: "I have come from far off, from the mountains, even as far as Lahaul and Malana, but I have always guarded you people."

Shanta, Chris and all the children join their hands and look up in reverence at Tej Singh who is now channelling their Devta. Although Shanta and the Goor are speaking in the local dialect, I can follow most of the conversation.

Shanta: "It seems you are annoyed with us, but today I am determined to get an answer from you."

Tej Singh's manner becomes even more fierce and I can feel the powerful energy emanating from him. The whole attic seems to be shaking and everyone is terrified. I notice that Harry bows his head, holding it in his hands in fright. Tej Singh's voice goes up several octaves and his body is shaking violently. His eyes redden and he begins sweating profusely.

Devta via Goor: "We gave birth to the ecosystem and have kept it all intact for you. I only believe in showering blessings on whoever comes asking … even the blind will get their vision back if they ask! But nowadays money rules the minds of the people and all of you have lost faith in us."

Shanta: "No, no, Devta! We have complete faith in you! Forgive us for any wrongs that we may have committed."

The Devta's accusations seem to have touched a raw nerve and almost instantly the room becomes supercharged. Everyone begins to tear up; the girls, Shanta, Chris, and even my cameraman. It is incredible, the language of the Devta is alien to us, yet the emotion has managed to overpower this barrier. Shanta has tears rolling down her cheeks as she beseeches the Devta:

Shanta: "Devta, we only depend upon you. Please help us! Even if you do not answer, I will not go to any other Devta for guidance. You are supreme for us. Please forgive us for our misdeeds! Please help my daughter!"

Finally, the Devta responds to Shanta's main query.

Devta via Goor: "Bhoot and preta run for their lives on seeing me. I have suppressed them over the ages. But, I can see that an evil eye has been cast on your daughter."

Shanta: "Devta, please tell us what we should do! We will do as you command. Please help my daughter!"

Devta via Goor: "Don't worry, she will be fine. She needs to take a dip in the holy water from the temple and sip it for three months and do a purification puja. I will guide you."

Shanta: "Thank you, Devta. Your will is our command. Once Leela is alright, we will invite you to our house for a meal."

Tej Singh's body stops shaking, his eyes and head roll back and he sighs deeply. His trance is over. Silently he picks up the flowers that were offered to the Devta and begins handing them to all present. However, when he reaches me something changes. He begins to tremble again, blowing air around me forcefully several times. His eyes are ablaze and seem to be looking through me. Tej Singh has gone back into a trance and is addressing me directly! Shanta quickly comes and stands beside me. The powerful vibration from Tej Singh makes my hair stand on end.

Devta via Goor: "I see a problem. You have a problem."

Shanta: "Devta, please tell us what the problem is."

I am flummoxed and uncertain how to deal with this. I automatically join my hands in unthinking supplication.

Devta via Goor: "You have been suffering from a mysterious ailment for years…"

I try to follow what he is saying but am at a complete loss. Shanta explains the Devta's words to me and everyone looks at me curiously. I am amazed. How does Devta Naag Dhumbal via Tej Singh know something that I have not shared with anyone here?

Shanta asks me: "Is that right?"

"Yes, I have had a chronic health condition for the past ten years."

Devta via Goor: "You feel unwell, but it is not a physical ailment. You are the victim of an evil eye."

Shanta: "You know it all, Devta. Please cure this lady!"

Tej Singh continues to shake in front of me and his eyes have a glazed look. He continues to address me directly.

Devta via Goor: "I don't know whether I will be able to ease your problem."

Shanta: "Devta, we know you will be able to cure her. Please have mercy on her!"

Devta via Goor: "I give you my blessings and now prophesy that within six months you will be cured of the evil eye that has been cast on you."

I am completely overwhelmed and inexplicably find myself shedding uncontrollable tears, much to my extreme embarrassment.

Devta via Goor: "And when you are cured, know it is my doing. If not, you have the right not to have faith in me."

Shanta: "Thank you, thank you, Devta! Devta, you are great!"

Suddenly Tej Singh becomes still and shuts his eyes. The trance is over. Tej Singh sits down right where he is, drenched in sweat, looking exhausted. Harry runs and fetches him a glass of water and Shanta beckons me to switch off my camera and sit beside her.

Everyone's attention is now on me much to my discomfort. Shanta asks me kindly, "So, what is your illness, Anu?"

Unlike the openness that people here enjoy, I am unused to discussing my issues in public, so to protect my privacy I keep it brief: "Well, I've been keeping unwell for the past ten years, but it was only last year that a doctor in London diagnosed my ailment as chronic fatigue syndrome." There is another barrage of questions from Shanta while the others look on interestedly, so I disclose a few more details of my condition that is mostly still unrecognised in India; there are specialists in a few countries abroad who specifically treat this condition.

"Tej Singh said much more that I couldn't understand. What else did he say?" I enquire of Shanta.

She looks at Chris and when he nods, she says in a concerned tone, "The Devta warned that you have an enemy, someone who wants you to have problems. This person is indulging in black magic to achieve this goal."

I am flabbergasted by this information and totally at a loss for words. Chris comes and puts an arm around me saying, "Don't you worry, Missy, you will be fine now that the Devta is looking out for you."

Shanta adds comfortingly, "Have faith in our Devta. Remember when Goor-ji was blowing air around you? That was actually the Devta blowing the evil spirit away." Shanta further impresses upon me that the Devta did not seek anything from me except my faith in him and his powers. According to Shanta my visit to Halan is not coincidental but fated. "You were destined to get your problem cured here." This intimate poochh session has become more intimate than I had imagined and more difficult to process.

I turn the conversation back to Leela. Shanta tells me that this is her third poochh with the Devta on this subject. Shanta had initially consulted the Devta in a village poochh where he had asked her to return. The second time she consulted him was when the rath was out at which time the Devta had told her that he would finally come to her home to deal with the problem.

Leela says, "The Devta said that someone had done an oprah on me." I nod, indicating that I had heard of this before.

Chris adds, "This black magic is a common spiteful practice in the valley."

Leela continues, "Devta said that someone had given me food to eat that had been cursed so that I would go through these problems."

I ask Leela if she suspects anyone, but she has no idea about when it could have happened.

"Are you worried?"

Leela shakes her head. "No, not anymore since I know what the problem is. And, the Devta has also given me the cure." She is satisfied and has full faith that her troubles are soon going to vanish.

All the girls agree with Leela, but I want to know what the youngest thinks about it all. Harry's first encounter with his uncle in trance was at a village festival when Harry was four years old. He remembers it as being terrifying. "I thought he would come and kill me," he tells me with a grin. It was his mother who helped him traverse this aspect of their culture. "Mom explained that who I saw was God, and he would always look after me."

Shanta looks at her son adoringly, saying, "Harry is an active and enthusiastic participant in all our cultural festivities as long as they do not clash with his studies."

Chris adds, "Our children have been part of this unique culture from the beginning by attending fairs and seeing all that is going on with the Devtas, who are a part of daily life here."

Tej Singh stirs from a short doze, opens his eyes, stretches his arms and lets out a huge yawn. I notice that his facial expression has completely altered and has gone back to its original congenial look. I ask if he is up to chatting and he readily agrees.

As is usual, with post-trance amnesia, Tej Singh does not remember what transpired in the poochh. He goes on to recount his story.

Tej Singh is not just a shaman, he comes from a family of pandits wherein both his father and mother were practising pandits. "Becoming a pandit was a turning point in my life as I had to follow a lot of rules and restrictions. Then, during my initiation ceremony in the temple, I got into a khel possessed by Devta Naag Dhumbal."

Although Tej Singh is a medium of Devta Naag Dhumbal, he has not been officially chosen by Devta Naag Dhumbal who already has a customary Goor. Tej Singh takes over the shamanic duties whenever the official Goor is occupied.

Tej Singh remembers going into trance at the age of twelve. It was during an early trance that he first jumped into the ceremonial fire at a village festival. This preceded his initiation as a pandit. Shanta also remembers the early signs that made her family realise that of all her brothers Tej Singh would take on his father's mantle as Naag Dhumbal's Goor.

Like his father, Tej Singh walked into the ceremonial fire on three occasions. "It is only during an intense trance that I stay in the fire, as long as I am in khel, sometimes for a minute, sometimes five," he says proudly, grinning at my astounded expression. "There is never a hot or burning sensation, and, you know, when the khel is over and I come out of the fire, not a single hair is burnt or even singed."

Tej Singh further reveals that he goes into trance for three different Devtas. He has jumped into the fire as Devta Agni Pataal and channels Devta Vasuki Naag. "It is not in my control which Devta decides to come into me," he declares.

"So, which Devta came into you today?" I ask.

"I don't remember," Tej Singh says, but Shanta points out, "Anu, remember Goor-ji blew air over you?"

I nod.

"So, definitely Devta Agni Pataal had come to him because it is this Devta who usually blows air to ward off evil spirits."

Tej Singh nods his agreement.

I ask Tej Singh about his Devta propitiation ritual, which I had not seen much of since Tej Singh had disappeared into the tiny temple here. It is not dissimilar to what I have heard before: "I speak some secret mantras, offer incense to the Devta and inhale it. Then I pray to a few special Devtas and the khel happens if the Devta so desires," he reveals.

He remembers his shaman father being consulted whenever someone in the village fell sick. Like his father, Tej Singh feels that his main role is to be a healer. "And he is a proficient one. He is very good at driving evil spirits away from those possessed."

I ask about the Devta's remedies for victims of spirit illness. "Usually, the Devta blows some air or sprinkles holy water on victims of spirit illness, or orders them to bathe in holy water. However, there are times when the evil spirits are too malignant to respond to these simpler cures and need special attention. I can see the dimension that these ghosts exist in, but they are invisible to everyone else," Tej Singh explains.

"My senses are most heightened in the night when I can see them clearly. They are strange creatures, some of them are hairy and walking on all fours like dogs, others are human-like but with strange mutations." We are all agog as he continues with his fantastic story: "They all have one thing in common: they only exist as shadows. During khel I become entirely powerful and can see them even in pitch darkness. Of course I do not remember, but I am told by others that I am able to see them."

Shanta reminds me, "Even today the Devta via Goor-ji spotted an evil spirit around you and blew him away."

She stands up and shoos us all downstairs to begin Chris's birthday celebrations. Meru has been waiting patiently for us to emerge. He notices my heightened pallor and takes me aside to find out what transpired. "Later," I tell him, and both of us join the family in the living room, which has been cheerfully decorated with balloons and streamers. A glowing Chris watches his six children lovingly bring out a cake with candles too many to count. Together we all sing the birthday song and even Tej Singh joins in.

The birthday celebrations and mood of gaiety are a complete antithesis to what had occurred earlier in the afternoon. Tej Singh, a man who jumps into fire or makes an entire attic tremble, is simply being a loving brother-in-law and uncle.

It is easy to see what has rooted Chris to this place, and before I leave, I take him aside and bluntly ask whether he is a believer.

"It is hard to be a disbeliever when you have seen miracles happen before your very eyes," he tells me. "You know, Anu, I've even carried the Devta's rath a couple of times and definitely felt the energy."

Chris comes to see us off. He tells me to have faith. "There is something very special amongst these people that I cannot explain but have experienced over the years, just as you did today."

My mind has begun to work in a completely unfamiliar direction. I wonder if I have really been affected by an evil eye. My rational mind rejects the idea, but deep within me the seed of doubt has been sown. I had experienced a strange energy when Tej Singh addressed me, a presence of something that I could not put my finger on. I didn't know what to make of it.

My illness was something that had been unknown to everyone in that room until the Devta pointed it out. That is a mystery to me. Never through my documenting could I have foreseen becoming so personally involved. From observing from the sidelines, I have been thrown dead centre.

Needing more clarity, I decide to investigate the research on spirit illness. On our walk down, Meru is noticeably subdued. After some prompting, he says, "Anu, I always tease you about your walking legs," then suddenly blurts out, more accusatory: "But you never told me you had a health issue!" I calm him by explaining that I've learned to pace myself in both work and life, based on the energy I have available.

I leave Manali planning to be back soon after some research and reviewing the footage, besides listening to the interviews, reading the transcripts, etc. More than that I need personal time to process my experiences and to try to make sense of them. Above all, I need to rest and recuperate, for the experience in the attic has left me strangely disoriented.

12
Divine Possession

Back in Delhi, after this second schedule of filming, I contemplate my experiences at length. My observations, experiences and research thus far have left me in no doubt about the validity of the trance the Goors I have met had experienced. However, I am still mystified by the notion of divine possession. Once again, I busy myself researching spirit possession in books and research papers. Yet again I find myself overwhelmed by the vast volume of research and writing that exists on this subject.

Spirit possession occurs upon the belief that demons or spirits can take control of a human body. It was fairly common in ancient belief that a human being might become possessed by a supernatural power. Indeed, virtually all cultures have some tradition of belief in the existence of spirit entities and spirit possession.

An eminent anthropologist, Erika Bourguignon, observed that spirit possession beliefs are geographically and culturally pervasive. After sampling 488 societies, she found spirit possession traditions occurring in 74 per cent of them. In other words, a five-year study examining contemporary cultures uncovered roughly 375 different traditions of spirit possession. This number would grow exponentially if one were to look at the thousands of cultures not included in Bourguignon's study.

In 1871 anthropologist E.B. Tylor published a volume entitled, *Primitive Culture*, which introduced the concept of animism to the study of religion. From the Latin animus, meaning 'soul' or 'life', animism refers to a belief in human souls as well as other spirits that may reside in animals, places, natural phenomena or inanimate objects. Although they are invisible and intangible, non-human spirits are believed to be sentient and therefore can be interacted with as if they were people. From an animistic perspective, spirits can be negotiated with, appeased or commanded by someone with unique abilities or who knows the proper procedures. Tylor theorised that all cultures develop along a predetermined path and that animism constitutes the most basic and primitive form of most cultures.

The father of modern anthropological studies in comparative religion, James G. Frazer, argues for the universality of spirit possession in his famous work, *The Golden Bough* (1890) noting that "the belief in temporary incarnation or inspiration is worldwide".

His description of possession is corroborated by the fieldwork of other eminent anthropologists, including Alfred Metraux who wrote: "People possessed start by giving an impression of having lost control of their motor system. Shaken by spasmodic convulsions they pitch forward as though projected by a spring, turn frantically round and round, stiffen and stay still with body bent forward, sway, stagger, save themselves, again lose balance, only to fall finally into a state of semi-consciousness."[1]

A century ago, T.K. Oesterreich, in what was the first cross-cultural study of possession,[2] argued for the "constant nature" of spirit possession throughout history and across cultures. Oesterreich postulated three principal external ways in which spirit possession manifests itself:

---

1 Alfred Metraux (1977)

2 T.K. Oesterreich (1966)

1. Where the physiognomy of the person changes (such as distorted features of face or body);
2. Where the person's voice changes (such as when a feminine voice is transformed into a bass one); and,
3. Where the person adopts an ego-personality that is opposed to the normal one so that the person speaks with the voice of the possessing spirit, not their own.

It is astonishing to me that such phenomena have been observed and studied extensively over decades, yet how little we know about them. These early accounts of spirit possession by Frazer and Oesterreich closely describe what I witnessed during several episodes of divine possession among the Goors; the exaggerated body movements, the contorted facial expressions, the sudden intrusion of an unfamiliar personality and the amnesia following the episode.

Iamblichus, a third-century Neo-Platonist philosopher, notes that there are different types of divine possession, which are often dependent on the particular deity who is considered to have possessed the individual. Iamblichus asserted strongly that those who are truly possessed by gods do not act according to sense perception, nor are they conscious of themselves in terms of being able to apply their personal knowledge or experience. To prove his point, Iamblichus listed "evidence" or "characteristic signs" that demonstrated that those possessed did not utilise normal human consciousness or sensation. These signs included anaesthesia and resistance to injury. For example, many were not burned when fire was applied to them on account of their "divine inspiration". He noted that even those who were burned did not react to the pain "because at this time they are not living the life of an animate being".

Divine possession was an important phenomenon in the early polytheistic Greco-Roman religion. Plato, the fourth-century Greek philosopher,[3] distinguished between the prophetic

3 Plato (1952)

(mantikê, inspired by Apollo), the mystical (telestikê, inspired by Dionysus), the poetic (inspired by the Muses), the erotic (inspired by Aphrodite and Eros), and divinely inspired trance possessions like that of the Oracle of Delphi.

Oracle temples were dedicated to specific deities and were spaces that individuals as well as state delegations frequently visited to seek guidance. The oracle was obtained through a prophet or prophetess who was thought to be "inspired" or "possessed" by a god, goddess or daimon, a type of semi-divine spirit. The most famous oracle was Pythia at Delphi who became "inspired" or "filled with a god" and whose body became a medium for the god Apollo's voice. Her temple is still a huge tourist attraction.

While Christianity subscribes to the idea of spirit possession, such possession is believed to be demonic, not divine. The Church holds that possession derives from the devil, or Satan, his lesser demons and the fallen angels. In the battle between Satan and heaven, Satan is believed to engage in "spiritual attacks" including demonic possession against humans by the use of supernatural powers to harm them physically or psychologically. Prayers for deliverance, sprinkling of holy water on the possessed person's house or body and various sacraments and exorcisms are generally used to drive the demon out.

Roman Catholic doctrine states that angels are non-corporeal spiritual beings with intelligence and personal will. Among these are "fallen angels", or demons, who are able to demonically possess people without the victim's knowledge or consent, leaving them morally blameless.

Likewise, in Islam, spirit possessions are deemed to be of demonic origin. The belief that spiritual entities, particularly jinnis,[4] can possess a person or thing or place, is widespread. Such

4 In Arabic mythology, a jinni is a mystical spirit that resides on Earth. Invisible to human eyes, this enigmatic being can take on different shapes and wield supernatural abilities.

entities are referred to as marrid, or 'demons'; bhut, or 'ghosts'; jinn, or 'invisible beings'; or shaytaan, 'satanic beings'.

According to traditional Islam, possession by a jinni can happen for various reasons. Ibn Taymiyyah[5] asserted that a jinni might sometimes haunt an individual because the person has harmed it. Another cause for jinn possession, according to Moiz Ansari,[6] is that the jinni falls in love with a human and thereupon possesses them. Some women have reported that during the time they believed they were possessed by a jinni, the entity tried to have sexual intercourse from inside their bodies. And thirdly, according to Moiz Ansari, it occurs when an evil jinni simply wants to harm a human for no specific reason. Such a jinni will find the opportunity to possess the person when they are vulnerable, when in a highly emotional state or when they are unconscious.

In the Hindu belief system, there is a commonly held perception that spirit possession is more common in folk aspects of Hinduism, while classical Hinduism pertains to abstract philosophies about the nature of existence and prescriptions for formalised rituals. However, a careful reading of the shastras, or "ancient texts", reveals that spirit possession was not only a part of Sanatan Dharma[7] but until the medieval era and even later in local literature, it was quite acceptable and commonplace.

Professor Frederick Smith in his excellent book, *The Self Possessed: Deity and Spirit Possession in South Asian Literature and Civilization*, observes that linguistic references to possession are found in the oldest Vedic texts, the Samhitas, around 1500–1000 BCE, where the Sanskrit words avesa, grahana, and pravesana indicate different modes of possession. The word avesa from the

---

5 Ibn Taymiyyah, *Majmu'a Fatawa Ibn Taymiyya* (Cairo: Dar ar-Rahmat, u.d.)

6 Moiz Ansari, *Islam And the Paranormal: What Does Islam Say about the Supernatural in the Light of Qur'an, Sunnah And Hadith,* 2006

7 Sanatan Dharma means "eternal law" in Hinduism

Sanskrit root viś meaning "to enter" has been used in the sense of possession in a benign and desirable context. In effect, avesa is friendly, benign or self-motivated possession, while pravesana is possession or absorption generated from outside.

He opines that "the non or scant recognition of possession in pre-modern India has been due to the long-standing aversion to it among the educated Judeo-Christians as well as educated Hindus for whom possession has fallen outside the realm of both reason and social accountability". As a consequence, despite their ancient roots and historical continuities, belief in spirit possession has tended to be marginalised in mainstream scholarly, religious and nationalist discourses. Nevertheless, in the everyday contexts of lived religion, "possession is the most common and most valued form of spiritual expression in India".

Moreover, in regional Indian and subcontinental languages there are many common terms used to denote possession: hava lagna or bhavana in Hindi; chadna in Bengali; bharhoawa, "to weigh or mount" in Marathi; avesh in Tamil; avecam or arude in Sinhalese, and so on. All indicate broadly the same phenomenon.

The Japanese scholar of Sanskrit and Buddhist literature, Minoru Hara, in his study of the Mahabharata lists nearly sixty semantic contexts in which avesa is found in the text.

Of the various instances of possession found in the Mahabharata there is none as graphic and remarkable as the case of Aswatthama who, when possessed by Bhairava, the ferocious form of Shiva, goes on to massacre the Pandava camp. Another sacred text, the *Linga Purana*, describes Shiva's possession of the body of a dead Brahmin, Lakulisa, using his yogic powers (pravishtayogamaya).

But not all possessions described in Hindu texts are by deities. There are also accounts of possession by ethereal spirits of various natures, capabilities and competencies as well as the invoking of a particularly powerful spirit for a specific action. Consider the following excerpt from the Aranyaka Parva of the Mahabharata:

> The danavas inform Duryodhana that his divinity is a gift from Shiva. They tell him that other asuras will take possession (praveksyanti) of Bhishma, Drona, Kripa and others, and so possessed (avistah), they will fight his enemies ruthlessly. Pitiless, possessed by the danavas, their inner souls overwhelmed, they battle with their relations and cast all love far out … moreover, groups of danavas and rakshasas will take on lives in the wombs of the baronage and fight mightily with enemies. They also tell Duryodhana that whenever fear arises in him from Arjuna for that too they have devised a means: the soul of the slain Naraka will take the body of Karna in order to slay Arjuna. These Kaurava heroes, possessed, were overcome by passion and darkness, so sought the death of Phalguna (Arjuna). Thus, Bhishma, Drona, Kripa and the others were no longer friendly towards the sons of Pandu now that their minds were taken over by danavas (danavakrantacetasah).[8]

In other words, it was not just the Kauravas who were fighting the war but also asuras and rakshasas who had taken control of the army, an aspect clearly missed in popular readings of the Mahabharata.

The concept of possession is also enunciated in a different context in the Vedas and in the Upanishads where the idea is used to explain the mechanics of creation. The *Isopanishad* describes how the inert world was entered, permeated, possessed and animated by the Lord (Isa): *Isavasyam idam sarvam yatkimca jagatyam jagat.*

In a fascinating creation myth, the Aitareya Upanishad describes man as being possessed by deities but governed centrally by the primordial deity. It says:

---

8 *Mahabharata*, Johannes Adrianus Bernardus van Buitenen

> In the beginning this world was the Self, One alone, and there was no other being at all that blinked an eye. He thought: let me create a world. Elemental deities were created who became hungry and wanted a place to establish themselves and eat. First a cow was brought then a horse, but both proved inadequate, so man was created. Then the Atman told them to enter their respective dwellings. Fire became speech and entered the mouth; the wind became breath and entered the nostrils; the sun became sight and entered the eyes; the water became hearing and entered the ears; the moon became the mind and entered the heart; death became the in-breath and entered the navel … and so on. Then the Atman thought: those deities cannot function without Me, and He pondered from which place He should enter man, deciding to "split open the head at the point where the hair parts and enter through that gate" (*sa etam va simanam vidaryaitaya dwara prapadyata*).

The rishis who composed the Upanishads were clear that the world and human beings are animated by great acts of original possession where the divine enters into and controls the activities of this world, albeit from behind a veil, the rendering of which is the key to adhyatmic, or spiritual realizations. While some may look at this as doctrinal positioning, it has undeniable application in the ritualistic heart of Sanatan Dharma. Consider, for example, the popular ritual of nyasa for a deity, whether Vedic or Tantric.

The intent of nyasa is by using the power of mantra to correctly place the appropriate form of a Devta in various parts of the body, or object, or image. It is only after a successful nyasa that the sadhaka, or practitioner, enters a state of being possessed, or in communion, and is suited for further ritual engagement. Consider this excerpt from the nyasa to be performed:

> May Brahma be established in my organ of generation. May Vishnu be established in my feet. May Hara be established in my hands. May Indra be established in my arms. May Agni be established in my belly. May Shiva be established in my heart…

When executed by a trained sadhaka, the above is nothing but an invocation for possession, which results in the divine possession of the body. In Tantra too, nyasa constitutes an integral part of ritual purification of the five elements of which the human body is composed.

Spirit possession also occurs in the yogic context where an adept is able to enter another and take control of the latter's mind or body. The story is told of Adi Shankara, the eighth-century Vedic scholar, possessing the body of a dead king during a celebrated debate. The popular *Vetalapancavimshati*[9] is replete with stories of possessions of different kinds. In Patanjali's *Yogasutras*, a chapter deals with siddhis, or "supernormal powers" that are gained as a result of yoga, allowing the avesa, or "entrance", of one's chitta, or "feelings", into another's body.

In the *Yoga Vasishtha*, we find a brilliant passage where Vasishtha tells child Rama about how kundalini shakti is used to enter into different states, beings or other forms of matter. In another part of the text, Vasishtha describes that when prana is led into a state of stability by engaging in the practice of breath retention, one can enter the body of another person, known as pravisati. This is how a yogi is able to transform their shakti and enter into or possess another being or object and bring the same under their control.

9 *Vetalapancavimshati*, or *Twenty-five Tales of Betal* is a collection of Indian tales and legends. The stories are about the captivating adventures of King Vikramaditya who encounters an evil spirit named Vetala.

In Tantric literature, possession acquires a more central status, which ranges from the exalted references of samavesa to the more mundane but rampant instances of oracular possession. According to Tantric tradition, entering turiya, or "the fourth state of consciousness", is possible only when the perfection of samavesa allows the deity to inhabit, instruct, guide and direct the sadhaka on exactly how the worship is to be executed to its complete satisfaction. In short, by general agreement practitioners thought it was unlikely for a sadhaka to enter the highest states of liberation without being absorbed or possessed by a higher deity or the Supreme, in this case, Shiva.

Kathleen M. Erndl, a Hindu scholar, proposes that "divine possession is the most dramatic way to encounter the goddess experientially, and it also presents the greatest challenge to the Western worldview". In Hinduism, divine possession is acceptable and even expected. Erndl discusses at length that "Hinduism does not draw a clear dividing line between divine and human; gods can become humans and humans can become gods". When a woman or man is possessed, the Devta is taking over control of a human body, and that body is allowing itself to be possessed. This is acceptable in the Hindu worldview.[10]

The Kapalika text *Saivaparibhasa*[11] states, "Kapalikas, or Shaivite adepts, attain samayam, or 'equipoise', through samavesa. Just as spirits possess people in ordinary life, in the same way Shiva possesses those who are liberated."

My research into diverse communities across India shows that spirit and divine possessions cut across all religions yet are particularly common in indigenous and rural communities.

For instance, oracles in Buddhist Ladakh follow the practice of invoking deities and mediating a dialogue between the divine

10 *Spirit Possession: The Challenge to the Western Worldview* by Bowie Snodgrass

11 A valuable manual on Saiva Siddhanta

and the populace by becoming mediums of possession. These practitioners are prevalent within the gompas, the Buddhist monasteries and temples, as well as in localised traditions where divine possessions take place in the domestic spaces of the oracle. In the latter, the lhamo, "the female oracle", or the lhapa, "the male oracle", is often involuntarily possessed by local deities. When they are in their normal state they are often described as luya, or "empty vessels", in Ladakhi.

Among the Tibetans, the Nechung Oracle serves as a spirit medium of Dorje Drakden, Nechung Monastery's central protective deity. This role involves entering trance-like states, where the oracle is possessed by the protector deity, offering prophetic advice and guidance to the Dalai Lama and the Tibetan government on matters of national security and politics. The possession typically occurs during monastic rituals and public ceremonies, where the oracle dons a ceremonial hat and is surrounded by chanting monks and beating drums, allowing the deity to communicate through the oracle's voice. This sacred tradition, which dates back to the sixteenth century during the era of the fifth Dalai Lama, continues to play a vital role in Tibetan spiritual life, even in exile, where the Nechung Oracle offers blessings and prophecies to the global Tibetan community.

After the 1959 Tibetan exodus to India, the Nechung Monastery was re-established in Dharamshala, Himachal Pradesh, continuing to recognise the oracle as the official "State Oracle of the Central Tibetan Administration".[12] The fourteenth Dalai Lama reveals in his autobiography, *Freedom in Exile*, that it was the Nechung Oracle who entered a trance state and provided him with crucial guidance on how to escape the impending assault from Chinese forces targeting him and countless others. Through the oracle, Dorje Drakden not only urged him to depart but also laid out specific directions for him to follow to reach the Indian

12 Choedon (2021); Laycock (Ed., 2015)

border.[13] While there have been differing opinions on which deity possesses the oracle, for many followers both the Pehar deity and Dorje Drakden are one and the same whose core purpose remains unchanged: to provide divine insight and protection for the Tibetan people.

Often the phenomenon of divine possession includes groups of people becoming possessed at the same time as seen at mass possessions, mostly observed in specific festivals as in Theyyam performances in Kerala, the Siri full-moon ritual in Karnataka or the Deodhani Festival in Assam.

The Siri cult is a trance tradition of the Tulu people of coastal Karnataka. At the Ayaana Festival of this cult, a mass possession takes place on the full moon that corresponds with the spring equinox. The festival takes place at the shrine of Siri, the patron goddess of the Tulu community. The rituals begin with a prayer and offerings of sandal paste and areca flowers, which are given as prasadam to Tantric Brahmans (Brahman ritual specialists). The group begins reciting the legend of Siri in a rhythmic chant and forms two concentric circles, the men on the outside dressed in red lungis and the women clad in saris forming the inner circle. It is the women in the inner circle who are supposed to become possessed by the spirit of Siri during the course of the ritual. Their relatives stand in the outer circle and keep up a hypnotic chanting. As the ritual proceeds, the women scream, roll on the ground or dance frenziedly. This continues until daybreak or until the women are exhausted. The possession event has great therapeutic effect on the participants and also enhances their social standing.

Another instance of group possession is the Deodhani Festival in Assam. Over the three days of this festival, those who are present in and around the Kamakhya temple in Guwahati

13 Dalai Lama XIV, Bstan-'dzin-rgya-mtsho (1990). *Freedom in Exile: The Autobiography of the Dalai Lama*. HarperCollins Publishers.

are immersed in an ocean of sound from the relentless pounding of drums and clashing of cymbals at a volume that is not only raucously hard on the ears but becomes a pulsating force that pummels and vibrates the body. At times the rhythm resembles an immense heartbeat, which might be imagined as the heartbeat of Devi Kamakhya.[14] At other times it accelerates and intensifies, rising in a crescendo that elicits 'shrieking, howling and jumping' from the dancing deodhas, the shamans possessed by fierce incarnations of the goddess.

Between sixteen to twenty-one deodhas receive garlands of flowers around their necks from devoted spectators. They wield weapons such as slender batons, tridents and swords. The deodhas engage at intervals in wild and exuberant dancing, making triumphal gestures with their arms and hopping around on one leg. Pulling exaggerated and grotesque facial expressions, they roll their eyes, project their tongues and bare their teeth ghoulishly, each possessed by different aspects of Devi Kamakhya.

Theyyam, "the dance of the gods", is another powerful instance of ritual possession. Some forms of Theyyam involve several performers and constitute a group possession. Theyyam is said to be an assertion of low-caste spirituality as the low-caste performers when possessed are worshipped by upper castes to whom they are otherwise "untouchable".

Huge crowds gather as local gods take possession of the bodies of the dancers. Dressed in elaborate costumes and painstakingly applied face paint, the Devta enters the dancer only when he puts on the headdress which can be up to seven metres high. Sixteen burning torches that are continually filled with oil are attached to the performer's body. A chicken is beheaded and its blood mixed with turmeric, and water is splashed onto the dancer who screams and rushes to a sacred grove. The dance to the accompaniment of rhythmic drumming carries on through the night, rising to a

14 P.A. Dold (2011)

crescendo at daybreak. The dancers who are mediums of the gods for a day are worshipped and approached for blessings.

Many anthropologists have documented the pervasive phenomenon of spirit possession in the Pacific and Africa, the Middle East and many parts of Asia and the Americas.

It has been observed that the phenomenon of spirit possession often conforms to patterns particular to the culture where it occurs and can be viewed as voluntary or involuntary. In cases of voluntary possession, practitioners will use several techniques to invoke the spirits or gods "to fill" or "to mount" them, resulting in a state of spiritual ecstasy. Anthropologists refer to these techniques as "induction strategies". They may include prolonged periods of prayer, fasting or the consumption of hallucinogens. However, the most widely used induction strategy is music and dancing. In some religions, such as Haitian Vodou, it is expected that many of the congregants will become possessed during ceremonies that involve singing and dancing. Certain ecstatic forms of Christianity, notably Pentecostalism, may also be studied as forms of voluntary possession. During church services Pentecostals become filled with the holy spirit, which can manifest as an altered state of consciousness, speaking in tongues and other extraordinary abilities.

At other times the possession is unsolicited and unwelcome. The anthropologist Erika Bourguignon wrote of "positive and negative" forms of possession to distinguish the experience of someone possessed by a demon from that of an oracle serving as a mouthpiece for a benevolent deity. I.M. Lewis amended this distinction to speak of "controlled" and "uncontrolled" or "solicited" and "unsolicited" forms of spirit possession. The primary differentiation between a positive and negative experience of possession is whether the possession is desired and occurs in a ritualised context where it does not interfere with daily life. In many cultures, an experience of involuntary possession may be a sign that the person is a shaman, or medium, as in the Kullu

Valley. With time and training they are able to control when the state of possession occurs, making the spirits a resource rather than a nuisance.

Essentially the phenomena of spirit possession amount to connecting and communicating with the spirit world. In recent times, outside the mainstream religions, there has been a plethora of mediums and channellers who have claimed special abilities to contact the spirit dimension.

Celebrity mediums, such as Matt Fraser, Tyler Henry, Teresa Caputo, John Edward, Lisa Williams, have made their way into contemporary consciousness through television shows, books and workshops for training individuals to explore their own psychic and medium potentials.

James Van Praagh, one of the world's most renowned and respected spirit mediums today, explains: "A medium is a psychic who has fine-tuned their extrasensory perception and can interface with spirits in other dimensions. They are able to feel and/or hear thoughts, voices or mental impressions from the spirit world. A medium is able to become completely receptive to the higher frequency or energies at which spirit people vibrate."

These modern mediums tend to experience four primary methods of mediumship.

4. Spiritual Mediumship: This is the reception and delivery of messages from the spirit in the form of clairaudience, clairvoyance, claircognizance and clairsentience. Messages are usually delivered through speaking, writing or with support of physical divination tools.
5. Physical Mediumship: This creates a physical phenomenon. It can include table-tipping, noise-making, levitation, smoke-billet pictures and the creation of ectoplasm with the help of a visiting spirit. The physical medium and the spirit work together to create and produce a physical phenomenon.

6. Healing Mediumship: This brings the divine light energy of spirit through the body of the medium to transform them and others. This commonly happens through "the laying on of hands", but it also refers to forms of energy healing like Reiki.
7. Channelling Mediumship: The medium connects with only one spirit or the same group of spirits time and time again. Channel mediums make their vocal chords and hands available to the channelled spirit(s) to deliver messages through speaking and writing. Many channellers feel they are allowing their body or voice to be taken over by the spirit whom they are channelling.

A study of channelling phenomena was done by the Institute of Noetic Sciences (IONS) in California.[15] According to its director, Dr Helané Wahbeh, "Channelling means a lot of things to different people. We are defining it as accessing information and energy from beyond time and space. More specifically, channelling means being able to receive information from beyond our traditional five senses and that exists on a spectrum from intuition on one side to the other extreme in what people might call full trance, where the channels are acting as a vehicle for a disincarnate being to communicate through them."

Spirit possession is still widely regarded by medical experts as a mental illness. Anthropologist Michael Taussig has suggested that "medicalizing" possession as insanity has aided Western imperialism by framing the supernatural beliefs of indigenous cultures as a disease that Western colonisers must cure. As the West comes to better understand the beliefs of other cultures, some medical professionals have shifted their attitudes towards possession. Psychiatrist E. Mansell Pattison has suggested that mental health professionals should learn more about the

15 Wahbeh (2021)

supernatural beliefs of their patients and explore ways to integrate psychotherapy with traditional practices, such as exorcism.

Psychologists and medical professionals generally assume that spirits do not exist and that spirit possession is actually "a naturally occurring state of dissociation" in which an individual experiences a breakdown of their awareness, memory, identity or perception. Other symptoms associated with spirit possession, such as convulsions, are likewise assumed to have natural causes that originate in either the body or the mind. Psychologists have proposed that possessed people are actually suffering from a variety of disorders, such as epilepsy, dissociative identity disorder, multiple-personality disorder, schizophrenia, bipolar disorder, obsessive compulsive disorder and Tourette syndrome. Other explanations have included ergotism or toxins that the possessed has consumed either unknowingly or as part of a medicinal or magical practice. Psychoanalysts have suggested that spirit possession originates entirely in the mind and that demons and spirits are actually manifestations of impulses and desires that the possessed person has subconsciously suppressed.

More recent psychological interpretations of possession and exorcism caution against explanations that ignore the role of culture. Psycho-social interpretations regard possession and exorcism as phenomena that have psychological and social origins. With this turn towards social theories of the mind, some medical experts have challenged the assumption that everyone who experiences possession is necessarily unhealthy. Instead, it has been suggested that possession and exorcism may contribute to psychological health in cultures where these phenomena are common.

Generally speaking, anthropologists do not pathologise spirit possession but on the contrary interpret it as an appropriate even desirable phenomenon of particular communities.[16] The general consensus in anthropological field studies is that with

16 Kirmayer (1994)

some exceptions possessed persons are usually not psychologically disordered. Because many mediums or other specialists of possession ritual are highly valued within their particular socio-cultural contexts, e.g., as healers or oracles, spirit possession is viewed as an integral part of local cultural techniques that are functional for local medical and religious systems as well as regulators of social power relations.[17]

Dr Wahbeh concurs that "channelling is not a psychopathology. Channellers who have participated in our surveys do not have a clinical level of pathology. There's no increased pathology and dissociation or psychotic symptoms and they live pretty well functional lives."

Even today in the twenty-first century, humanity continues to interact with spirit entities. While contemporary culture regards spirit possession as something extraordinary, to many it is a relatively ordinary part of life. On 11 March 2011, a tsunami devastated Japan, killing nearly twenty thousand people. In the months that followed, many Japanese living in the vicinity of the disaster reported ghostly encounters with the spirits of those who had drowned. Some experienced possession by people and even animals that had died in the disaster. Japan's clergy, including Christian, Buddhist and Shinto priests, were all asked to help quell the unhappy spirits.

In June 2013 a primary school in the Philippines was forced to suspend classes after twenty students inexplicably began screaming, fainting and convulsing. Many interpreted the behaviour as demonic possession. Priests were summoned and blessings and exorcisms were performed. One theory was that the children had conducted a séance offering an invitation to demonic spirits. Another was that some palm trees that had recently been felled near the school had been a home for spirits who were acting out their vengeance by possessing the children.

17 Boddy (1994)

Whatever the explanation, what is important is the persistence of the belief and phenomena of spirit possession in modern urban societies where no active socio-cultural framework upholds such beliefs.

Which brings us to important questions: What about the spirits? Is spirit possession a phenomenon in its own right, mediated by otherworldly entities? A materialistic ontology would naturally deny this possibility. However, how do we reconcile this belief to the lived experiences of millions over centuries?

Answers to such questions have multifarious ramifications, and predominantly on our belief system.

Segment 3

Sacred Healing

"A psychotherapist in a traditional culture may be greatly aided by the continuing presence of the sacred in his society. The whole weight of the community's religion, myths and history prioritizes sacred therapy as the therapist proceeds to mobilize strong psychic energies inside and outside the patient which are no longer available in modern society."

– **Sudhir Kakar,** ***Shamans, Mystics and Doctors***

Goor Hardayal preparing to conduct an exorcism for a family in Shuru village, 2009

Goor Hardayal conducting a Chidra ceremony (village purification) in Shuru village, 2009

Anu Malhotra filming Goor Hardayal, while he conducts a personal pogle (divination ceremony) for her, 2009

Goor Hardayal beats himself violently with shangals (iron chains), while jumping up and down in an intense divine possession trance, 2009

Goor Rudramani ceremonially propitiating his deity, Jamadagni Rishi, Batahar village, 2009

The annual Ambika Devi festival in the village of Nao Pano, when a mass exorcism is usually held. A lady supposedly 'possessed' can be seen dancing wildly in trance, 2009

Local children at play with toy raths, 2009

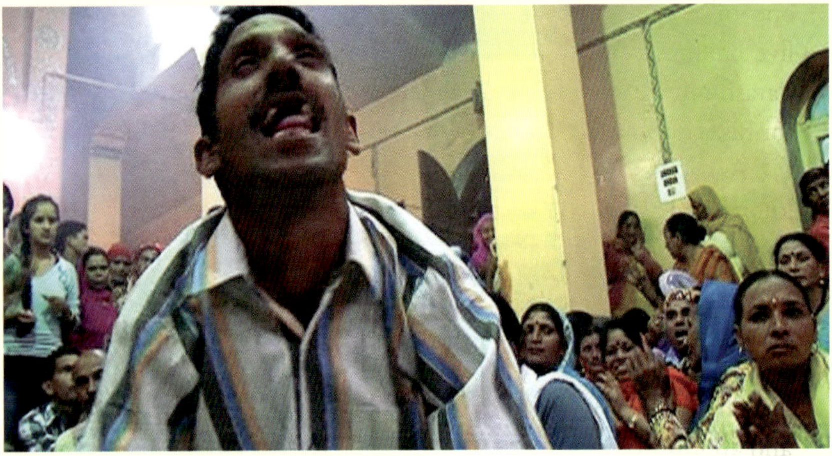

People in a trance at a mass exorcism in the village of Nao Pano during the annual Ambika Devi festival, 2009

The Myth of Rishi Jamadagni

The myth of the seven great sages, or the Saptarishi, is mentioned in various ancient Hindu texts. These sages, of whom Jamadagni is one, rule the current Manvantra, a cosmic cycle of creation and destruction. Jamadagni, whose name means "he that consumes fire", is believed to have descended from the great sage Bhrigu, one of the mind-born sons of Brahma. Rishi Jamadagni had five children with his wife Renuka, the youngest of whom was Parashurama, an avatar of Lord Vishnu. Rishi Jamadagni is revered for his wisdom as a sage and a warrior.

As a boy, Jamadagni persevered and attained complete knowledge of the Vedas without a teacher or guru. Without formal instruction he mastered the science of weapons and warfare.

According to myth, on a particularly hot and sunny day, Jamadagni was angered by the sun, and shot three arrows into the sky, terrifying Surya, the Sun God. To placate him, Surya appeared before Jamadagni as a Brahmin and offered him sandals and an umbrella to give him respite from the heat.

It is believed that towards the end of his life, Rishi Jamadagni meditated upon Lord Shiva and asked for an isolated, serene place for himself. Eventually, after years of meditation, Lord Shiva guided him to the village of Malana in present-day Himachal. He started on the journey with his wife Renuka, with two of his brothers following. Rishi Jamadagni realised that he did not want his brothers to come along, so he created a mist to misguide them. And so it happened that one of the brothers arrived at Lahaul and the other in the Banjar Valley. Malana was at the time the domain of demon Banasura. When Jamadagni arrived, a battle ensued between the Rishi and the rakshasa. The battle ended in a peace treaty whereby administration of Malana was to be handled by Banasura, while justice would be dispensed by Jamadagni. Even today, in the isolated village of Malana, the first sacrifice during all festivals is made to Banasura. The village has a temple dedicated to Renuka, and in the nearby village of Tosh, there is a shrine to Rishi Jamadagni or Jamlu Devta as he is affectionately called.

Another legend tells of a time when Rishi Jamadagni was returning from a pilgrimage to the Kailash Mountain, carrying eighteen idols of different deities in a kardu, or basket, on his head. When he reached the Chandrakhani Peak near Manali, Banasura, the great demon of Malana, who ruled on the other side of Chandrakhani, sensed the approach of the great sage. Rishi Jamadagni was Banasura's sworn enemy. As the sage approached, Banasura sent a harrowing wind across the mountaintop which blew the idols of the eighteen gods from the kardu, scattering them all over the valley.

13
Spirit Illness

In less than a month we are back in Kullu Valley. It has now begun to feel like home. The monsoon has turned the entire valley into a verdant wonderland. The mists have begun to settle lower, swirling about the tops of the tall pines. However, there are hours of sunny spells that make the greens glisten. The sunsets and sunrises are more vivid at this time of year as moisture-bearing cirrus clouds streak the sky. It will soon be time for the apple harvest, and the market is already filled with crates of early pickings. Rocky outcrops between the orchards are filled with rose hips and wildflowers.

But for the moment I am here to learn the names and ways of the dark and malicious spirits that bring illness and misfortune to the unwary here in these mountains.

The next day, as Meru and I walk in his orchard laden with apples, I come to the point and ask him about spirit illness and its prevalence in the valley. "Meru, I noticed that in all the poochh sessions that we have been to, many people came to the Devta for health related issues, and the Goor's, I mean the Devta's diagnosis, which is quite often nazar, bhootpret or oprah, are all black magic, right?"

Meru informs me that nazar is a common phenomenon, arising out of jealousy or envy. "See, Anu, another person's good looks, financial success, or marital happiness may cause so much envy to some people that they resort to putting spells or getting a tantric to do an oprah on their object of envy or revenge."

I ask if he has had any direct experience or has witnessed any instance of spirit illness. He reflects for a moment before responding, "Yes, I have a cousin who all of a sudden began to have severe health issues when she was eighteen years old, which could not be diagnosed by the doctor. Then she began behaving strangely, so we finally took her to our temple where the Goor put a poochh to our Naag Devta. The Devta said that someone had done an oprah on her because she was very beautiful."

"So, what cure did the Devta suggest?" I probe.

"I don't know, Anu, but I do remember that she had to go to the temple every day for a week after which she was cured."

Seeing the scepticism writ large on my face, he laughs. "Well, you too have been suffering from a strange illness for the past ten years, and the Devta told you that you have a nazar. Have you considered that it may be so?"

I have to admit that this has been on my mind, and thus my investigation into this shadowy world of spirit illness has assumed more significance. I request Meru to ask around to find instances of spirit illness and people who are willing to share their experiences with me. I realise that this enquiry may prove difficult as people are usually reticent about revealing such private matters, but I am hoping that Meru will be able to unearth something.

A week goes by without any news from Meru, so I send Avantika to track down Tuleram to ask if he would be willing to talk to me about spirit illness. The next day, Avantika returns beaming and excited, "Tuleram will meet us the day after, and guess what! He is doing a poochh for a child who is sick!"

Two days later we trudge up the now familiar slope through Old Manali to Tuleram's tiny cottage. We nod and wave to the smiling village folk who keep inviting us for chai. Tuleram waves at us from his balcony, shouting his usual cheery greetings, "Good morning, good afternoon, good evening!" He has been waiting for us. He gestures for me to join him on his veranda, and when I do, I notice a woman seated on the ground with an infant of about two years on her lap. The child looks angelic even though he is whimpering, and tears are streaming down his face.

Tuleram explains that the woman wants to consult the Devi about her child's ill health. "I don't know what's happened to Babu. He was fine, but two days ago he began crying incessantly," the woman tells me tearfully, clearly distraught.

"Have you taken him to see a doctor?" I ask.

The woman snorts and shrugging her shoulders, says, "The doctor checked Babu and said that there was absolutely nothing wrong with him! If that is the case, why has he been crying nonstop for two days?"

Tuleram cuts in, "Arre, don't worry, na! Mata will take care of it. Come, let me see what is ailing our little boy." He snaps his fingers in front of the child's face and stares at him intently, then closes his own eyes, muttering some mantras. Both the woman and I wait with bated breath and even the child stops crying. In a few minutes Tuleram opens his eyes and begins conversing with the woman. He sees my expectant expression, and says, "Babu has a nazar. But the Devi will cure him." He stands up, walks inside and soon returns with a bunch of leaves and a jar. Tuleram proceeds to chant mantras loudly as he rotates the bundle of leaves around Babu's head, then waves it over the child's head in an outward motion as if sweeping away something there. He flings the leaves over the balcony onto the hillside. Taking some sesame seeds from the jar with his right hand, he waves them over Babu's head. Opening his palm he studies the seeds. He hands them to the woman saying something which is obviously positive, for she smiles broadly and pockets the seeds.

When I ask about the procedure, Tuleram smiles and explains as best he can. "See, I waved the sacred bethar[1] leaves to absorb the nazar and then threw them away. The seeds divined that the nazar had gone, so Babu will be fine now. See how peacefully he's sleeping now."

We all look at Babu who has indeed fallen asleep. His mother smiles lovingly down at her sleeping infant. I look at Tuleram enquiringly, and he explains, "Madam, these are traditional cures which have been prescribed by our Devtas and passed down orally through generations."

The woman lifts Babu and stands up, saying, "Madam-ji, our Devtas are more powerful than the doctors." As she makes her way down the stairs Babu wakes up, looks around and is strangely quiet. Tuleram exclaims as he dismisses us, "Okay, Madam-ji, good evening, goodnight. I have to go."

Back at the cottage, while we are viewing the day's footage, Meru calls saying that he has found a friend who is willing to talk to us about a case of spirit illness and that he would take me to meet him the next day.

The next morning, we set off from Manali, driving along the left bank of the Beas for about half an hour to the village of Batahar to meet Chaman Lal Thakur. Along the way Meru informs me that Chaman is in his mid-fifties, is well-educated and financially well-to-do. "Chaman is a man of the modern world but remains rooted to his village life," says Meru.

Batahar is a charming village with cottages set amidst fields of maize and vegetables. There are apple orchards laden with fruit and brooks edged with yellow and white wildflowers. We head to a handsome stone-and-wood modern cottage set in a lovely garden of rambling roses, lilies and zinnias. Adjoining it are orchards of luscious red apples, ripe for plucking.

---

1 Bethar: A kind of juniper found on the higher slopes.

Chaman is waiting for us inside his cosy living room decorated with contemporary furniture, huge glass window frames and a splendid view of the mountains, fields and orchards. Charming and eloquent, he greets me warmly and we fall into easy conversation. I thank Chaman for agreeing to talk to me, and he grins. "Arre, Anu-ji, I know all about your project." Noting my surprise, he says, "The Banons are childhood friends, so Kishan was telling me about your film. And of course, I know Meru well, so I'm happy to help in any way."

After exchanging pleasantries, I ask Chaman about his experience of spirit illness. Chaman discloses, "It is common practice in our villages to periodically get a jhar[2] done for our children to remove a nazar. But, when one of my female relatives began behaving strangely, I saw spirit illness from close quarters. This lady who was usually soft-spoken and shy began unloosening her hair and dishevelling it. She would sit in a corner with a fierce expression in her eyes and make loud horrible sounds." Chaman's affable expression has changed to one of distress as he recalls the experience. He adds, "She was a newlywed bride and her strange behaviour was hugely alarming to her in-laws."

"What happened to her?" I ask gently.

Chaman responds, "Well, we had to take her to our village Devta who said that she was possessed by the Chettu Devta, a smaller village god who had come with her from her native village."

I ask Chaman to tell me more.

"Well, the Devta prescribed a series of cures, which were done over six months after which she was cured."

"And this lady never exhibited those symptoms again?" Despite my best efforts, my voice betrays my scepticism.

Chaman notes it, and says wryly, "No, never. In fact, she's a mother of two kids now."

---

2 A practice to cast off evil-eye or "nazar"

"So, Chaman, what were the remedies prescribed by the Devta for your relative?"

Chaman shakes his head, saying, "I don't really know, and we can't ask the family as it's a delicate matter." Seeing my crestfallen expression, he adds, "But I can try and get permission for you to film at our temple of Rishi Jamadagni and meet his Goor, Rudramani, who treated my relative."

Meru nods approvingly. "Yes, he would be the right person to answer all your questions about spirit illness."

I am keen to visit this temple and the Goor. Chaman promises to make enquiries and get back to me.

And so it is that a few days later I am back in Batahar. Chaman has obtained permission for me to document Goor Rudramani's poochh session, which takes place once a week within the temple itself. We walk down a narrow lane lined with a few traditional houses until we reach the outer wall of the temple where Chaman is waiting for us, all smiles.

The notice on the temple wall instructs women with their period not to enter the temple, a common taboo in most Hindu temples. In addition, all leather items like belts, wallets and handbags are strictly prohibited in almost all Himachali temples. Chaman explains that all the temples of the rishis follow stricter rules and stringent sanitation practices.

We take off our shoes and walk into the temple compound. There is a shallow tank in the floor in front of us into which water from a natural spring flows through a pipe. Chaman tells me that this is the Devta's sacred water with which we have to wash our hands and sprinkle our heads as a ritual purification before we enter the temple. Next to the pool is a small temple of Maha Kali where we pay our respects. We walk towards the contemporary gable-roofed temple of Rishi Jamadagni, which incorporates both the kath-kuni and wooden roof styles of architecture that are quite common in the newly constructed temples in the valley. Outside the temple is an alcove where instead of a statue two stones are placed like a chair, representing the throne of Jamadagni Rishi. There are other royal connotations like the two temple guards dressed in an ornate red uniform and holding silver staffs.

The guards do not allow me to enter the temple, so Chaman and I sit at the doorway from where I am allowed to film with my camcorder while he explains the proceedings to me. I notice that the temple hall is filled with about thirty locals, mostly women and a few older men. In one corner there is an ornately carved wooden seat, almost a throne, where a man dressed in a kurta, dhoti and topi is seated.

Chaman whispers, "That is Goor Rudramani who is also the pujari of Jamadagni Rishi."

Goor Rudramani seems unlike all the Goors I have so far encountered. To begin with, he has short hair, he does not have the customary dharj in front of him, nor does he have someone ringing a bell near him and most notably there are no bajantris. Rudramani is reciting something softly as his audience listens prayerfully. Suddenly Rudramani jumps with a start and begins to sway gently. He is in a trance. Everyone bows their head acknowledging the presence of their Devta who will now speak through his medium. Rudramani does not enter a violent trance; he speaks in a normal tone as the Devta.

Devta Jamadagni Rishi via Goor Rudramani: "I am Rishi Jamadagni, the form of the all-pervasive Lord Brahma."

Congregation: "Jai ho, Maharaj! Hail to our Devta!"

Devta via Goor: "There is much power in our ancient rituals. You must read our scriptures and recite prayers."

Congregation: "We have come to witness your glory, Devta. Please bless us!"

Devta via Goor: "Have faith in me! With true faith anything is possible."

A couple come to the forefront of the crowd of devotees and begin speaking to the Devta. Pradeep and Snehlata are from Kullu and this is their second visit. Previously Pradeep had been suffering from a nervous disorder and despite ten years of medication had shown little improvement. His condition had made him irritable, and his anger was stressing his wife and children. Initially he had been reluctant to come to the Devta here, but he had improved dramatically after his first visit.

Pradeep: "I'm feeling stronger, and my mind is at peace despite no medicinal aids. Thank you, Devta!"

Devta via Goor: "Your body has begun to heal, don't worry. Have you brought the mud I asked for?"

Snehlata hands Rudramani a small bag from which he pulls out some mud that the couple have dug up from their garden. Rudramani closes his eyes and runs his hands over the mud in quiet concentration. In a couple of minutes, to my astonishment, he begins to describe the house that Pradeep and Snehlata live in.

Devta via Goor: "Your new house is near a slum. You have a pathway in front of your home and a motorable road at some distance."

Snehlata: "Yes."

Devta via Goor: "It is a cement construction and is painted in white, yellow, green and red."

Pradeep: "Yes, it has been painted that way."

Devta via Goor: "And you have an iron gate?"

Snehlata: "Yes, we do."

Devta via Goor: "Did you conduct a puja ceremony when the foundation stone was laid?"

Pradeep: "Yes, we did."

Devta via Goor: "According to Vastu texts, you were advised to bury something below the stone. Did you?"

Pradeep and Snehlata: "No, we didn't."

Devta via Goor: "That's a pity. The location is a good one for your house but not for you. You will have to get a puja conducted as soon as possible to rectify your oversight."

Pradeep: "Thank you, Devta. We will do as you say."

Devta via Goor: "I promise you that your family, health, mental and professional problems will disappear after the puja."

Pradeep and Snehlata: "Thank you, Devta!"

The couple leave the hall and step outside. I rush after them in pursuit. Chaman requests they speak with me to which they graciously agree. Snehlata is all praise for the Devta, "Our Devta is very powerful. My husband had refused to come here many times before, but once he did, he felt miraculously better."

She becomes a little teary-eyed, and Pradeep admits, "Thanks to my wife's urging, I came here last month for the first time. The Devta wanted me to have a cleansing bath in his sacred spring water for a week, and that has made a world of difference. I feel calmer and have more control over my limbs. See, I can now hold my pen." He pulls out a pen from his shirt pocket and taking the piece of paper offered by his wife begins to painstakingly write on it.

"See, he can write now." His wife smiles.

Suddenly the calm of the temple compound is rent by loud blood-curdling screams. I race back towards the temple door to see what is happening. Expecting a commotion, I am surprised to see everyone sitting calmly. In the front of the crowd is a young girl sitting cross-legged, writhing in apparent pain and crying pitifully. She begins to flail her arms and whirls her dupatta over her head. As her actions gain momentum her screams become louder and more terrifying. I am completely shaken by what I am witnessing.

"What in heavens is happening? What is causing the girl to scream in agony? Why is everyone sitting quietly and not doing anything to help her?" I turn to Chaman in confusion. He gestures for me to calm down and watch.

The girl has stopped screaming. Instead, she is moaning and rocking her body back and forth. The temple helper stands and walks towards one end of the hall to where a few long iron chains hang. "The Devta's shangal," Chaman whispers, pointing. The helper lifts a seemingly heavy clutch of chains and walks to where the girl is sitting. He bends over and drapes them across her neck.

The girl bows her head and to my astonishment immediately quietens down and becomes still. Goor Rudramani speaks to the girl, and she listens in silence. Everyone sitting around also listens attentively.

Devta via Goor: "You are under the spell of Narsingh. He has possessed you."

Girl's mother: "Oh no! My Lord, what is to be done?"

Devta via Goor: "I have suppressed him for now with my shangal. To get rid of him you will have to drink the sacred water from my temple and take a weekly sacred bath. These will heal you."

I notice the girl lift her head, look at the Goor and nod her head. The temple helper takes the chains off her and she is given some holy water to drink. The girl adjusts her clothes, knots her hair and seems to be completely normal. She stands up, bows deeply and comes out along with her mother. I note that although her face is flushed, she seems fine albeit preoccupied. Both women leave the temple compound hurriedly. I am flummoxed, deeply affected by what I have just witnessed.

Seeing my expression Chaman indicates that we should leave and takes us back to his cottage. I rest a while, trying to process my experiences. Later, over a delicious lunch of siddoos, a local delicacy, we discuss the morning's events. Chaman explains that because the Devta had diagnosed the girl's condition as one of possession by Narsingh, "the Devta's shangal was put around her neck to subdue the evil spirit. You saw how she calmed down as soon as she came in contact with the shangal."

He tells me about the cure prescribed by the Devta: a weekly bath with the Devta's sacred spring water. After each bath the girl was to undergo a jhar with a sprig of bethar while the Goor would recite certain mantras.

"How long will she have to do this?" I ask.

Chaman shrugs his shoulders, saying, "Till the spirit is exorcised, which can happen in one session as it did with my relative or it could take a few months."

Chaman is reticent about making enquiries regarding the possibility of me speaking to the girl or her mother but suggests that he would set up a meeting for me with Goor Rudramani. "Rudramani-ji will definitely be able to answer all your questions as he is a learned scholar and very articulate. He has studied many ancient Hindu texts and knows our mythology and customs well."

I agree it is a good idea, and take my leave, thanking Chaman for being so helpful. He promises to revert soon.

Back in my cottage I mull over the extraordinary day. Dismissing spirit illness as superstition or at best psychosomatic illness would have been an easy explanation for what I had just witnessed and have been hearing about anecdotally, yet I cannot dismiss the lived experience of many in the valley. I am determined to investigate this intriguing phenomenon.

Chaman calls the next morning and cheerfully informs me that Goor Rudramani is willing to meet me the day after. It is a warm afternoon as I make my way through the narrow streets of Batahar past the temple where the event had occurred to a modest brick-and-mortar house surrounded by apple orchards on three sides. Goor Rudramani meets me politely on his sunny veranda, and we sit on the floor and begin our conversation, with the Goor questioning me closely about my documentary. He has a serious manner and speaks chaste Hindi. After satisfying himself with the intention, approach and content of the documentary series, he relaxes and agrees to be interviewed.

I begin by asking how Devta Jamadagni Rishi had first come to Batahar. He tells me that there were originally twelve seats of the Devta in Kullu Valley that had grown into many more. In Batahar, ancestors of the village had found the Devta's dharj while digging foundations to construct a house. One of the people standing there fell into a trance and the Devta revealed himself to them. A temple was built on the spot, and over the years the size of its congregation swelled.

Rudramani says he sees himself primarily as a social worker in his dual role as Goor and pujari of Devta Jamadagni Rishi, a role he assumed more than twenty-five years ago. He first went into trance when he was twenty-eight years of age whilst attending a religious festival where devotees were singing kirtans. He was singing the holy song of Jamadagni Rishi when he suddenly felt a strange shaking creeping over him. He went into a trance. Later he was told that he had jumped into the holy fire that was burning and that he had stayed in the fire for four to five minutes. Afterwards he had no singes or burns and no reason to believe that he had jumped into the fire other than the clear testimonies of several eyewitnesses.

His father was the Goor and pujari of the Devta, but Rudramani was chosen by the Devta even while his father was alive. He tells me that he kept going into trances until the Devta declared that Rudramani would act as his Goor, and during meditation would instruct him on his role and practices. Rudramani also received pointers from his father. "My father taught me to always keep my intentions pure towards our Devta and not to be tempted by greed of any sort. He taught me that we are here to serve, and it is our duty to look after the Devta's devotees and ease their woes."

I mention that his state of trance seemed quite different from those I had witnessed so far. Rudramani explains that there are two types of divine possession: one that begins at the feet and travels upwards—as had happened with Tuleram, Hardayal and Tej Singh—where the Goor's personality dissolves gradually; and another that happens in an instant through the head and is likened to being hit by lightning when the Goor instantly goes into trance. Rudramani says he mostly experiences the second type of divine trance possession. He informs me that it is not necessary for a Goor to shake much during a trance. "Violent shaking is more likely to happen when the Devta is angry and the shaking represents his rage, but I usually experience gentle body movements though I am told my voice changes."

Yes, I do note that Rudramani's own voice and style of speaking are different to what I had heard a couple of days ago at the temple.

I now turn to my main query about spirit illness. Rudramani says, "Well, you see, there are two sorts of maladies in the world. Some of these are physical ailments only for which the Devta asks the person to consult a doctor. However, there is a second sort of ailment that may seem physical but is related to mental, emotional or spiritual issues. There are many non-physical dimensions to illness, which medical science does not know or recognise, and these can only be diagnosed and cured by the spiritual powers of the Devta."

Rudramani informs me that spirit illness is rampant in the valley and delineates three categories: the mild forms are of the nazar; more serious are oprahs done with the help of a tantra practitioner; and the most serious are possessions by ghosts, evil spirits, demons, minor gods or nature spirits.

I ask about the girl I had seen at his temple and the cures that he had prescribed. Rudramani corrects me, "It is not my prescription, it is the Devta's remedy. And my Devta is well-known for being an effective healer." The soft-spoken Goor explains that the cures commonly prescribed by his Devta are drinking and bathing in the sacred water that comes from a natural source; tying protective threads or especially made amulets into which mantras have been chanted; specific pujas; observation of certain taboos; cleansing of self and home with bethar, or other specific cures.

I recollect Kala Devi's case in Shuru, Deepak's case with Tuli and other such incidents related by several locals that my crew and I had spoken to. There also appears to be various sorts of possessions like Chaman's relative who was said to be possessed by a Chettu Devta or the girl in Batahar who is supposedly possessed by Narsingh. Clearly, there is much to understand and explore. Meru tells me that ridding someone of demonic possession often requires a tanqt, or "an adept who has specialised knowledge of exorcism". Not all Goors have this bhootvidya, or "knowledge of ghosts". However, Goor Hardayal does. Meru asks Hardayal if we can meet him, and he invites us home for tea.

The next day we set off for Shuru for our second visit to Hardayal's house. He and his family greet us warmly and we settle down on his veranda. His wife Kamla serves us milky tea and biscuits while his daughter, Shanta, and son, Devi Chand, also hang around, excited by the cameras.

After finishing our refreshments, I begin questioning Hardayal about spirit illness. He pretty much reiterates what Goor Rudramani had told me. "Inexplicable illnesses, bodily pains, mental instability, problems in business or problems in conceiving children often bring people to the Devi. Sometimes the Devi tells them that their problems are medical and advises them to consult a doctor. If the Devi feels that a person's problems are related to strife or tensions at home, she may just counsel them and advise the person or family to mend their ways. On the other hand, they could be afflicted by an evil eye, black magic or possessed by evil spirits. In that case the Devi tells them what needs to be done."

When I ask about Chettu Devta and Narsingh, Hardayal tells me that a major deity like Shiva, Vishnu, Brahma or any of the rishis would never harm a person. "However, all the major Devtas in the valley also have their own gann,[3] or "clique of less powerful spirit entities". Some of these gann may be demonic and can be manipulated through devotion, rituals or a sheep sacrifice to possesses or harm someone. In fact, whenever a sacrifice takes place during a religious festival, it is done as an offering to appease one of these gann," says Hardayal matter-of-factly.

I ask him how his Devi cures possession, and he says, "That depends on the power and intensity of the being that possesses the person. Some of these spirits can be appeased with iron

3 Gann: A group of lesser spirits who are devotees of the Devta and who reside in every village and temple

objects. If the entity is not very powerful the Devi would accept a coconut sacrifice, but if it is a powerful being it would require a sheep sacrifice."

I am curious about the efficacy of the Devi's cures. Hardayal laughs loudly. "It is a matter of faith. If the ailing person has full faith in the Devi and her remedy it is bound to cure them, but if their mind is sceptical, it will not work. It's all about faith."

Hardayal's older son pipes in with a recent incident. He discloses that recently a girl with a debilitating health condition was brought to the Devi on a stretcher. She could not eat and was nourished through a glucose drip. Doctors across Himachal had given up on her as most of her organs were failing. Finally, the family brought her to the Devi. During a poochh it was revealed that the family's Kul Devta was upset with them for some misdeeds by the girl's father. "The Devi prescribed a puja to propitiate the Kul Devta and a few other specific pujas. With every puja the condition of the girl improved. Finally, the Devi visited their home where the Kul Devta was propitiated and a few months later the girl ran up our temple steps fully cured. She now lives a normal life. Is this not a miracle?"

There is clearly a lot of anecdotal evidence about the efficacy of healings by Devtas. I tell Hardayal that I would really like to meet anyone he may be treating for spirit illness. Hardayal thinks for a while and tells me he is currently treating a family and will be performing an exorcism in a few days. I ask him if I could film the event, and he says, "Well, only if the Devi allows you, and you will also have to meet Bhimi Ram, the head of the family, and take his permission."

A day later I am in Bhimi Ram's modest house in Parsha village where he lives with his large family. Bhimi Ram greets me warmly, confirms that he has received a call from Hardayal and is open to talking to me. With the natural openness so typical of the locals he begins describing the misfortunes that had begun befalling his family a year ago. "It all started with my granddaughter falling ill. She was admitted to the hospital and soon her little brother followed. We were running around doctors and hospitals as someone or the other was constantly falling ill; my daughter-in-law, my wife and even I fell sick." It was when his grandson was bitten by dogs twice in the same week that Bhimi began to suspect there may be more to his problems than just medical ills. So, Bhimi Ram went to Sharvari Devi to seek her advice.

The Devi detected that a malevolent spirit had attached itself to the family and their home. She had asked them to get a tana mana, or exorcism, performed. Bhimi is confident that all his problems will be resolved with this exorcism. I am grateful when he graciously gives permission to film the proceedings. But would the Devi be agreeable as well? The gods of Kullu have been very cooperative so far, but I know I will be on tenterhooks until I hear from Hardayal.

14
An Exorcism in Shuru

The night of the exorcism arrives. The Devi has given me permission to film the proceedings, much to Meru's surprise. "You are very lucky, Anu," Meru comments wryly. "The Devtas and people of the valley are usually very secretive and reticent towards outsiders about their occult rituals. You are probably the first outsider to be allowed to film an exorcism."

A full moon peeks above the silhouettes of mountains, slowly illuminating the surroundings. As we drive to Shuru village I breathe in the cool air deeply, attempting to quell my excitement and trepidation. I am hoping that everything goes as planned and we will be able to document the exorcism without any last-minute objection from the Devi or the family.

Sharvari Devi's temple looks magical in the moonlight. My crew has set up our lights filling the courtyard with brightness. Bhimi Ram sits surrounded by his huge family of about fifteen people of all ages including infants and children. Meru and I greet Hardayal and Pandit-ji who just nod and gesture towards one side indicating that we stand there. Meru instructs us not to speak with the family, not to ask questions of anyone and to be as silent and unobtrusive as possible. I settle myself in front of the courtyard on the temple steps alongside Meru. We watch as Hardayal and the pandit go about the preparations, as they had done for the poochh session. They bring out the Devi's dharj and bell, juniper leaves, flowers, a plate of rice, incense sticks, a pot of holy water and the Devi's shangal. I notice Hardayal's son, Devi Chand, standing in one corner holding a sheep. It is apparent that the animal is going to be sacrificed tonight, and I begin to feel queasy. Meru sees my expression and pats my hand reassuringly.

An ominous mood settles around us as Hardayal takes his place on the low platform in front of the temple, the dharj, the shangal and other puja paraphernalia placed around him. The pandit sits beside him holding the bell in one hand and a dagger in the other. He begins to ring the bell, and Hardayal ritually invokes the Devi in the same manner as he did on the day of his poochh session. He chants mantras, inhales the juniper smoke deeply, and plucks a shaft of hair from his head. Soon the Goor's body begins trembling and swaying, signifying the onset of a trance.

I zoom into Hardayal's face and note that his eyes have rolled up and his usual congenial expression has transformed into a dark one. The family too is watching intently; the children huddle closer to the adults, perhaps feeling the change in energy. Hardayal leans back and his cap falls off; the family members join their hands and bow their heads, knowing that the Devi has now possessed her medium's body. Hardayal's trance intensifies, his body shaking strongly as he begins channelling his Devi in a strident voice. After the usual iteration about herself and her powers, the Devi begins conversing with the family.

Bhimi Ram: "Mata, please have mercy on us! My family has been suffering for the past two years. Only you can help us now. Please, Devi!"

Sharvari Devi via Goor Hardayal: "Yes, yes, I can see all the misfortunes that you have been through, and I have already told you about the reason. But, if you do as I say, we can solve it now."

Bhimi Ram and family: "Of course we will, Devi; you are most powerful! We will do as you say. We know you will take our troubles away."

Devi via Goor: "You are all my faithful disciples. For you I will take your troubles upon myself!"

Bhimi Ram and family: "Jai ho, Mata! You are great!"

This type of conversation carries on for a while. Most of the adults speak openly to the Devi expressing their anguish, and the Devi responds to them all. I notice that Bhimi Ram's mother is crying, a couple of children bury their heads in their mother's shoulders while the infants sleep peacefully in their grandparents' laps.

The sacrificial sheep is brought to Hardayal. He puts a tilak on the forehead of the animal and blesses it, then his trance begins to amplify, and he begins shaking violently. I note that his eyes have glazed over, and his persona has become frightening. Hardayal picks up the shangal and begins to flagellate himself on his back with great force, his body jerking violently while he is still sitting cross-legged. He begins shouting, assuring the family of the Devi's power to protect them.

Devi via Goor: "Even terminally ill patients come to my abode, and walk back cured. Today I will cure you too."

Bhimi Ram: "We have full faith that you will cure us all, Mata!"

Devi via Goor: "Have no fear! I have consulted your Kul Devta, and soon your issue will be resolved."

Bhimi Ram's wife: "We have no fear, only faith in you, Devi."

Devi via Goor: "Your troubles will soon be over; such is my power!"

Bhimi Ram and family: "Devi, be praised. We are completely dependent on you!"

Hardayal jumps up, carrying the iron chains, which make a loud clanging sound as he is still shaking violently. His trance intensifies further as he begins flagellating himself again, jumping up and down. The energy in the compound is electric, and as Hardayal circumambulates the family, I find my hair standing on end. While he is jumping up and down and beating himself,

Devi Chand brings the sheep and a twig of bethar to Hardayal who then stops jumping but is still trembling as he stands in the centre of the family huddle. Hardayal takes the bethar twig, waves it around the family and then pats the twig on the sheep. He does this thrice. Meru whispers into my ear, "He is transferring the malevolent spirit from the family into the sheep."

The breeze seems to have halted abruptly, and an oppressive atmosphere seems to have sucked out all the air from the courtyard. I find that I am holding my breath as I try to steady my camera shake.

Hardayal's body continues to twitch. He comes towards the sheep and picks it up. I am amazed at how effortlessly he lifts up the sheep as it is quite large and looks like it may weigh nearly a quintal. Hardayal continues shaking and jumping while making another circumambulation of the family, holding the sheep up above his shoulders with both hands. The family sits huddled closely, intently watching Hardayal's every move. I find myself clutching Meru's arm as terrified as the children must be who thankfully stopped looking a while ago.

Once he circles the family, he stops in front of his platform. What he does next horrifies me, and I almost drop my camera. Hardayal brings the sheep up to his face, screams ferociously, bites into the neck of the animal and throws it high into the air! The sheep somersaults in the air and lands on the floor from where it is immediately picked up by Hardayal who bolts off with it into the darkness like a wolf with prey. I notice that like myself many members of Bhimi Lal's family look shocked as does my crew. Avantika is holding her head and staring with her mouth wide open. My heart has stopped beating and I find myself trembling. I close my eyes and try to calm myself by breathing deeply.

There is pin-drop silence. I start zooming in to focus on some of the faces of the family sitting in the courtyard, but my shaking hands negate the effort. Ten minutes later Hardayal comes back. It is clear that the sacrifice has taken place. He walks up to the family and begins to bless them all one by one by placing the bell and bits of juniper leaf on their heads. He seems calm, presumably out of trance, and sits down on his platform, handing out rice to everyone as the Devi's blessing. The mood at the temple compound has changed and become significantly lighter. I see that Bhimi Ram and some members of his family are even smiling after what they view as a successful ceremony.

Then Hardayal abruptly leaves the premises, but Bhimi Ram and the family crowd around the pandit asking him about the fine points of the proceedings. They are speaking in Kullvi and Meru indicates that we should leave and give them more privacy.

We drive back to my cottage in silence. I cannot help replaying the images of Hardayal and the sheep over and over again in my mind. I am still shaken and disturbed and say so to Meru who gives me a perspective. "See, Anu, sacrifice for us is not a superstitious act, rather it's a sacred offering to our Devi." When I mention the plight of the sheep, he snorts and says with irony, "We all eat meat, right? So, instead of being brutally slaughtered for a meal that's ordered on a whim, not to mention having been cruelly reared and there is so much wastage, here we offer a well-taken-care-of sheep to the Devi as a sacred act." I realise that Meru's logic is impeccable and that my distaste is fundamentally hypocritical.

Even though it's 2 a.m., the crew and I continue discussing what we witnessed. My cameraman admits that although he had meant to film the scene from a few different angles, he had remained rooted to one spot in morbid fascination. Avantika is typically more vocal: "I was petrified, and when Hardayal bit the sheep and flung it over his head, I almost fainted!"

The crew and I take the next day off to unwind and to view the extraordinary secrets that we had filmed the night before. In the camera close-ups, we note Hardayal's frightening expressions, his state of extreme trance, his seemingly spontaneous flagellations and the final fearsome act, which even in the bright light of day sends shivers down my spine.

Two days later I am back in Shuru sitting on the terrace of Hardayal's home, which has a spectacular view of the valley below. While we sip a delicious tea, Hardayal chats with Meru in his usual, cheerful manner. It is difficult for me to reconcile this jovial man with his easy laugh and witty quips to his shamanic persona.

I ask him about the night of the exorcism of which the pandit has fully informed him. Hardayal tells me that according to him the exorcism conducted by the Devi had cured the possession. But I want to know how the possession occurred in the first place. He tells me that every village home in the Kullu district has a special space where their Kul Devta is worshipped. In this case the family had failed to consult their Devta before installing him in the shrine of their house. As a result, the Kul Devta had become upset and a malevolent spirit was able to take up residence in their house. The spirit had caused all the family's misfortunes, ill-health issues and discord. The family would now do a poochh with their Kul Devta, Bir Nath, and follow his instructions on where his altar in their home should be placed and how he would like to be installed.

I ask him about the process of the exorcism, and he explains, "The Devi uses the shangal to amplify her power and beat the spirit into submission. When waving the bethar twig and circling the sheep around the family, the Devi transferred the evil spirit to the sheep. And when the sheep was sacrificed, the spirit was exorcised."

When I ask him about his biting the sheep and throwing it in the air, he says sheepishly, "Madam-ji, I don't remember anything, but I guess the fierce form of Kali appeared and took the sacrifice herself."

I ask emphatically, "But Goor-ji, do these exorcisms really work?"

Both Hardayal and Meru look slightly offended at my question. After all I am questioning a custom and belief followed by generations of Himachalis, and that have stood the test of time and faith. Hardayal objects, "We have grown up witnessing or experiencing the results of our rituals, otherwise why would we still believe in them and follow them? There must be some benefit, isn't it!"

Meru bypasses our uncomfortable conversation by telling Hardayal about my ill-health that Tej Singh's Devta had divined. He explains that I was suffering due to an evil eye. I'm embarrassed when Meru suggests, "Anu, why don't you check the diagnosis with the Devi? I'm sure Goor-ji can organise it." Hardayal is most keen to help me. He also sees it as an opportunity to address my scepticism. He tells me that he will do a pogley for me and reassures me that divinations such as pogley and rice readings are conducted when a seeker has not completely surrendered in faith to a Devta or a Goor. Meru encourages me to do it, and out of curiosity I agree. Hardayal obligingly agrees to conduct the pogley the same evening and asks us to return at 5:00 p.m.

We drive down to Manali for a Chinese lunch and return thereafter. We wait near the temple compound until Devi Chand comes to fetch us. We walk with him to another part of the village where there is a small, cemented platform that also serves as the Devi's sacred stone. Hardayal awaits us, wearing his shamanic robe, and I see puja essentials such as holy water in a steel pot, plates filled with flowers, ash and juniper leaves.

He asks us to seat ourselves and begins laying out the pogley items. He tells me, "Please state your query for the Devi."

I say, "I have had an illness for the past ten years and doctors have not been able to cure it completely."

"Doctors are like that only!"

"Please ask the Devi to tell me the cause of my ill health, Goor-ji."

He smiles and says cheerfully. "Don't worry, the pogley will reveal the cause of your problem."

Hardayal sits down and begins making small balls from a mound of cow-dung and ash placed on the platform. He fills one with juniper, one with flowers and leaves one empty. He then closes his eyes and begins muttering some mantras. A few minutes later he declares, "O Devi, if this lady's ailment is merely physical and curable by a doctor, choose the ball with juniper leaves. If hers is a case of an evil eye, choose the ball with flower petals, but if her case is incurable, let the empty ball rise to the surface."

Although I have entered into this enquiry in a spirit of curiosity, I find myself slightly anxious. What are the pogley balls going to reveal?

Hardayal drops the three balls into the pot of water and I am surprised to see two balls float up. Hardayal grabs the floating pogley balls, places them in front of me and asks me to open them. I open the first ball to find that it contains juniper leaves. Meru opens the second ball, which holds flower petals. I look at Meru, who exclaims, "See, Anu, two balls came up together. This means there are two causes of your ill health: a medical issue along with an evil eye." Hardayal nods, agreeing with Meru.

"So, what's the cure, then?" I ask Hardayal.

"Well, let's ask the Devi with another pogley," he responds obligingly.

Hardayal proceeds to make three more pogley balls and once again closes his eyes, mutters mantras and declares, "O Devi, please indicate to us the appropriate cure for this lady: if you will cure her, choose the ball with flower petals; if she requires medical treatment, choose the ball with juniper leaves; if she is to do nothing, let the empty ball come up."

He drops the three balls into the pot and once again two balls float up together. Hardayal offers me the two balls and I open the first to reveal flower petals while Meru opens the second to reveal juniper leaves!

Hardayal tells me, "The Devi has answered your query. She has diagnosed that you have both a nazar as well as a medical issue and that you require both the Devi's cure and medical treatment." He discusses this with Meru while I digest the pogley proceedings. We had witnessed a couple of pogley sessions where each time only one ball had floated up, so what are the chances of two balls popping up simultaneously, not once, but twice, I wonder.

"What would the Devi's cure be, Goor-ji?" I ask.

Hardayal replies, "For that you will have to ask the Devi in her poochh session."

Meru explains that it is only during a poochh session when the Goor would go into a divine trance that this question could be answered by the Devi. Hardayal, standing up, adds, "You can think about it and come to any poochh session, but for now let me tie the Devi's protective thread on you." He fishes out a red mauli[1] from his bag, closes his eyes and begins reciting some mantras over it. He knots the thread, blows into it several times, continuing his whispered mantras, then ties the thread around my left wrist. He says gently, "Madam-ji, this will make you feel better. The Devi will protect you now but keep this sacred thread on until it falls off by itself."

Incredibly, I feel a sense of lightness and reassurance. This ritual resonates with me as I have had these protective threads tied several times at religious ceremonies. I marvel at this aspect of human psychology; our subconscious belief systems have so much power over our emotions. I thank Hardayal profusely and we take leave.

Once back in my cottage I contemplate my journey thus far. Not only am I exploring the culture and experiencing the unknown, but there is also a lot of self-exploration involved too. I had powerful experiences at Batahar and Shuru, but little did I know there is more to come. I am about to have my strangest experience yet.

1 Mauli: A sacred Hindu thread, usually tied around a worshipper's wrist after prayers

15
A Mass Exorcism

In the course of making this documentary I had been speaking to a lot of people about how I wanted to explore and understand the phenomenon of spirit illness, and Chris was one of them. One day he called to ask if I wanted to see a mass exorcism. I didn't quite understand what he meant, so he clarified: His daughter was married into a family belonging to the village of Nao Panao in the neighbouring district of Mandi, and every year on the Devi's birthday celebration a mass exorcism takes place in the temple. Chris said dramatically, "I hear that a lot of people who are possessed and cannot be cured go there where they are cured for good!"

I was intrigued and asked Chris to obtain permission to film the event. He promised me that he would have his son-in-law do a poochh with Ambika Devi and come back to me. When I mention this to Meru, he is sceptical as he does not think we will receive permission to film the exorcism.

But a week later, much to my surprise and delight, Chris informs me that we have the Devi's permission to film the event. The next afternoon we are on our way to the village of Nao Panao ready to expect the unexpected. The village is about forty kilometres from Manali. It is a pretty drive to Mandi alongside the dancing Beas. En route, Chris tells me the myth of Ambika Devi.

Legend has it that Ambika Devi, an aspect of Shakti, had been brought to the village of Doogri in Mandi from a neighbouring district by her pujaris for reasons that are now lost in time. They brought her mohra, or seal, but lost it somewhere in Rangedh village. A local woman found the mohra lying half-buried in a field and tried to pick up the shiny object, intending to sell it in the market. But, as she reached down to pick up the mohra, it turned into a snake. The news spread like wildfire in the village, and others who tried to pick up the mohra met with the same fate. It was not until a man of pure intentions came to pick up the mohra that it could be lifted off the ground. He understood that the object was imbued with the divine and was not something to be hidden or sold off.

As he picked it up, a girl in the crowd spontaneously went into a trance and Ambika Devi introduced herself. She informed them of her desire to take the mohra down to Nao Panao. The men of the village gathered with fire torches in the night to escort the mohra in a basket down to Nao Panao. As the news spread, the original pujaris of Ambika Devi came forward and received the Devi at Nao Panao. This legend is enacted every year on her birthday. Like all "living" mythologies that have power over popular imagination, I wonder about the impact of this myth on the mind of the local communities.

We reach the Nao Panao temple in the early evening where Chris's son-in-law is waiting to meet us. Much to my surprise Ambika Devi's birthday is celebrated on a considerably large scale by local standards. The area around the temple has been decorated with colourful buntings, banners and glittering tinsel strings. The usual festival stalls have emerged, selling inexpensive clothes, children's toys, bangles, cheap jewellery, gifts and other fripperies. A medley of music from religious to Bollywood songs blares from tinny speakers. There are numerous stalls selling eats like pakoras, jalebis, various kinds of mithai, chholey bhaturey, ice cream and of course chai. The atmosphere is festive, and crowds of people throng the area. The temple complex is a modern construction. Wide marbled stairs lead us to the main hall under a tall pyramidal dome painted pink and white.

Near the entrance inside the large hall is a huge alcove in which are two statues of Ambika Devi, one as a little girl and the other as her aged avatar. Both idols are beautifully draped in sparkling cloth and dupattas adorned with real jewellery and multicoloured flowers. Strong incense smoke and fragrances waft out from the Devi's alcove as we pay our respects to her. Chris informs me that devotees could pray to whichever form of the Devi they felt more attracted to. He adds quite seriously, "You know, the expressions of the statues often change to reflect the Devi's emotions."

Several people are sitting around along the sides of the hall. Chris recognises a woman who is trying to pat a young boy to sleep on her lap. He chats with her for a bit in Kullvi and tells me later, "She says that her son suddenly stopped walking, despite there being no medical cause for it, so she is here to consult the Devi about it." I look around and see that most people in the hall seem to be despondent. "They are all here to seek the Devi's healing grace," Chris declares.

While my crew begins talking to anyone who will agree to speak about their issues, Chris and I step outside for a cup of chai. As dusk settles, it is time for the festivities to commence, and we find that decorative lights have come on, adding gaiety to the setting. I watch as crowds pour into the temple courtyard dressed in their festive best. Women and girls are mostly wearing salwar-kameez suits in bright shades with glitzy dupattas and jewellery, while men are mostly in trousers, shirts and Kullu topis. Musicians are beginning to assemble in a performance area adjacent to the temple and are putting up speakers. Most people are going into the temple hall, making their offerings to the Devi and coming out again to enjoy the festivities outside. I am beginning to doubt that any exorcism could happen amidst this gaiety.

Inside, devotees begin to settle down around the hall, which to my surprise is already half-full, mostly with women. A woman is playing the dholak and others are singing devotional songs, clapping to the beat. The entire room seems to be participating, singing, clapping and swaying or just nodding heads to the rhythm. "It's a scene not unlike most temple festivals or jaagrans[1] in India," I comment, to which Chris says, "Wait and watch, Anu."

The singing and drumming gather pace, becoming more fervent, and the ambience in the hall seems to pick up charge. A pandit walks around the room with a smouldering dharj of juniper, which is wafting its typical pungent aroma and thick smoke. Another couple of women begin drumming dholaks and many others join in the loud singing. The sound and energy in the hall go up notches.

A slim, attractive woman wearing a fluorescent-green salwar-kameez stands up, walks to the centre of the hall and begins to move to the music. I think it is a bold move as women in the valley rarely take centre stage. Initially the woman sways gently, but soon her dancing becomes more and more energetic. Her eyes are closed, her long hair comes loose from her bun and swings around her shoulders, and within fifteen minutes her dancing has become frenetic. She flails her arms over her head and jerks her body about in wild abandonment. Her eyes are closed, and her expression is one of being completely oblivious to her surroundings. I am mesmerised. However, most people around me are not paying any attention to her, as they continue to sing and drum loudly.

A stocky older woman wearing a light-pink salwar-kameez, who is still seated, starts to make strange sounds. She begins swaying, and then while still sitting pulls herself forward with her arms towards the temple alcove. Every once in a while, she stops

---

1 Jaagran refers to "keeping awake, watchfulness (at night)" as part of a religious ceremony. It is a Hindu ritual predominantly observed in North India, which includes all-night vigils, along with songs and dances to pay homage to the deities.

her forward movement and swirls her body waist up in circles, hair flying upwards. She lets out a loud shriek and beats her arms forcefully onto the ground, breaking her red glass bangles.

As I stare at these incredible scenes, Chris whispers, "These women are in a trance, Anu, they are possessed." His voice breaks my spell, reminding me to switch on my handycam. I immediately zoom into both women's faces alternately and realise that Chris is right: both women are moving spontaneously in wild abandon, uncaring of the mass of onlookers. It is extraordinary behaviour for a Himachali woman.

The next person exhibiting peculiar behaviour is even more intriguing. A young man goes down on all fours bucking like an animal! He sticks his tongue out and begins making distorted faces whilst bucking uncontrollably. His eyes are closed, and he makes little jumps, impersonating a dog.

Meanwhile, a few other women have begun dancing, each in their own distinctive, peculiar manner. Another man stands up and begins jumping up and down making weird faces. The dancing woman in green falls, and I rush to her in concern. I sit down beside her, realizing that she has fainted. Surprisingly no one else, including Chris, has bothered to step up to help her. I lift her head and sprinkle some water onto her face. I shake her gently, and ask in Hindi, "Are you all right?" The woman opens her eyes, looks through me blankly and once again shuts her eyes and begins moaning.

While I am trying to make her take a few sips of water from my bottle, Chris comes across, saying firmly, "Leave her, Anu. Come with me." He takes me by my arm, dragging me to one side, and barks in annoyance, "What do you think you're doing? She doesn't need your help. She's possessed. Don't interfere!"

Suitably chastised, I look towards the woman and see her making her way out of the hall walking quite normally. I follow her, and Chris comes after me. She sits down, ties her hair into a bun and drinks water from my bottle. She looks around, seemingly tired, but quite alert now. I seize my chance to speak to her. It is quite noisy outside, and I have trouble making myself understood, so Chris exasperatedly steps in as interpreter and addresses her in Kullvi.

The woman's name is Tara, and she has come here from a neighbouring village. Tara has an attractive face, but her eyes have a resigned and dull expression, and I soon understand why. "I've been getting into this trance condition for the past ten years. Whenever it happens others tell me that I behave strangely, which I don't remember," she says despondently.

Tara tells Chris that for years she has been falling into this debilitating trance state once a week. She has seen doctors who have been unable to diagnose her condition. All her medical tests turned out to be normal. Tara has visited many other temples, none of which has given her any respite. When she learned that the Devis of this area are known for their powers of healing, she began coming here three years ago. She felt an improvement and a little stability after her very first visit and the trances began to occur only once a month. "The Devi also told me that someone from my village who disliked me had put an oprah on me and that Narsingh had been set upon me to torment me until I'm finished," reveals a disheartened Tara. She stands and I escort her into the temple where she goes and sits with her companions.

Meanwhile, Chris has struck up a conversation with the lady in the light-pink salwar-kameez who until a short while ago had been dragging herself on the floor in a state of trance. He introduces me to Meena who, unlike Tara, is glowing and quite cheerful. She speaks Hindi, so I can follow her story. She tells us, "I was possessed by an evil spirit six years ago and started behaving like a crazy woman. I would beat my children. I would run away from home and was often found roaming around the village listlessly. Everyone in the family was terrified of my madness. I began coming to the Devi here and within three years was cured."

Meena also reveals a curious aspect of her experience. Once her trances were gone, she built a shrine for Ambika Devi at her home. She discovered during the course of her treatment that the Devi had bestowed some healing powers on her. She began to experience the divine possession trance of the Devi in her home and at religious gatherings. At present, as ordained by her Devi, Meena has begun holding biweekly poochh sessions at her house, where through her the Devi offers cures for minor ailments.

"How do you differentiate between the earlier trances and the Devi's trance?" I ask.

Meena's face brightens. "There's a world of difference. In the earlier trances I would go crazy and feel very ill, but when the Devi comes into me it is unmistakable. The Devi also speaks to me and has reassured me that as long as I keep my faith and serve her sincerely, I will continue having these healing powers." Meena adds that whenever she goes into the Devi's trance, she feels a great sense of positivity and well-being, although of course she never remembers what had transpired during her trance or what she had advised people during her poochh. "I'm much happier now; all the pains in my body have disappeared and helping people has added a positive dimension to my life."

It is all very intriguing. Tara's and Meena's states of possession have all the hallmarks of hysteria, or what has been described as a psychodynamic response to powerlessness, which is especially true of women in patriarchal cultures. To this is added another layer of meaning through Meena's channelling of the Devi's healing powers. I find myself more and more fascinated by this confluence and convergence of the psyche and spirit worlds, between imagination and alternative realities.

While I have been filming at the temple, my crew is stationed a few kilometres away in the village of Rangedh where Ambika Devi's mohra had first appeared in a field. I see later, from Avantika's vivid descriptions and the footage, that the Devi was being readied for her journey downhill. Her small rath is oval-shaped and shaded by a huge chhattar, or ornamental umbrella, made of silver. A red silken cloth cascades down from this chhattar, draping the entire rath. Ensconced in this lush palanquin is a single mask of the Devi wearing a benevolent smile and lots of real jewellery.

Ambika Devi is to travel downhill in a basket just as she had the first time, carried by a man of the same lineage as the one who had first carried her. She is flanked by Sadhu Ram, her eighty-year-old Goor, who has been her medium for the past fifty years.

Sadhu Ram begins the aarti by waving a thaal[2] containing a diya, tikka, flowers, rice grains and sweetmeats, and ringing the bell continually. He chants prayers, joined by the Devloo, all of whom are wearing yellow flowers in their Kullu caps. Once the aarti is done, he carries the Devi's rath in his arms and steps outside where a multitude of devotees await the Devi. They offer her flowers and begin lighting their mashaals, or fire torches, while the bajantris play the Devi's sacred tunes.

The men recreate the Devi's first journey downhill by leading the way with flaming torches, lighting the way for the Devi and her entourage. It is a dramatic sight: the darkness of the night lit by dozens of blazing torches. The haunting music fills the air and the fervour and excitement are palpable. "It was one of the most exciting and magical nights of filming for me," Avantika tells me later, her eyes shining.

The hall inside the temple is packed, the singing and drumming reaching higher and higher levels of fervour. Many more people are now exhibiting strange behaviour. Bloodcurdling screams resound in the hall, and I clutch Chris's arm. A young girl in a cream salwar-kameez is screaming and rolling about on the floor. She stands and tries to run away, but her family ties her dupatta to her waist to stop her. The girl's face twists in a grimace of pain as she continues screaming hysterically. Another young woman in red, lying with her head in a family member's lap, begins screaming

2 Thaal: Ceremonial plate containing ritualistic paraphernalia

and writhing as if in great pain. Another woman begins slamming her chest with her hands, yelping loudly, while next to her a young boy is jumping up and down, eyes wide open with a stupefied expression. Meanwhile, Tara and Meena are still dancing, and the man impersonating a dog continues his antics. All seem to be lost in another dimension. I am completely overwhelmed, pained by the scenes that I am witnessing. The heavy smoke, smells and sounds are affecting me, and I have to step outside. Little do I know there are more distressing scenes to come.

Chris takes me to a chaiwalla for a cup of chai, and I take deep breaths trying to clear my head of those awful screams. "What the hell is happening inside, Chris?" I burst out accusingly.

Chris pats my hand gently and says, "People who are ill or possessed wait all year for this particular festival, Anu, with a steadfast faith that they will be healed by Ambika Devi. Their strange behaviour is part of the healing process. Is it not incredible that these people are not ostracised in their communities? Instead, they find acceptance and support here. You are disturbed because this is not your worldview and neither have you witnessed anything like this before. But, for us living in the valley, all this and our connection to our Devtas are a part of our living experience. Our children have been involved with our Devta culture since birth, so it is very natural for us."

We hear excited shouts and turn to see people pointing to a long line of flames along the slope of the adjacent mountain, as if the entire road has caught fire. The Devi will be arriving in fifteen minutes! We move quickly inside the hall to scenes of even wilder abandonment. The singing, drumming and screaming have reached a crescendo, and an intense sense of anticipation fills the hall.

The Devi's procession arrives. Men holding torches and women holding flowers line up on both sides of the pathway to welcome their Devi. The bajantris are playing loudly and the men cheer their Devi on with ecstatic shouts of "Jai Mata Di! Jai Mata Di!" as the Devi's rath reaches the temple precincts. The men throw their torches in a heap, chanting loudly. It is an extraordinary sight, and the ambience is electric and emotionally charged. Chris says in my ear, "These mashaals will burn all night, signifying the burning of all the evil spirits exorcised today."

The procession enters the temple with the bajantris blaring their horns and the drummers drumming a frenzied beat to announce the arrival of the Devi. She is welcomed with great enthusiasm with all the devotees shouting "Jai Mata Di" in unison.

When Sadhu Ram takes the Devi's rath inside the temple alcove to join the other idols, the bajantris begin playing full throttle. Abruptly the music stops, and there is silence. Surprisingly even the women who had been screaming and dancing moments ago quieten down. In the sudden absence of sound, I hear my heart thumping from the high-decibel singing, drumming and chanting. But soon enough the earlier scenes of screaming and hysterical behaviour start again, and this time with even greater ferocity, if that were possible. Just as I am wondering about the next step in the Devi's healing modality, I see a few of the Devloo walk into the crowd, holding shangals. Each man goes up to one of the supposedly possessed women or men and puts the heavy iron chains around their necks. The men begin to shout at each of these people and then holding the shangal in both hands begin shaking the person violently. I am horrified and feeling faint in my head and stomach.

The boy on all fours looks absolutely helpless like a deer caught in a trap, and my heart goes out to him. One of the Devloos comes towards the girl in pink who is still tied at the waist with her dupatta. She is sitting close to where I am standing, so I have a bird's-eye view. The girl is still thrashing around and screaming wildly, but as the man roughly throws the chains around her neck she quietens down. Her head and eyes, however, are still rolling around. The man tucks his forefinger under the girl's chin, lifting her head with a jerk. He questions her roughly, "Who are you?

Who sent you? What do you want?" He shakes her vigorously with the shangal between every question.

Chris whispers in my ear, "He is questioning the evil spirit that has possessed her."

Initially the girl says nothing and just moans loudly. After several shakings she says something to him, still looking dazed. He questions her a little more, which Chris interprets for me, "The spirit is replying. It has agreed to leave the girl's body; that's what the man is ascertaining."

After this violent exchange the man removes the chains, pats her head and moves on to another person. I can hardly believe my eyes when I see the girl sit up, tie her hair and nonchalantly turn towards her relatives and begin speaking to them normally. I film her at length and there is no mistaking that the girl is behaving normally, and her eyes are quite clear and focused.

"See, the spirit has been exorcised," claims Chris jubilantly.

The shangal treatment is meted out to all the afflicted. They are shaken up, questioned roughly and the spirits supposedly possessing them are threatened with dire consequences if they do not leave those bodies.

In most cases the men and women seem to begin speaking after being shaken vigorously and their family members watch without seeming worried. Many of them resume normal behaviour after the session with the shangal, ostensibly exorcised. There is one exception. One of the younger men was shaken for a long time as he would not speak. He kept screaming and looked at the man shaking him with wide open eyes filled with absolute terror. I am completely overwhelmed and find that I am crying. What if he genuinely has a mental condition and is not "possessed", I wonder. I am deeply unsettled and decide to leave.

It's 4 a.m. and the festivities outside are still in full swing. People are dancing to songs that are being played on loudspeakers while others continue to eat and drink. I am disoriented by the stark contrast of these scenes of merrymaking compared to what I had just witnessed. On the drive back to my cottage I am unable to shake off the bizarre scenes that play in a loop in my mind. I don't sleep much that morning, dozing fitfully in between disturbing memories and fevered dreams.

16

Lifting a Village Curse

Meru comes over to my cottage the next day to ask about my experiences at Nao Panao. When I relate the incidents that took place at the temple and question the efficacy of the healing modality, he pretty much echoes what Chris had said: "Anu, these practices are a normal part of life here. We believe malignant spirits do exist who either possess people on their own or are manipulated by people to harm others, and we have implicit faith in our Devtas. We know that they can heal any physical, mental or spiritual illness."

Meru is right. I am looking at his world through my urban lens; one that is defined by a completely different perception of reality.

He moves on to give me some good news, his eyes twinkling. "Goor Hardayal called to ask if you would like to see a chhidra in Shuru."

"What's a chhidra?" I ask.

He explains that often curses can be put on entire villages. The malice of a few can cause problems for the entire community. Whenever a curse on a village is divined by a Devta, a chhidra, or "forgiveness and cleansing ceremony", needs to be performed. I jump at the opportunity and ask Meru to request Goor Hardayal to ask his Devi if I may film it. I am beginning to feel confident about the blessings of the gods on my project.

Sure enough, Sharvari Devi is agreeable, and a few days later Meru and I are once again on our way to her temple in Shuru village. There is a feeling of festivity in the air as the Devi's brother, Devta Shandil Rishi, will also be arriving shortly. Meru informs me that the two deities share an intimate sibling relationship and that these visits are common. Shandil Rishi is always there for the Devi in times of need or celebration.

Devi Sharvari's rath has been beautifully decorated and placed in the courtyard in front of the temple. Twelve silver masks depicting the Devi are stacked one above the other with six chhattars or "little umbrella-like ornaments", placed over them. Pandit Tikaram greets us warmly, and I ask him the reason behind conducting this chhidra. Tikaram explains that about a hundred years ago a temple of Lord Shiva was shifted from its original place to another. For some reason the construction of the temple was not completed, and hence even the Devta was not installed. All this happened several generations ago, but the dosh, or "sin", was inherited by every successive generation and all the village folk. "This dosh has had dire consequences for us, like too little or too much rain, rising ill health and conflict between villagers and the diminishing faith in their Devi. So, the Devi told us to conduct a chhidra to be released from the dosh."

Soon we hear the familiar beat of the drums from afar, announcing the arrival of Devta Shandil Rishi. Meru and I begin walking in the direction of the sound. A short distance away is the now familiar sight of women lining the path with thaalis of flowers to receive the Devta. The Devta's rath reaches the centre of the village where a huge crowd of villagers is waiting. The music blares, the drums play an energetic beat and there is great bonhomie and jubilation. Soon the throng makes its way to the temple.

Hardayal and Pandit Tikaram stand by Sharvari Devi's rath, held aloft by four kahars, awaiting the Devta. Clad in his cloak, his long black hair falling to his shoulders, holding the sacred dharj and bell, Hardayal looks every bit the powerful shaman that he is renowned to be.

As soon as we spot the Devta's rath rounding a corner, the Devi's rath rushes towards it. Meru says, "See, the Devi is happy to see her brother." The Devta's rath also runs towards the Devi's rath and they meet fondly. Hardayal bows deeply to the Goor of Devta Shandil Rishi, a scrawny old man with salt-and-pepper hair.

They walk together to the temple courtyard where the palanquins have been placed side by side. A huge crowd has gathered to watch the proceedings. Both Goors stand in front of their raths and propitiate the four directions and the joginis, or "nature spirits". Then they ritually invoke their Devtas and go into a divine possession trance. After the usual self-introduction and a pronouncement of their Devta powers, the Goors stand up and perform the Devkhel. People are standing everywhere: on the stairs of the temple with me, on the rooftops of their homes, looking out of windows and in the temple courtyard.

A man walks towards the temple with a sheep and hands it to Hardayal who ties it to the railing of the temple compound. I feel a sense of déjà vu and dread: not again! Meru, noticing my distaste, nods slowly, "Anu, now you will see how the Devi accepts the sheep sacrifice."

One of the Devloo members steps towards the sheep with a plate of red vermillion, flowers and rice, and begins to prepare the sheep for presentation to the Devi. He marks its forehead with vermillion, places flowers in its ear and then places petals and rice all along its body. Hardayal steps forward, mutters some mantras and pats the sheep's head. The sheep looks forlorn but calm. The atmosphere is pregnant with anticipation: how will the Devi accept the offering?

The Devloo member takes a small pitcher and pours water on the sheep in a straight line from its head to its tail. He lifts the animal a few inches off the ground and drops it. He steps back, and the whole congregation waits for a sign of the Devi's acceptance.

"Only if the sheep shivers will we know that the Devi has accepted the sacrifice," Meru whispers.

I too begin to look intently at the sheep. Within minutes it shakes its head, and the water, flowers and rice grains fly in every direction. I look at Meru questioningly and he gestures that this was not a shiver. The Goors, pandits and Devloos who are standing around the sheep join their hands in prayer and wait patiently. The sheep stands and looks around. The men and onlookers wait for at least fifteen minutes in pin-drop silence, broken by an occasional bleat from the sheep. The gathering grows tense as time passes.

"What if the sheep doesn't shiver?" I whisper in Meru's ear.

He shrugs his shoulders. "That means the Devi does not accept this particular animal, and this sheep will be set free," he explains. "Another sheep will be presented to the Devi in that case."

Irrationally I find myself hoping for this particular sheep's life when it suddenly shivers, and tremors reverberate through its entire body. It is a fait accompli, and the entire congregation seems to let out a collective breath.

Meru nudges me and I turn to see that the Goors are leading their respective raths out of the temple compound. The bajantris lead the way making joyous music while the crowd follows. We reach the dilapidated Shiva temple where another huge crowd has gathered on the street and on surrounding balconies and terraces. The raths are placed in a clearing nearby on a huge silken cloth and their accompanying paraphernalia is laid around them. Meru tells me, "The entire village has to participate in the chhidra, no exceptions." I look around and see that everyone does seem very involved in the proceedings.

A couple of Devloo members pick up two small red sacks filled with rice and tie them to the sacrificed sheep's limb. They place this bundle on the platform in front of the old temple. Then the Devloo members tie a sacred red thread to the sheep's leg and unspool it until it reaches one end of the temple where it is tied to a pillar. A sickle is placed beside it.

The Goors sit in front of their respective raths and begin the ceremony. They ritually invoke their Devtas and move into a state of divine possession trance, though neither of them starts shivering in the way that Goors usually do; they both appear entirely normal and rational. Later Meru explains, "It is up to the Devtas how they choose to express themselves, depending on the situation."

Hardayal stands, picks up the ball of sacred red thread that is tied to the leg of the sheep and passes it around to the two hundred or so people there. Each one holds the sacred thread with their fingers. "It is essential that all the villagers of Shuru hold it as they are all part of the dosh," Meru explains.

Hardayal begins to chant some mantras while a plate of barley is passed around. At the end of every mantra, everyone present including Hardayal throws a fistful of barley at the leg of the sheep standing on the temple platform. When the mantras are over, Hardayal takes up the sickle and cuts the red thread and then the leg of the sheep in half. Meru whispers, "This signifies that the villagers are now released of the dosh and all the misfortunes that were to come as a result of it." There are smiles all round with a palpable sense of togetherness and communal understanding.

The chhidra is over and it is time to feast. Pandit-ji brings out some halwa and offers it to the two raths and then to everybody present. The sacrificed sheep will be cooked and distributed to all the village folk as prasad, or "consecrated food".

It is time for my crew and me to return to Delhi. I have a lot to digest, footage to view, interviews to translate and so on. However, a day before my flight, I receive a call from Chaman. "Anu-ji, you were enquiring about various aspects of spirit illness. Would you be interested to see something different?"

Of course I would be interested! So, the next morning I find myself driving with Chaman to Sohel village situated quite close to Batahar.

After a steep drive uphill, we arrive at a car park surrounded by extraordinarily large deodar trees. The Devta of Sohel is also

Jamadagni Rishi, whose kardar awaits us under one of the ancient deodars. The kardar walks us to the temple, which is also shaded by the giant trees. We sit on a platform, and he proceeds to tell us the story.

A young girl from an adjacent village had suddenly developed a disability in her legs and could not walk. Medical diagnosis eluded the family, and the sudden nature of the affliction aroused suspicion. The family went to consult Bhaga Sidh Devi of Peeni village. This Devi had a Goor who was just a young boy yet to step out of his village. The boy Goor went into a trance and declared that someone intending to harm the girl had made a human figure of iron and stuck it with a nail onto a tree in the village of Sohel.

"The family brought the boy Goor here to Sohel. He immediately walked up to a particular tree and went into a trance after which he was able to find the iron figure nailed to the tree and take it off. Incredibly the figure had a pin stuck in the legs!" says the kardar animatedly. He tells us that the boy Goor advised the family to throw the figure in the river and sacrifice a sheep to appease the malicious spirit who had been invoked to harm the girl. After these rituals were performed, the family informed the kardar that the girl was indeed walking again.

I am keen to see the tree, so the kardar leads Chaman and me down a narrow slope to where an ominous-looking, gnarled, ancient tree stands in a grove. As we approach it I see that its trunk is studded with tiny metal figures of humans, animals and birds. The kardar informs me that joginis reside in this tree, so people with mannats, or unfulfilled wishes, come and nail metal symbols onto it for the fulfilment of their desires. I am intrigued and want to know more about joginis, but the kardar brushes me off, saying, "Madam, I don't know much about joginis. You need to talk to a Goor who communicates with nature spirits."

Driving back, I ask Chaman about nature spirits, but he too reiterates the kardar's advice. Later I call Meru, inform him about my day and ask him the same question to which he says, "No, I don't know much about nature spirits, but I can ask around and see which Goors have the requisite knowledge and experience so that you can meet them when you're back next."

Just when I thought that I have mostly finished with my documentation, the subject of nature spirits and Goors who can communicate with them is presented to me. It is as if veils keep being lifted off this incredible world to reveal more layers beneath. My final schedule in Manali promises to be an interesting one.

17
Spirit Healing

The music is loud and raucous with frantic dhol beats. Flashes of bright light pierce the lingering smoky haze in the hall. I watch Tara dance in wild abandon, her long hair swishing from side to side. Meru whispers in my ear, "Look carefully, Anu!" I step closer to Tara peering at her face and recoil in shock. The woman dancing is not Tara Devi, it's me!

I feel the beat of the music thudding in my bloodstream and my head begins to pound; the huge crowd of onlookers begins to clap and cheer me on. A sweet lethargy spreads through my body. I close my eyes and begin to enjoy the experience.

A malevolent scream breaks my blissful state, and I open my eyes to see a vile-looking man approach me holding a shangal in his hands. I hear shouting and find Avantika shaking me out of my slumber in the editing suite.

As I examine the footage I keep going back to the scenes from Nao Panao: Tara's swirling hair, Meena jerking her head violently and the shangal treatment meted out to most of the possessed women and men. I intend to immerse myself in research on the phenomenon of sacred healing in India and other cultures, but before that I want a psychological perspective from Dr Sudhir Kakar who has spent considerable time studying the practices of shamans, gurus, ancient medicine men and various mystics.

We meet at the India Habitat Centre, New Delhi, where I show him a rough cut of some of the healing rituals that I had encountered. Dr Kakar is most interested to hear about the mass exorcism in Nao Panao, intently watching the footage on a monitor in the room.

Dr Kakar explains that the "trance" that the women in the video were exhibiting was a state of disassociation produced by the rhythmic music, clapping, swaying and drum beats. The state of disassociation allowed these people to exhibit what they were feeling inside.

He explains: "The main thing is you never hurt yourself in this state because you are not unconscious, you are quite conscious all through." I tell him that the women I filmed had been brought there to get rid of the bhoot that possessed them.

Dr Kakar tells me that this bhoot stood for bad impulses, forbidden thoughts, aggressive feelings and sexual desires that these women felt—emotions that are generally understood to be "bad", unacceptable or negative—so, for social and psychological reasons these feelings are repressed. At some point they rise to the surface and are expressed in different physiological and emotional ways. When these expressions are attributed to a bhoot, it allows the person to escape responsibility for those forbidden feelings and desires. Sacred healing by a Devta is very effective for people who want to believe their "bad thoughts" come not from them but from some outer force referred to as a bhoot, pret or any spirit. "Spirits are outside of the person, not inside; so, as long as you believe that, it is a very valid way of producing a cure," he says.

He ascribed the relief they felt when the shangal was placed on them to the punishing of their guilt, which made them feel better. I told him that the afflicted were mostly young or newly married women whom a Narsingh supposedly haunted. Apparently, this Devta liked pretty women, especially those wearing the colour red.

Dr Kakar opines, "Well, in most patriarchal societies that have a strong sense of hierarchy and family and a strong sense of morality, these two bhoots are very common for young girls: the bhoot of sexuality and the bhoot of anger against those in authority in the family, the in-laws mostly. So, you may get a bhoot that abuses in-laws because the woman can't do it herself; then there is the sexual bhoot who expresses all kinds of sexual desires because the girl can't do so herself; or the sexual bhoot may also express sexual fears the girl has."

Clinical psychology works on the premise that when you put your feelings outside, you heal inside. Anger, anxiety, depression, fear and many other feelings are unhealthy only if they remain buried inside, unexpressed.

Together we watch the healing process that involved shaking the women with the iron chains. Once again, I find myself shaken and disturbed by the visuals. Dr Kakar too watches in silence. He finally speaks, concluding that the relief felt by the women came from the perceived transference of their tabooed impulses to a different entity. Feeling that she was not held responsible for her behaviour herself was very relieving to the victim as guilt was a difficult cross to bear. Having found expression and expiation, the impulses would disappear for a short while, but if the woman's triggering circumstances did not change, the symptoms would reappear, and the problems begin again. I tell him about Meena Devi, who was not only cured but had begun to hold poochh sessions herself.

"Yes, well, that is a very good way of keeping herself healed for good by keeping the Devi's good energy with her. Devi, for me, means the good parts of your psyche or the good energy that you experience, and you are making sure that those bad thoughts such as the bhoot don't come back again."

I felt the community of spectators was also imbibing the healing energy that made this a therapeutic experience. The ritual involved an acceptance of the outliers of the community and hence sensitised people to the problems of others. Instead of alienating the fringe elements, they saw them as victims, empathised with them and supported them through the event. They considered the practices in the temple as valid, authentic and effective.

Dr Kakar agrees with me. "These sacred ceremonies are much more effective than many modern treatments because firstly people believe in them, secondly the whole community is involved and thirdly their sacred gods and goddesses are involved. Therefore, sacred healing is much more effective for these communities."

It has been a fruitful meeting and Dr Kakar has given me many insights. However, I still want to explore these healing rituals from lenses other than the psychoanalytical and social ones. I remember a friend mentioning an anthropology professor who had spent many years in the mountains in the state of Uttarakhand.

Professor William Sax is an American who has been returning to India to study remote cultures since 1977. I make a few phone calls and am soon able to track him down. Fortunately, he is in India, and even more fortuitously he is in Delhi. I set up a meeting.

When I meet him at a university campus, he turns out to be a tall, affable man, notwithstanding his fierce-looking moustache. He has a look of peace in his eyes and a genial smile. He speaks Hindi fluently having studied it at the Banaras Hindu University as, he tells me, he had felt it would be a travesty if he neglected to learn the language of the cultures he was studying. His linguistic skills amongst other things help him understand the local perspective. He is deeply committed to studying the ways of ritual healing of the shamans of Uttarakhand and has studied them for ten years. His studies are published in his book, *God of Justice: Ritual Healing in Central Himalaya*.

Having lived in the mountains of India, Professor Sax has a pragmatic approach towards the evolution of these sacred healing practices. "It is as effective as medicine, sometimes it works, sometimes it doesn't." He recalls a case of a fourteen-year-old village girl who was suffering from continuous stomach aches.

The doctors could not diagnose the cause, so the family went to the local shaman. "He determined that there had been a lot of quarrelling within the family. The shaman performed rituals to bring the family members together to recognise and confront the tension between them. They managed to resolve their issues by joining together and doing the ritual, and the girl's symptoms disappeared and never came back."

He continues, "Now, what here was causing the symptoms, what was happening? If you ask the villagers, they will tell you that it was a curse within the family; one family member had cursed the other and it was affecting the girl. If you ask a psychologist, he will tell you that she was having some kind of problem within her own psyche. I as an anthropologist would say there was a disturbance in the social field of the family when their relationships were upset. They were unhappy, which was causing tension within the entire household. This negativity expressed itself in one of the family members who was perhaps a more sensitive soul. Though the therapy may have been focused on her, it was actually directed towards the family as a unit, and that's how I think these rituals work."

According to Professor Sax, sacred healing is simply a valid healing technique that is accessible to many people and needs to be understood and appreciated. Faith is an essential part of healing even in modern Western healing systems, but one that is rarely understood or acknowledged.

I say, "I guess these cures are effective because they manage to impress the psyche, like a placebo effect, right?"

He nods and adds, "It is also a well-accepted fact that modern medicine and other forms of medicine are found to be more effective when the patient has faith and belief in the treatment. The placebo effect in healing is well recognised in modern medicine. These ritual techniques are connected with the community's mythologies and are very strongly connected with the land and the sacred history and geography of the land. So, their environment, their identity, their belief systems, their ancestors, all of these are brought together in sacred healing, hence their effectiveness."

Professor Sax continues, "Deity possession and what it means depend on whom you ask. A psychologist will tell you that possession is a state of altered consciousness that can be measured and is associated with certain changes in the brain and perception. If you ask an anthropologist like me, I will tell you that deity possession in this part of the world is a cultural technique that has been developed for solving individual and collective problems, mostly health-related problems but also other sociological problems. Of course, if you ask the villagers, they will say that the god or the goddess possesses them. However, the very few scientific studies that have been done on shamanism have shown that ritual healing has a rate of success that is comparable with that of psychotherapy."

Both the psychologist and anthropologist seem to have settled on broadly the same rationale, namely, that the efficacy of sacred healing lies in its addressing the psychological and social roots of the illness.

Shamanic healing, like faith healing and other traditional healing systems found all over the world in tribal communities as well as in every mainstream religion, takes into consideration the values, emotions, beliefs and social interactions of a person in their healing practices. Social customs, moral controls and role expectations give rise to all kinds of pathologies that vary from culture to culture. This is especially true for women who invariably bear the heaviest burdens of social and moral expectations and also receive the least support.

It is an unstated but implicit understanding in sacred healing that all illness, even when it appears to be of organic cause, is rooted in a social problem. Also, no matter what the perceived cause, illness is viewed as a state of mind, a subjective experience. This is exactly what modern medicine defines as psychosomatic illness. The only difference is that sacred healing views all illnesses as being of the mind and spirit, which further has its roots in imbalances in the body politic. This understanding of illness and the techniques used for treating illness are far more sophisticated than have been appreciated by modern science.

The shaman as well as the sick person are an embedded and integrated part of the community that forms one large sociogenic organism. Faith is fundamental to effective healing, which is why the Devta via Goor constantly reiterates the power of the deity and berates the people for not having enough faith. The Goor invokes the community's shared cultural story to make the sick person as well as their relatives more receptive. Dr Sudhir Kakar in his book *Shamans, Mystics and Doctors* (1982) writes: "The whole weight of the community's religion, myths and history enters sacred therapy as the therapist proceeds to mobilise strong psychic energies inside and outside the patient..." Throughout history, humankind has attempted to contact the divine through ritual and sacred ceremonies. Rituals can be defined as choreographed actions through which a person or persons communicate with a higher power, placating it, or worshipping it and drawing it down for the benefit of a person or situation. Rituals and ceremonies are used to heal, empower, bless or sanctify.

The action is believed to have the power to transform the world either objectively (by making divine beings change circumstances in one's favour) or subjectively (by altering perception so that reality changes). Sacred ceremonies and sacred rituals are an attempt to invoke spiritual presence and blessings through action. A sacred ritual typically has a lot of history behind it. Rituals have been done for centuries, without alteration. As a result, they're imbued with the power that comes from this repetitive practice over time.

Often a ritual is a composite of different types of rituals:

1. Contagious, involving contact with an object possessing the desired quality, such as the banyan or pipal tree, which symbolises long life, or a full moon, which symbolises virility.

2. Invocatory, involving singing songs in praise of a particular deity or reading a story that extols the greatness of the deity.
3. Social, involving only married or unmarried women who gather around and support each other during the ceremony.
4. Sympathetic, involving placement of fertility symbols in and around the house.
5. Transactional, involving fasting, food taboos, all-night vigils, and charitable acts.

Sacred ceremonies, on the other hand, while requiring some structure, rely more on intuiting spiritual direction and guidance. For instance, in the common practice of puja, the deity is contacted through flexible ceremonies of offerings of flowers, incense, money, food or even nothing at all. What is important is the devotee's faith and intention, his desire to align his spirit with that of the deity.

The Devta system follows a composite of ritual and ceremony. The rath, the dropping of cap, etcetera, follow a set form, but trance possession requires the intent and alignment of not only the Goor but also the participating community.

There are a number of rites, rituals and performances that spring from native lore, mythology and customs. These require knowledge and appreciation of the context. As for the text and texture, be it a folk-play or a tale narrated by some village elder or a song sung during some festive occasion, the theme, motifs, the manner of presentation, mimicry, the stimulus, the language and the play on/of words, jokes, pun and the accompanying actions all are of great meaning to the native audience as they are enacted in a cultural context.

While the larger scientific community and modern medicine have remained critical and sceptical about spirit healing practices, the Fifth Plan Document records that India has more than half a million traditional healers. A gross estimate[1] suggests that more than 90 per cent of the Indian population has used these practices at some point in time. There is now mounting empirical evidence that these traditional therapies work. Surveys conducted in India show that more than 90 per cent of urban respondents believe that the traditional therapies are effective in the treatment of physical and mental illnesses (Purohit, 2002).

The reasons for their efficacy are many. Traditional healing is holistic, taking into consideration the values, emotions, beliefs, social interactions and spiritual orientation of the person. Kleinman (1988) states: "In all Asian cultures, the body-self is not a secularised private domain of the individual person but an organic part of the sacred, sociocentric world, a communication system involving exchange with others, including the divine. The person in these therapies is seen as embedded in a social hierarchy and network of relationships." Healing occurs through broadening of the network of relationships (Kapoor, 2003) so that the social world is linked recursively to one's inner experiences.

Through instruments of myth, the healing process connects people with their past and future, with the living and the dead, with demon and divine, broadening their range of connections. Rituals and ceremonies solicit the indulgence of ancestors and departed relations who are held as part of the wider support group. This helps people situate their problem in the larger social matrix and moves them away from a narrow, myopic and consequently overwhelming view of their problem. This sharing of their burdens triggers healing.

The healers need some technique to trigger the healing process. These techniques involve the communication of subliminal messages from the healer to the person, messages that are communicated through symbols, legends and myths that arouse positive healing emotions. Kakar (2003) also emphasises that it is

---

1 VHAI (1991)

the unquestioned faith in the paranormal powers of the healer that is at the core of positive outcomes.

Armed with this new more holistic understanding of sacred healing, I set off once more to experience and study the last frontier of the most secret and esoteric part of Himachali shamanism: nature spirits.

Segment 4

The Divine Feminine

"The natural world is a living, breathing entity, and every part of it is interconnected and interdependent. The Gods and Goddesses of nature are the guardians of this delicate balance, and it is our responsibility to live in harmony with them."

– ***The Yajur Veda***

Top left: *Goor Inderchand wearing his traditional ceremonial cloak, 2009. Cutting hair is taboo for all Goors*
Top right: *Goor Inderchand invoking divine possession by his deity Jamadagni Rishi, 2009*
Middle: *The Goor and the villagers of Vashisht escort their Devta Vasishtha to Beas Kund for a pilgrimage, 2009*
Bottom: *Goor Inderchand channelling his deity, Jamadagni Rishi, during a village dispute, 2009*

Deities visiting the Raja Rupi Palace, home of the erstwhile king of Kullu, Maheshwar Singh, 2009

Raja Maheshwar Singh greeting deities who have come to offer their respects to him as the chief kardar of Lord Ram. The rath bends towards him in greeting, 2009

Top left: *Lord Ram's rath being escorted to the Kullu Dussehra grounds by dozens of raths of Devtas and Devis who are visiting from all over the Kullu and adjoining valleys, 2009*
Top right: *Goors Tuleram and Hardayal participate in the Jagti ceremony held post the Dussehra Festival in Kullu, 2009*
Right: *Anu Malhotra filming the Kullu Dussehra, 2009*
Bottom: *Goor Devi Chand ceremonially escorting Hadimba Devi's rath through Old Manali village, during Hadimba Devi's birthday festival, 2021*

Goor Devi Chand (extreme right) stands alongside two other Goors, ceremonially propitiating their deities during Hadimba Devi's birthday celebration, 2021

***Middle:** Goor Devi Chand, late Goor Tuleram's son, who took over as Hadimba Devi's Goor in 2018. He is speaking as Hadimba Devi to the locals, during Hadimba Devi's birthday festival, 2021*
***Bottom:** Goor Devi Chand offering flowers as blessings of Hadimba Devi during the ceremonial procession of her birthday festival, 2021*

The Myth of Lord Raghunath

Raja Jagat Singh ruled over the prosperous kingdom of Kullu in the sixteenth century. As a ruler, he had informants in every nook and cranny of his kingdom. And so it happened that he heard whispers about a peasant named Durgadutta who was said to be in possession of numerous precious pearls. In truth, these were "pearls of knowledge", for Durgadutta was otherwise just a poor villager. But the Raja coveted Durgadutta's treasure. He sent his guards to Durgadutta's house and ordered that he hand over the pearls or be hanged. Seeing that his fate was sealed Durgadutta set himself and his house on fire. As he immolated himself, he cursed the king, "Whenever you eat, your rice will appear as worms, and the water you wish to drink will appear as blood."

Because Durgadutta was a Brahmin, his curse came to pass. The Raja began to hallucinate and could not eat or drink. Finding himself doomed, the Raja sought advice from a Brahmin. The holy man told him that to lift the curse, he must retrieve the idol of Lord Raghunath from Lord Ram's kingdom in Ayodhya. The king at once despatched a Brahmin to Ayodhya to steal the idol.

One day, an opportunity presented itself, and the Brahmin stole the deity from the sanctuary of the temple. Concealing the idol in his bundle, he hastily set off for Kullu. The people of Ayodhya immediately noticed that their beloved idol was missing. Remembering the stranger from Kullu and noting that he was missing, they set off in hot pursuit. They caught up with him on the banks of the Sarayu and asked him why he had taken the idol of Lord Raghunath. The Brahmin recounted the story of the Kullu king.

However, the people of Ayodhya refused to part with the idol and took it back from the Brahmin. But when they tried to walk back to Ayodhya with the statue, it became incredibly heavy, and they were unable to lift it. They saw that when they tried walking in the direction of Kullu, it felt as light as a feather. Realizing that it was their deity's wish to be installed in the kingdom of Kullu, they gave the idol to the Brahmin.

Upon reaching Kullu, Lord Raghunath's idol was consecrated as the reigning deity of the Kullu kingdom. Raja Jagat Singh washed the feet of Raghunath-ji and drank the charanamrit, the water with which the deity's feet are washed. The curse was lifted, and Jagat Singh declared himself as Lord Raghunath's regent and first servant.

18

A Himachali Wedding

The volume is getting louder and louder, both of the music blaring from the speakers, and of the cheers. The revellers are completely immersed in the celebration. The younger ones are buoyant with energy apparent in their kinetic moves, bouncing on their feet, hands moving rhythmically to the up-tempo beat. The older of the lot are more tuned into the melody, making slower, more deliberate moves, mostly with their hands. They are all united in their happiness as they dance. It seems like the entire village of Goshal is dancing.

I had returned to Kullu upon an invitation, much earlier than originally planned. I had been occupied with editing my film in Delhi, when Meru had called, inviting me back to Kullu for the biggest festival of all—the big fat Indian wedding! Immersed in between "match cuts" and "sequences", this invitation to a Himachali wedding caught me off-guard. I was scheduled to return later in the year, in October, to investigate nature spirits as well as film the famous Kullu Dussehra, but on an impulse I agreed. I was keen to attend a traditional valley wedding.

Packing my bags, I head once more to the mountains. The next day I drive to Goshal, looking forward to the usual lively village buzz, but strangely enough, the main street is empty.

Where is everybody? The looms are silent and still, the fields are quiet and the lanes vacant. I walk to Meru's house, and here too, there are only cows that greet me with loud moos. As I pause, wondering where everybody is, I hear the sound of music carried by the breeze. I follow the sound to discover what is probably the entire population of Goshal gathered in a ground near the temple.

As I draw closer, clouds of smoke laden with delicious aromas waft towards me from giant copper pots on wood fires. People greet me warmly as I am by now a familiar face among the residents of Goshal. I wend my way through the crowd of village folk, many of them scurrying about busily. The women folk are wearing their more festive salwar-kameezes, mostly in bright reds and pinks, heavily embroidered with gold and silver threads. Some of them are sitting around a huge wok frying bhaturey, while some are kneading great hunks of dough, which yet others are industriously rolling out. Further on are large pots and cauldrons being stirred only by the men under the supervision of an older gentleman.

On an open area are pitched gay shamianas, colourfully striped party tents in red, yellow, green and blue. Under this sit the musicians and around them are the natti dancers stepping joyously to the beat. Around them are some enthusiastic locals matching them step for step. I spot Meru, busily giving instructions to some men.

He greets me with a huge smile and a hug. Meru's neighbour's son is getting married to a girl from another village. Today, the baaraat, or the groom's procession, will leave for the bride's village and the main ceremony will take place there. I presume that it will take place in the evening, but Meru tells me that it will happen two hours from now and that we will reach there before lunch. "This is Kullu," Meru smiles playfully, "we do things differently here." I ask him where the groom is and he tells me that he is taking a bath after his batna, a ceremony where the groom or the bride is given a rub-down with herbal pastes. As we talk, two men come up to us and complain to Meru that I have not broken bread yet. I explain that I've had a heavy breakfast, but Meru looks sheepish at being found wanting as a host. And so, I sit on the mat with Meru to partake of a deliciously flavoured meal of daal and rice.

As we eat, I ask Meru to tell me about the uniqueness of Kullu weddings. But for once the usually expansive Meru has little to offer. "Well, our weddings are just like weddings anywhere," he says. I know this cannot be true; everything in Kullu is rooted in ancient culture. I am right, but it is not Meru who has the answers this time.

"Well, we had the jagra yesterday, and I don't think they celebrate it like that in the plains." I turn towards the voice and find myself looking at a bright-eyed, chubby-faced school student, sitting right next to me.

Seeing he has my avid attention; the boy introduces himself as Gaurav Rana and launches himself into a detailed description of the events of the previous day. "Nothing in Kullu can begin without the blessings of the Devta," he pronounces firmly. "The jagra is when the deity arrives in the home of the groom or the bride. The musicians lead the way and the whole Devloo accompanies them."

Meru joins in saying, "In our time, uh, I mean when I got married, the Devta's rath itself would come home, but now instead we have the Devta's nishan (the insignia), the bell and the dharj. The Devta's kataar, a small dagger that represents the deity, is brought for the groom." As in the jaagrans in the plains, songs of devotion are sung for the deity but that is where the similarities end. In the Manali jagras, a bonfire of a special sacred wood is lit and is kept burning through the night.

Gaurav is on a break from his boarding school which is in another district. He is brimming with enthusiasm. "I have seen you shooting at the Hadimba Devi festival. What have you shot so far?" he asks excitedly. He is delighted to hear that I am documenting the unique culture of the valley. Gaurav tells me that when he went away to hostel, he went through an intense phase of questioning the whole system. He says he comes from a family that is deeply involved with their Devta, Srishti Narayan, an aspect of Lord Brahma in the village of Aleo. Members of his family, who are in the hotel business, often carry the palanquin of the Devta. He tells me that his questioning phase was now over, as his enquiries had helped him shed new light on their belief system. "I realised that what we have here is special. Not everyone experiences living gods that they can communicate with," he tells me earnestly.

I ask him whether other educated youngsters in the valley are also involved with the Devta system. He thinks for a while and says, "Fifty-fifty", gesturing with his hand, "but speaking for myself, I understand now how real and sensible it is." The conversation with Gaurav has offered me an interesting insight into how the younger generation responds to what is, in effect, a clash of civilizations.

Meru and I move to his home. It will be a while before the baaraat leaves and till then I shall seek answers to some of my many questions. We climb up to the central room with the stove. Meru's mother makes an appearance only to inform us that she is off to attend the feast, and that Nisha, Siya and Shivam are already there. Meru makes some tea and we settle down for a chat.

"Well, we mostly have arranged marriages here," he begins. "The horoscopes of the bride and the groom are matched and then the families decide whether the match is good. They may also consult the Devta if there is any doubt. Regarding the marriage itself, the very first ritual is the channda, where the family of the bride or the groom requests someone from the village to personally go to every house in the village and inform them about the upcoming nuptials and invite them to the wedding."

Here in Kullu, the village functions like one clan. The person getting married is a child not of one family, but of the entire village. Therefore, the responsibility of a wedding is not the job of a single household but of the entire village. The villagers call a meeting where responsibilities are allocated, from food to cooking to looking after guests and organizing events. Only the finances are borne by the groom's or the bride's family, but there too, villagers often help each other out. "In fact, food itself involves multiple responsibilities. We get the huge copper pots that you saw from the village mandhar. Then some people undertake to bring the raw materials. Others oversee the quantity of food to be cooked; some of us serve it and even the pots and pans are washed by us."

It sounds absolutely wonderful to me, and I ask Meru if I can pitch in somehow. But Meru tells me that I am a special guest, and the villagers would not dream of making me work for them. "Your only job is to eat and drink heartily," he chuckles. "The women cut the vegetables and knead the dough to make the bhaturas. But the main cooking is done by the botis. A boti is a special Brahmin cook. They cook for all big events, and there are about five to seven of them present today."

This was exactly what I had noticed at the temple ground this morning—the women only prepared the bhaturas while the other preparations were made by a group of men under the supervision of an older man who I now realise must have been the senior-most boti.

We chat for a while until we hear the horns being blown and hurry back to the ground. The natti dancers are performing and the crowd has swelled considerably. The groom comes out dressed in a sherwani[1] and dhoti, wearing a traditional turban, his face is covered with the customary sehra.[2]

The natti dancers are now in full swing. The groom shakes a leg with them before he begins the walk uphill with the rest of the baaraat. As he sets off, he is handed two things by the pujari—a coconut and the Devta's kataar. Meru tells me that the coconut is blessed by the Devta and the kataar belongs to the Devta. As

1 Sherwani: A knee-length formal men's jacket
2 Sehra: A veil over the bridegroom's face, traditionally made of flowers and tinsel

he carries the kataar on his wedding day, the groom is considered an avatar of the Devta himself and so he will not touch anyone's feet or greet anyone with folded hands on this day. When the procession reaches the road, a car decorated with a web of flowers awaits the groom. He gets in and then everybody else also begins to get into various cars. I climb into mine and tail the wedding cavalcade to the nearby village of Kulang where the bride lives.

The baaraat stops at the main road of Kulang and is disgorged from the many vehicles, making a great commotion on the road. Then the baaraatis set off on foot up to the village. Once they reach flat ground, the musicians begin blowing the horns. I imagine the bride in her home, hearing the horns and feeling a frisson of anticipation and nervousness. Four men arrive carrying what can best be described as a giant wok. It has two rods jutting out from two sides. They place it on the ground and to my amazement the groom climbs in. "Oh, they have hired a kadata!" Meru says smiling. This kadata is the groom's palanquin of yore. Today it is a novelty, even in the valley.

The marriage party, bearing the groom in the giant wok, reaches the shamiana where the bride's family awaits. We are far behind it all and by the time we catch up, the bride and groom are garlanding each other with flower garlands as they stand on a makeshift stage. As soon as the garlands are exchanged, loud music starts to play, and everyone begins dancing. Once the dancing is done, everyone heads towards the eating area. The scene resembles the one at Goshal with enthusiastic youngsters serving guests who sit on mats on the ground.

I have been watching from the sidelines with Nisha by my side. Suddenly, Meru appears with a young, bearded man who looks familiar. Meru introduces me to Inderchand Goor of Jamadagni Rishi, the Devta of Kulang. Meru reminds me that I had witnessed him solving a village dispute, along with another Goor, last year.

I still cannot place the man smiling at me, perhaps because his hair is tucked into his topi. Meru whispers in my ear, "Anu, this is the Goor that I was telling you about … Inderchand is supposed to be adept at communicating with nature spirits."

I immediately request if I may interview him. Inderchand shakes his head, looking doubtful. Meru pulls him aside and patiently explains my project to the young Goor.

Meanwhile, Nisha urges me towards the vedi where the holy fire is burning. There is an air of solemnity and people are quiet as the pujari recites mantras. The bride and groom are seated side by side and the rituals that follow are exactly as those followed at any North Indian Hindu wedding.

The wedding ceremony comes to an end and the bride's family bid her a tearful goodbye. Even though I am in Kullu for the express purpose of documenting and studying the Devta culture, I find myself increasingly captivated by the deep sense of community that binds the hill people. I have already observed how each village functions as a familial unit during marriages, deaths and all social and religious rituals, sharing responsibilities and even financial burdens. Illnesses and personal problems like divorce and alcoholism are all seen as concerning the greater body politic and are dealt with as a community. Unlike in the cities, the elderly are never concerned about being alone or abandoned. Though there are differences of caste and economic status within, these differences have not widened into an unbridgeable chasm and the society seems amazingly egalitarian in spirit. Perhaps this explains the general sense of well-being, the good cheer, contentment and self-confidence that I am so struck by each time I come here. There is a marked lack of envy, resentment or competitiveness among the poorer members of the community, for they are included in all celebrations and ceremonies.

My musings are cut short by the arrival of Meru. I eagerly ask if he had managed to prevail upon Inderchand with our request. Meru nods in the affirmative and I give him a delighted high-five. Hopefully, Inderchand is my gateway to understanding the world of nature spirits.

19

Goor Inderchand, Medium of Nature Spirits

The October skies shine a brilliant blue over the Kullu Valley. The leaves of the poplar trees are shades of burnished brown and bright yellow. Although it is hot under the sun, the air is cool. I sit on the balcony of my cottage in Shanag village and look appreciatively at the magnificent mountains surrounding this upper tract of the valley.

I see Meru's car drive up and gulp down my coffee as I rush downstairs to join him. Today, he is taking me back to Kulang village situated in the upper valley, to meet Goor Inderchand.

Meru and I drive up the busy road that leads to Rohtang Pass, past roadside shacks displaying snowsuits and gum boots for hire. En route lies the village of Kulang, with its wonderful views encompassing the surrounding rocky ranges, cedar forests and the aquamarine Beas flowing below along the valley floor.

Leaving our car at the end of the road, we walk up around a huge waterfall to Kulang, a traditional hamlet, straggling scenically up the mountainside. There are cows tethered to front yards and bales of straw hanging from the first-floor balconies. As usual, at this time of day, women are busy with their household chores and those working on their balconies lean out to watch us. One lady calls out to Meru, smiling and waving at him. Meru responds with a greeting and begins chatting with her. By now I'm accustomed to this slow progress through a village, as locals always make time for pleasantries, a practice that I find so endearing and enjoyable. These social niceties are an essential glue that keeps the community well connected.

Meru tells me that several members of Inderchand's family had served as the Devloo of Devta Jamadagni Rishi, as pujaris, kardars and sometimes as Goors. Jamadagni Rishi had earlier been the presiding deity of Kulang before the arrival of Devta Parashar Rishi.

We make our way to Inderchand's small, traditional wooden home, painted cobalt blue, where a lovely young woman opens the door. Devkala, Inderchand's wife, greets us enthusiastically and invites us to sit on her tiny balcony. She says that Inderchand will be back shortly and busies herself making masala chai for us. Whilst serving us tea, the chatty Devkala regales us with her love story. "We had a love marriage! I first met Inderchand when he came to my village to visit an aunt. We were both teenagers ... but we fell in love."

The two continued to meet secretly for a few years, until Inderchand gathered the courage to approach Devkala's father and ask for her hand in marriage. "But my parents refused ... they didn't want me to marry a Goor ... because a Goor's life is very hard, Madam-ji," she tells me, momentarily pensive. However, love is a force that cannot be denied and the lovers decided to take matters into their own hands. Taking his parents into confidence, Inderchand rode late one night to Devkala's house, on his motorcycle. "I was waiting for him with a packed bag ... He gave me three missed calls, as a signal, and I came down from my room stealthily and we eloped!" Devkala trills excitedly, her face shining at the recollection. "We are now celebrating nine years as husband and wife," she declares proudly.

Just then Inderchand arrives, apologising profusely. He is of medium height, a mite chubby, fair-skinned and with light hazel eyes. He sports a longish beard and is wearing a kurta-pyjama and a sleeveless Kullu woolen jacket. After another round of chai and general chit-chat, Inderchand settles down to tell us his story.

"I became a Goor when I was just twelve years old," Inderchand says. "My fate was predicted by Devta Jamadagni Rishi, who was visiting Kulang from Mandi district when I was born, and sure enough by the time I turned twelve, I was chosen as a Goor by our Devta Parashar Rishi."

Inderchand began to experience signs when he was only seven or eight years old, which greatly upset the child. "I would get mysterious headaches, often feel dizzy and began suffering from aches and pains. When musicians played music for Devta Parashar Rishi, I would lose consciousness and go into a low-intensity trance."

It was a confusing time for both him and his parents. The physical ailments adversely affected Inderchand's life and became an impediment to his completing his education and following his dreams.

There were other, more frightening experiences too. "My deity, Devta Parashar Rishi, has a mystical connection with snakes—they act as his guards. So, my mother often found snakes on my bed and in the house! They never harmed us, but the experience was quite frightening for me and my parents."

The young Goor recounts his most eventful day, "One day, I began shaking uncontrollably and ran off to the temple of Parashar Rishi in the village. I am told that I banged my head thrice on the temple wall and my cap fell off."

The Devloo present, who witnessed Inderchand's actions, realised that he had been chosen as a Goor. However, the rest of the villagers were sceptical, given his young age. "They could not understand how I was chosen at such a young age and quite out of the blue. They made fun of me … advising my parents to have better control over me and on what they thought was my spoilt, attention-seeking behaviour. They even advised my parents to get me admitted to a mental institution," says Inderchand, matter-of-factly.

I have begun to note that although the Devta culture is one of faith and belief, it is not a blind, unquestioning acceptance of religious form. Not all odd behaviours or phenomena are of divine or demonic influence. The faith of the people is tempered by a healthy scepticism. Every medium is tested rigorously for authenticity based on perceived results before he is accepted as a Goor.

Inderchand continues, "When the taunts became unbearable, I stopped attending all the Devta's festivals. But you know, the Devta did not give up on me. On all festive occasions, the Devta's rath would come to my house … and I would simply go into trance."

Devkala adds proudly, "His words during trance always proved accurate. Finally, the villagers had no option but to acknowledge my husband as the chosen Goor of our Devta."

This soft-spoken and gentle-looking man has now been a Goor for twenty-one years and is highly respected in his village and beyond. Interestingly, he is also a professional photographer and supplements his income by taking pictures of tourists. Inderchand says, "I always had a fascination for photography and managed to learn it quite well. So, during the tourist season I go to Rohtang Pass and take portraits of tourists. It doesn't earn me much, but I love doing it and it also allows me to be outdoors, in the high mountains."

I look at Meru pointedly, as I want to turn the conversation to the subject of nature spirits. When he does, Inderchand invites us to witness a poochh session to be held a few days later. He will, of course, need to first receive permission from his Devta to film it.

Meru and I return to Kulang on the appointed day, and we walk towards the temple of Parashar Rishi. I recall the incredible tale that Inderchand had told us about its origins when we had last met. The story is told that a few decades ago, the Devta had instructed his Devloo to go to a specific spot where he wanted his temple built. The Devta had told them that he would give them a sign as to the design of the temple he wanted constructed. When the Devloo arrived at the spot indicated by the Devta, they saw a spider's web spun in the design of a temple.

Thereafter, this small wooden temple with its low-hanging gabled roof was constructed based on the pattern of the spider web. It is nestled in a small grove and has quite a different ambience from most other temples that I have visited so far. Unfortunately, the carved wooden door of the temple is locked, so we are unable to look inside.

We look around the deserted premises for Inderchand and soon spot him walking towards a huge tree. He is wearing his shaman's robe and holding a dharj spewing clouds of dense smoke, the distinct pungent aroma of juniper wafting from it.

Inderchand makes three rounds around the tree, murmuring mantras under his breath. He then walks to a clearing between another small copse of trees and gestures for us to join him. A small group of people is already seated on the ground in the clearing. As we approach, I'm immediately struck by Inderchand's complete change in demeanour. His usual gentle presence has been replaced by a stern, authoritative air. He sits on a small, cemented platform, surrounded by six men who have come to speak with their Devta.

Inderchand begins the ritualised process of going into trance. Although I have witnessed this process multiple times over the past year, I am still powerfully fascinated. After the mantras, the ringing of the bell, the deep inhalation of the smouldering juniper in the dharj and the plucking of his hair, Inderchand leans his head backwards and his cap falls off. He loosens his long, wavy hair which is nearly down to his waist. Inderchand picks up the bell, ringing it for a long while, murmuring prayers as his unfocused eyes gaze upwards. To me it seems as if he is taking an inordinately long time to go into trance, but just as I begin to think that it is not going to happen, I notice that his hands have started to tremble. I move closer with my camera as his body begins shaking.

Inderchand's head suddenly begins to thrash about violently in all directions, his hair flying wildly. He begins to speak in a loud guttural voice, completely different from his usual soft-spoken tone, and his body language becomes aggressive.

Goor Inderchand/Devta Parashar Rishi: I am omnipresent, in the clouds, the wind, the water. They are all part of me. I am here to protect the earth…

Men: Praise the Lord!

Goor Inderchand/Devta Parashar Rishi: Don't worry, I will protect you. I will see to it that you do not face any problems.

Men: Devta, you are great … please help us…

He pronounces the Bharata,[1] the usual preamble to the actual poochh, where the Goor recounts the Devta's history; declares his mighty powers; demands absolute faith of the onlookers; praises the Devta and reiterates their faith in him. I am completely riveted by the incredible transformation of Inderchand and the powerful energy that seems to envelop us all. Eventually one of the men poses a question to Inderchand, who tilts his head up, eyes closed and begins breathing deeply.

Meru whispers in my ear, "He's asking for rain in this area…"

My pulse quickens as this is exactly what I want to investigate. I poke Meru in the ribs to continue telling me what is being said, but he is looking beyond me. I turn to see three elderly local village men walking purposefully towards us. I can see that they are visibly upset.

One of the men goes up to the cameraman and stands right in front of the lens, yelling angrily, "Stop this filming right away!

1 Bharata refers to the tradition of singing ballads that celebrate the heroic exploits of the deity to invoke the Devi/Devta, and may have influenced the development of theatrical performance in Hindu culture.

How dare you … this is our personal ritual." I interject and explain that we have their Devta's and Goor's permission to film, but the men are adamant and literally hustle us out of the clearing. As we are leaving the premises, I look back and see that Inderchand and the men have continued with the poochh, as if nothing had transpired.

I am taken aback by this turn of events, as this is the first time I have faced hostility in documenting the Goor culture, but Meru puts the incident into perspective. "You realise that you are probably the only person to film so many of our ceremonies, rituals … and even some occult practices. Our people, especially the older generation, are uncomfortable about revealing these things to outsiders. They have only accepted it because our Devtas have given you permission to do so. So, let's just be grateful for the doors that have been opened so far, and forget the few challenges along the way." Words of wisdom from Meru!

However, I am adamant about investigating nature spirits and the abilities of certain Goors to communicate with them. I pester Meru till he finally calls Inderchand the next day and fixes a time to meet him.

A few mornings later, we are back in Kulang at Inderchand's home. He apologises for the setback to our filming of his poochh. "I was told about what happened after the poochh. Sorry, those men did not know that the Devta had given us permission for you to film." Inderchand asks us to accompany him to the forest adjoining the village, where he needs to pluck some juniper leaves. We walk to the edge of the village, alongside a gushing stream and make our way to a shadowy forest of dense deodars.

En route, I ask about yesterday's poochh. "Those men were shepherds who were worried about the recent lack of rain in the higher regions where they graze their sheep. They requested the Devta for rain," Inderchand explains. "The Devta has promised them rain in the next few days."

"But will it rain?"

Inderchand looks confused, "Of course, it will rain … if the Devta has said so!"

I remember a similar incident last year, when the locals had requested Hadimba Devi to prevent rain from ruining her festival. Tuleram had responded, in divine possession trance, that it would stop raining. And it had.

When I mention this to Inderchand, he looks at my unconvinced expression and says patiently, "Anu-ji, this is a common phenomenon for us." He explains that praying to and propitiating nature is an essential aspect of their local culture. "We were initially a community of herders before we became largely agrarian. Therefore, we are dependent on the natural elements. Sometimes we have to ask for rain or to stop it. If the river floods, we ask for respite; if there is massive snowfall, we ask for it to stop. We ask about general weather forecasts or for a good harvest. Our Devtas have always helped us by mediating with nature spirits."

We walk up a rocky path alongside a stream and reach a secluded spot with a small waterfall and a huge rock beside it. Inderchand stops there, saying, "I love coming to serene places like these in the mountains … with streams and trees … when I meditate here, I draw power from these sources by communicating with the spirit of nature."

I want to know more about this, so Inderchand explains, "Nature spirits are present in all the elements … water, air, fire, earth and the atmosphere … every mountain, every tree, every river and every rock. That is why we honour and worship spirits of mountains, who protect our villages; spirits of lakes, which are sources of power; spirits of forests and even spirits of waterfalls. Above all, we revere the power and the benevolence of Mother Earth, and honour and worship her."

Inderchand further explains that a universal web of energy supports all life, from humans to all elements of the environment. Since we are all interconnected, a mutually supportive balance is essential for our survival and well-being. Shamans, in trance, access the world of spirit, to bring back insights on how people may achieve this balance and live in harmony with nature.

I am deeply humbled by Inderchand's profound insights. A Himachali shaman has explained to me the fundamental, ecological principle of interdependence, where man and nature are viewed as one biotic community. And this is his experiential knowledge … something that we, in the modern world, have forgotten.

Keen to explore the subject further, I ask Inderchand a flurry of questions. However, he begs our leave to continue his task, and addresses Meru, "Why don't you take her around your village and show her all the sacred spots where nature spirits reside?" Meru agrees, and Inderchand amiably takes our leave and begins walking up the mountain.

Back in Meru's cottage the next day, over a flavourful cup of black mint tea, he tells me about the numerous deities present in his village Goshal. "Anu, we worship three main deities—Goshali Naag, Vyas Rishi and Gautam Rishi, who are actually the ruling deities of nine villages in this area. We also have several family Devtas and Kul Devtas, who are guardians of our homes and families."

I want to visit Goshal's main temple, but it is still under construction. "The temple was very old and quite beautiful, but it needed intervention … leaks had begun to appear. The Devta demanded a new temple and then the nine villages gathered to fulfil the command," Meru explains.

It is intriguing to know how a new temple is constructed in the valley. Briefly explaining the elaborate process, Meru says, "We have traditional artisans who undertake this work. They are called thawris, and because this is a sacred task, they live in the temple premises till the major work is finished. The Devta chooses the day that the work will begin and is consulted for every major decision. It is of utmost importance that things are done according to the Devta's will. Every major event is marked by a puja. The first puja is conducted when the trees are chopped for wood. The next ceremony is held when the foundation stone is laid. The Devta chooses the single slab of wood that goes across the roof. When all the work has finished, a suitable day is chosen and the Devta's idols are consecrated in the sanctum, with a ceremony known as a pratishtha, like what we have in all Hindu temples. Our pujaris conduct a havan and a few secret rituals, amongst other ceremonies necessary for a temple pratishtha. The whole village gathers for this event and a feast is organised for all."

I bring our conversation around to what is of utmost interest to me: nature spirits. Meru informs me that nature spirits go by various names, depending on where they reside and their typical impact on humans. To illustrate his point, Meru takes me for a walk around his village, pointing out various sacred spots.

It is always a delight to walk around Goshal, which has largely maintained its traditional appearance and peaceful ambience. I lament to Meru that the traditional wood homes with their slate roofs look so charming as opposed to the newly constructed cement houses.

"I know, Anu, I think so too, but our older homes require much maintenance, and the new homes are more comfortable. We have also got used to electricity, heaters and washing machines." He laughs.

We walk to the farthest corner of the village, till we reach a large tree with a huge canopy and a stone platform at its base. The wide trunk of the tree had several small birds made of thin metal sheet nailed to it. "This is Athara Peede, an ancient tree, worshipped mostly by those from a lower caste. And it has special energies," he tells me.

I ask Meru about the metal birds.

"People ask this tree for mannats, and when their wish is fulfilled, they offer these iron birds to the tree spirit," he says.

We offer the tree some flowers and a prayer before leaving. I ask Meru to tell me more about this practice, but he confesses to not knowing much more.

"Actually, these practices go back to our hoary past … you may not find anyone who knows much about it … we just follow the tradition." He shrugs.

We now walk in another direction towards the edge of the village where we reach a clump of tall bushes. Meru points out some small stones piled one atop another beneath the bush.

"This is Pataal Devta," Meru says, explaining that there are in fact four Pataal Devtas in his village, one of them being the Agni Pataal Devta. "So, it is known as Pataal which means, deep inside the earth, so actually it's an earth spirit." He takes me to another sacred spot of the Pataal Devta, where a small shrine had been built with lose stones, under a bush.

Meru now takes me to a cemented compound in the village which has another small shrine made of loose stones. I notice a pile of dry husk piled up in front of the shrine, as well as several stalks of maize stuck between its stones. "This is the shrine of the Chettu Devta," Meru says. "He is related to the fertility of our fields, and so we offer a bit of the first harvest to him … in fact, we consult Chettu Devta about the right day to sow and when to harvest."

Finally, we make our way around the village and begin climbing the mountain looming behind it. Meru is taking me to the abode of the Daani Devta, a mountain god. Meru explains, "Our Daani Devta is a fatherly figure who looks after the entire village. He is propitiated by special feasts in April and November, when a rot, a thick wheat roti, is offered to him from every house in the village."

He goes on to explain that Daani Devta is considered to be an aspect of Lord Shiva, who looks after this village. Shepherds, especially, pray to him and offer him a sacrifice for their safety when they graze their sheep up in the mountains. "Some generations ago, we were mostly shepherds here. There was very low production of crops, so we did not have adequate vegetarian food. We had no fertilizers, and winters, as you know, are very severe with heavy snow. Sheep were the only asset we had, so that is what we used to offer. It continues as a tradition, but we do look after the sheep and rear it lovingly as long as it lives," he adds hastily as he knows my repugnance towards animal sacrifice.

I know by now that an animal sacrifice is an act of faith for the people here and the animal sacrificed also provides them with essential food. This practice is intrinsically tied to the geography of the region as well as their occupations and faith.

We finally reach a small plateau halfway up the mountain, where a tiny shrine made of loosely packed stones sits serenely in the late-afternoon sun. This was the symbolic abode of Daani Devta. We pay our respects and offer some sweets that Meru has carried. The view from here over the valley and Goshal village is magnificent, and we sit awhile in appreciative silence, drinking it in.

I ask Meru about other nature spirits.

"We do have many more spirits like Than, Keu and Narsingh Devtas, who are bahans (vehicles), attendants or bodyguards, of the bigger deities. So, the sacrifices that we make to our main deities are also offered to them, so that they also are satisfied." I ask him to explain further, and he replies, "These are smaller gods. But if they are unhappy or dissatisfied, they tend to create problems for us like weather issues, bad luck or diseases. In fact, some of them also have demonic qualities so they can even be propitiated by people and persuaded to harm others."

I ask how the local villagers come by this understanding. Stupid question obviously, as Meru rolls his eyes and says, "Through our Devta of course! The Devta tells us which smaller god is angry and how to appease them." I ask Meru if he personally believes this, and he responds exasperatedly, "I have experienced and seen the results of many such rituals, I know what I am talking about."

He jumps up saying, "Chalo, let's go now." He takes some leftover ladoos and proceeds to place them around the shrine, informing me, "See, I'm leaving these for the joginis." Noting my blank expression, he explains, "Joginis are nature spirits found in all natural places. They live in areas of wilderness ... in forests, lakes, streams and mountain passes. They only reside in clean areas, and we have to keep their areas very clean, or they get offended."

Meru is unable to offer a better explanation of joginis and later I find that understanding them is problematic, given the diverse perceptions that most locals have of them. Some describe them as the "pre-pubescent" aspects of the goddesses Durga, Parvati and Lakshmi, some link them to the mythical courtesans who occupied the court of Indra Devta, the Lord of the Lords, while others just refer to them as "the energies that power our deities".

We visit Goor Inderchand, hoping he can shed more light on joginis. According to Inderchand, "Joginis are girl Devis ... the powers of the earth. They must be propitiated after we propitiate the Devi." He takes us to a huge tree, close to the temple complex, which has a cemented base with a few flowers strewn on it. "This is the space of the jogini of this tree," he points. He asks me, "Didn't you see me stop and pray here, whenever we took our Devi's rath out?"

Meru reminds me of all the occasions that I had seen Goors sprinkle water and rice in the four directions, whilst moving out of their temples in their Devta's procession. "Yes, Anu-ji," Inderchand says, smiling at me, "it is the joginis that we honour ... for it is their energies that power our raths."

Inderchand continues his explanation over a cup of tea at the adjoining chai stall. "It is very important to keep the joginis happy ... because if they get angry, the weather becomes unfriendly, or people start falling sick. Then the Devi rebukes us and tells us to look after the joginis by ensuring that we keep their spaces clean, praying to them and making offerings to them."

"And now I have to rush..." says Inderchand gulping down the last of the tea and collecting his belongings. Meru and I hurriedly extract from him an invitation to come to his house the next day so that we can continue our conversation.

The following morning, Meru and I return to Kulang to learn more about Goor Inderchand's understanding of joginis.

Sitting on the veranda of Inderchand's house, we listen to him as he explains, "There are sixty-four types of joginis, Chaunsath Jogini, who are present in all the elements of water, air, fire, the atmosphere, and the earth. They are the powering divinities of this ecosystem." He elaborates, "We have to be careful to keep their abodes absolutely clean and not disturb them by shouting or whistling in their areas, or they can get upset and create havoc in our lives."

Inderchand goes on to tell us about a recent incident where a woman from his village had come to see him complaining about poor health and listlessness, which the doctor had been unable to cure. Inderchand had conducted a divination session wherein it had been revealed that the woman had angered a jogini inadvertently. Apparently, the woman had desecrated the jogini's sacred abode by dumping garbage there and was now suffering her displeasure. Inderchand is going to help the woman appease the jogini by conducting a few specific secret rituals.

I literally beg Inderchand to allow me to film this ritual. Knowing how important this was for me, Meru says something to Inderchand in Kullvi. Inderchand looks thoughtful, and then nods his head in assent. Later, Meru reveals that he had requested Inderchand to first ask the lady if she was willing to allow us to film the ritual and to then contemplate my request.

I am on tenterhooks for two days until Inderchand calls Meru to tell him that the woman had agreed to the filming. A day later, I return with my crew to Kulang. I am a bit hesitant this time as we had literally been thrown out of Kulang the last time, but Inderchand assures me that I will not face resistance, as this is a personal issue and did not involve the village Devta.

He introduces me to Mira, the local woman who has been stricken by a jogini. Mira is a short and stout woman, with a weather-beaten face and an unsmiling expression. She seems distraught and does not speak much. Together we walk to a deserted clearing up in the village, with a small stream flowing nearby. On Inderchand's prodding Mira, hesitantly says, "I am suffering from poor health, listlessness and am finding it hard to focus on work. I went to the doctor and took his medicines for a few months, but there was no improvement. When Goor-ji put a sacred thread on my wrist, there was a little relief. Now I want to be cured completely."

Inderchand is to appease the wrathful jogini through some secret rituals. He is carrying a silver plate and several other effects for the purpose. "These are to appease the three Devi's—first Saraswati, the goddess of learning, then Lakshmi, the goddess of prosperity, and finally Durga, the goddess of power. See, joginis are of three types, namely, tamasic (requiring sacrifice), rajasik (a middle path) and satvic (pure). We will appease all three, as we don't know what kind has afflicted Mira."

He lays out three flat stones and begins to prepare the yantra, a sacred device. He draws three patterns with powdered rice, specific to each Devi. On top of each of the stones he adds elements that each Devi favours—cow dung for Goddess Lakshmi, vermillion for Goddess Durga and sacred water for Goddess Saraswati.

Inderchand then places flowers on the three yantras. "I have prepared these to attract the three kinds of joginis who worship these goddesses," Inderchand declares. He has already divined that Mira has been afflicted by a water-based jogini and is now attracting her to reveal herself. He propitiates her with holy water and then offers a coconut sacrifice near the stream. He waves the water of the coconut all around and then puts some pieces of the coconut on the Devi's yantra. When Inderchand senses the jogini's presence, he plucks a stem of the bethar plant, which is said to ward off all evil, and uses it to sprinkle the holy water around Mira. He exorcises her in this way three times, before sending the woman on her way. Mira walks off, throwing a flower in her wake for the jogini. She is required to keep walking and not stop till she reaches home, so that the jogini does not follow her again.

I am keen to speak to her, but Inderchand makes it clear that stopping her would interfere with her treatment. He now picks up the three stones, offering the first in the direction of the sun, the second to the north and the third to the south. The puja is now over. I ask Inderchand whether the ritual had been successful, and he tells me, "As long as Mira will be respectful to the jogini's sacred spaces, she will be safe."

I am curious to know how Inderchand knows these things. "Who taught you all this?"

Inderchand smiles and responds, "Madam-ji, this knowledge comes to me instinctively. I receive it from my Devta when I meditate, and then I just follow those instructions."

My conversations with Inderchand and Mira have left me even more mystified than before about these jogini spirits. The vast layered complexities of Dev Bhoomi seem to me to be as the woven patterns of a pattu shawl, intricate, and mystifying.

20
Joginis

Of all the facets of Dev Bhoomi that I have encountered so far, I find myself most intrigued by the joginis. It seems logical that societies that have remained sequestered from the mainstream and whose daily lives are closely intertwined with nature, would have retained sensory capabilities that their urban counterparts may have lost access to.

I decide to visit Pandit Rohit Sharma to see if he has better insights to offer on the subject of joginis. Pandit-ji greets me effusively and is eager to be brought up-to-date about my filming. After going over my experiences since our last meeting, I ask about nature spirits and joginis.

"In the Devi Bhagavat,[1] it has been said that the Devi who came into being with the creation of the universe is Mother Nature herself. Our village goddesses are the power and energy of Mother Nature, and they control the forces of nature and have power over man and beast," says Pandit-ji, in evident enjoyment of the subject. He continues, "For example, Siya or Pujarli Devi is

1 Devi Bhagavat: A religious tract that elucidates the idea of the Divine Feminine

the deity of crops because she came out in the siya,[2] the furrow, of a farmer, and worshipping her yields good crops. Phungnis are the deities of rain. Whenever there is a drought, people worship them by sacrificing a lamb."

Pandit-ji explains that each village in the valley has innumerable open-air shrines and propitiation spots dedicated to gods or spirits of nature and disease—vankhandinis,[3] banbirs,[4] bataals,[5] narsinghs,[6] jalbataals,[7] choupatiyas,[8] and others. Each of the nature deities have their own distinct character and function.

"Joginis are the controllers of the four directions. We venerate our joginis before starting on important journeys, and even our Devtas need the joginis' energy to move their rath," Pandit-ji declares. Seeing my bemused expression he explains, "See, when the rath is built, the wood is energised by a jogini. A new rath is made whenever the Devta demands it. The entire procedure is complex, but to put it simply—after the demand is made, the Goor is taken to a forest. There he goes into a trance and is guided to the tree chosen by the Devta. The jogini of that tree must first be appeased through a ritual. The tree is then cut and brought to the temple along with the jogini herself, who infuses the wood of the rath with power … that's how the raths move on their own."

It is indeed a complex cosmology. There is no single overarching God as in the Abrahamic religions. Instead, there is a multitude of

---

2 Siya: Synonymous with Sita, one of the main protagonists of the epic Ramayana, who was found in a siya (furrow) in a field and is considered to be the daughter of Mother Earth

3 Vankhandini: God of the Forests

4 Banbir: A hero and a god and often also a demon

5 Bataal or Betal: An incarnation of Bhairava, serving as the leader of all spirits, ghouls, and all types of pisachas.

6 Narsingh: A demon-god who lives in a walnut tree

7 Jalbataals: Water demons

8 Choupatiyas: Demons and the gods of the crossroads

deities and spirits in a delicate balance of power, much like it is in the physical world.

Pandit-ji goes on to inform me about jogini-sthaans.[9] "These are wilderness spots, unspoiled forests and high-altitude lakes which are inhabited by a profusion of joginis, making them powerful sacred energy areas. In fact, our Devtas make regular pilgrimages to some of our high-altitude lakes to replenish their powers," he discloses. "In a few days, Devta Vasishtha Rishi is going to bathe at Brighu Lake."

I ask him why and he says, "Arre, Devtas also have to replenish their energy, na."

Pandit-ji goes on to tell me the significance of the legendary high-altitude lake.

The Brighu Lake is named after Rishi Brighu. According to the myth, it was there that he composed his treatise of Vedic astrology, the *Brighu Samhita.* He also meditated intensely on Lord Shiva's name. Impressed by his devotion, the Lord granted him one boon. The Rishi asked Shiva to create a lake in that very area in Brighu's name.

Meru adds, "Anu, Brighu Lake is at an altitude of 4,300 metres and it is frozen most of the year. Since it is rarely visited by people, it is a pure place and a strong jogini-sthaan. Its sacred waters hold healing and rejuvenating powers."

The idea that even deities needed to replenish their power was enough for me to decide to document the sacred pilgrimage.

The next day, Meru and I drive up to Vashisht. The village of Vashisht has grown to be like Old Manali, full of backpackers and German bakeries, although the firangi gatherings are not as large. At the heart of the market is the Vasishtha Temple devoted to Vasishtha Rishi, one of the great Saptarishis who is said to have meditated at that very spot. According to a myth, Vasishtha Rishi was the guru of Lord Ram, who is worshipped

---

9 Jogini-sthaans: Sacred places where joginis reside

as Lord Raghunath in Kullu. And so, a Ram temple is located right beside Rishi Vasishtha's temple. At one end of the compound is a temple with a kath-kuni-style gabled roof. On other side are the famed hot springs of the area, known to have medicinal properties.

I tell Meru about the time when, after my trek with Nitin and Sonia, all three of us had come here to soothe our weary muscles. It had been almost midnight when Sonia and I had bathed in the ladies area. The large, cemented shallow tank was surrounded by high walls and was open to the sky. From a wide-mouthed tap streamed a steady flow of steaming hot mineral water, straight from the source. I remember dipping in the almost scalding water several times, and then between dips, lying on my towel, staring up at the velvety skies, bursting with stars. It had been a magical experience, and the dips had miraculously melted my knotted muscles. When I woke up the next morning there were no painful reminders of our arduous trek.

Meru says smilingly, "See … that's the magic of nature, Anu."

We walk into the compound and find people bustling about busily. We try to get in touch with the pujari or the kardar, but it seems that nobody has a moment to spare. The pujaris are conducting the evening puja and the kardar is busy with arrangements for the pilgrimage. We manage to speak to some villagers and gather patches of information. The Devta was to leave for the trek the day after. We manage to get hold of one of the younger priests and try to talk to him. He does not show much interest until I mention that I had been sent by Pandit Rohit. Meru tells him about my documentary and asks him to check whether we can shoot the procession. He goes into the temple and comes out twenty suspenseful minutes later. "Pujari-ji says that we will let you know tomorrow … after asking the Devta," he informs us before rushing off.

This time, somehow, I feel confident that we will get permission to film. We had been informed that at least 200 people would accompany the rath. I tell my production manager to organise camping gear for us—tents, sleeping bags, water, canned food and snow apparel, as the Brighu Lake area is still snowed in.

I am excited at the prospect of doing this high-altitude trek. However, the gods have other plans for me. The next morning Meru drops in unexpectedly. "Anu, I am sorry, but I can't accompany you for the trek," he says sheepishly.

I am hugely disappointed as Meru is not just my interpreter, he is largely responsible for explaining my project to the locals, in language and manner that persuades them to speak to me.

"Why?" I demand to know.

Meru explains, "Because I have to go to Jogini Falls. We have to conduct a ritual to our Kul Devi, Mahamayi."

My disappointment gives my tone a sharp edge. "Ok, but why do you have to go to the Jogini Falls for that?"

"Because, my family has to go to Jogini Falls," he explains. "Mahamayi lives in the waterfall, that's why. She is the jogini of the Jogini Falls. We go to her for important things like offering the hair of our children when they are first tonsured, or if we want to ask for a specific mannat."

Meru explains that his mother had asked Mahamayi for a mannat last year and now that the wish has been fulfilled, she needed to propitiate the Devi and offer a feast in her name. "She has decided to do it this week during these navratras. Yesterday, the pujari confirmed the puja for tomorrow," Meru says.

My face falls as the Brighu Lake trek is also starting tomorrow. Meru then offers the perfect solution, "Look, why don't you film the Jogini Falls ceremony, as it is very unusual. Send Avantika and Rinku, the cameraperson, for the trek with your handycam." He adds teasingly, "In any case, it will be too difficult a trek for you." Seeing my revived spirits, he laughs. "Yes, you can film it."

I can hardly believe my luck that a traditional ritual for a nature spirit, in this case the spirit of a waterfall, would happen so propitiously while I'm in the valley!

That decided, I find myself heading to Goshal on a wonderfully clear and sunny day. Meru, Nisha and the twins await me, along with Meru's mother and his sisters, Kaushalya and Neetu. The women are all dressed in their traditional pattus, with colourful scarves tied around their heads and even the twins show off their new clothes to me. Everybody seems happy and excited, especially the twins who are rambunctious, as always. After general chit-chat over mint chai, everyone picks up one of the several bags that have been packed for the feast and we set off.

As we walk through the village, we find a number of Meru's cousins, a few neighbours and other women awaiting us with flowers in their hands. These are their offerings for Mahamayi and blessings for Meru and his family, who respectfully accept them.

We walk through a lane and stop in front of a wooden house, which belongs to Meru's uncle, who is the pujari for today's ceremony. Meru knocks and a man steps out, holding a bell and dharj, which are Jogini Mata's nishans. With him is a man leading a sheep, which I realise, with dread, is going to be offered as a sacrifice to Mahamayi.

The pujari now leads our procession, muttering prayers under his breath. Meru points eastwards to the massive cliffs rising from the base of the valley, across the Beas. The magnificent Jogini Falls is visible from Goshal village, about two kilometres away, adjoining the village of Vashisht. It's a lovely walk, passing by gurgling streams and through cool, shady copses.

We cross a wooden pedestrian bridge over a stream and stop to watch village children splashing about in its clear waters. Meru's mother tells me that the stream is known as Anjanu, named after Lord Hanuman's mother, who is believed to have mediated on Lord Shiva somewhere here. We pass orchards where white butterflies flutter over the undergrowth of wild flowers. Tree leaves glisten under the bright sun, dancing in the breeze. "Idyllic," I think, as a feeling of pure joy pervades me.

Soon, the steep mountain climb begins. The sound of the waterfall beckons us enticingly. We are all feeling the heat under the strong October sun and are looking forward to reaching our destination.

The sound of the waterfall gets louder, and we take a turn around a bend to a clearing right beneath the waterfall. I gaze in delight at the beautiful spot and the spectacular waterfall. Jogini Falls is huge, with a wide cascade of water, which drops from around 150 feet through multiple levels. The water thunders as it crashes down upon massive rocks, sending up huge sprays which sparkle with iridescent light. The rocky cliff behind it rises majestically into an azure sky, towering above the tall deodars which grow sporadically around the lower slopes at the base of the waterfall.

Jogini Mata's shrine lies at one corner of the grassy clearing. It is a small brick and cement structure and has a tiny entrance where the pujari lights a metal diya. We remove our shoes and wash our hands before making our way to the shrine.

"Our Jogini Mata's sthaan is sacred and very pure and we have to keep it absolutely spic and span ... because all joginis demand complete cleanliness and personal hygiene," Meru shouts in my ear, as the sound of the falls is deafening.

We stand at the entrance of the shrine and pay obeisance to the goddess of the waterfall. I look inside and all I can see are flowers and a few red chunnis. Apparently, Jogini Mata does not have an idol, but is represented symbolically, as befits a nature spirit.

Meru goes down the slope where there are three other structures, two rain shelters and another shrine, a modern construction, also devoted to Jogini Mata. When we join him, he is busy cooking rice in large pot. When the rice is ready, he places some on a plate and gestures to the pujari, who picks up the ghanti and dharj and begins walking further down the slope. He is followed by Meru's mother and the man with the sheep. They walk down to a place where the rocks form a natural cave right beside the falling water. Inside are a few stone slabs with flowers placed on them, and an upright standing stone marked with a huge slash of vermillion. Meru tells me, "This is the space of the Keu Devta who is the Devi's guard. So, the sacrifice is not offered to the Devi, it is offered to Keu Devta."

The pujari ties the sacred red thread all around and offers the rice in three directions towards the stream. I am reminded of the Goors offering flowers in three directions and make a mental note to enquire further about this rite. Meru takes the puja thali prepared by the pujari and begins to apply the mix of vermillion, rice and flowers on the sheep. That done, we wait for the sheep to quiver, a sign that this particular animal is acceptable to the deity.

Meru's mother joins her hands and prays fervently for the sheep to be accepted. It is taking a while, and Meru seems to be getting slightly impatient. But his mother is steadfast in her prayers and suddenly, the sheep shakes. Without missing a breath, the man who had brought the sheep takes it aside and slays it with a single, clean movement. It is all done so quickly, I barely register it.

After the sacrifice, the girls stand in a row and Meru washes their feet and the pujari ties the sacred red thread on their wrists. Meru's mother ties red ribbons around their waists, joking and laughing all the while as she hands out some money and halwa to each of them. It is exactly like the kumari puja performed in many homes during the navratras where the virginal female is worshipped.

Now it is time for the havan, and the pujari has begun preparing another puja thali with rice, vermillion, flowers and a cup of water. Meru, who has substituted his jeans and t-shirt for a dhoti and kurta, strikes a coconut to the ground and sprinkles its water all around. The pujari assembles a few pieces of wood and lights a fire to conduct the havan. He offers a few spoons of ghee to the fire and then hands everyone a potpourri of assorted grain to offer to the fire. It is a brief ceremony with no spoken mantras by the pujari. Instead, everyone offers their own prayers to Jogini Mata. Meru collects some of the black ashes from the sacred fire and dots everyone's forehead with the consecrated soot.

Everyone now crowds around the pujari in excitement. My suspicions regarding the cause of this excitement are proven correct when Meru informs me that the pujari will be conducting a question-and-answer session, using grains of rice to determine the answers. Indeed, the pujari, looking relaxed, is perched on a stone and muttering mantras over a handful of rice grains.

Meru's sister rushes forward and he places a few grains in her palm. Neetu peers at her palm and counts the grains carefully. Suddenly, she whoops in delight, a wide smile gracing her elegant face. Meru chuckles. "She must have got an odd number of grains!" Seeing the questioning look on my face, he adds, "Remember, you saw it at Hardayal's poochh—an odd number of grains means a positive outcome whereas an even number denotes a negative one."

He urges me to ask about whatever has been on my mind. I go to the pujari and hold out my palm. I get five grains of rice in my hand—the jogini has looked kindly upon my wish.

And now it is time for the feast to commence! We make our way uphill to a grassy knoll, where lie two rows of black stones. The stones have their centres scooped out and resemble car tyres. Everyone settles down behind the stones. Seeing my puzzlement, Meru laughs. "Look carefully, Anu, these are plates!"

Nisha explains, "Anu, these stone plates have been here since long, no one knows how they came to be here, but they were probably put here so that we don't have to lug plates up here!"

She begins washing the "stone plates" thoroughly. This is certainly a first for me and I take my place at my designated stone, while Nisha and Meru's sisters serve us rice, dal and curry. We eat, enjoying the pristine surroundings and the thunder of the waterfall.

After the repast, I ask for a little water to clean my "plate", but Nisha tells me to leave it as is. "The leftovers will be eaten by the birds. Whoever comes here next will clean the plates to their own satisfaction." I am constantly amazed at the sensitivity to nature that is built into the everyday life of the people of this mountain culture. It is a common-sense approach to ecology that we urban dwellers have lost connection with.

The sun shines brightly illuminating the massive cliffs facing us. I am feeling languorous, so we decide on an hour's rest before heading back to Goshal. I wander up a wildflower-strewn path until I discover a huge flattish rock. I climb upon it and sit down to visualise once again and commit to memory the gorgeous view of Jogini Falls—the thundering waterfall, tall cedar trees, the meadows strewn with grey rocks and white wildflowers.

I lie back on the rock and gaze at the natural beauty surrounding me. I realise that the myth of Dev Bhoomi perfectly reflects its earth-centred religion and culture.

It is apparent to me that there is no part of the lives of the people of Kullu that is not tied up with the spirits of this, their land—their mountains, forests, rocks and lakes. There is nothing that is not alive, conscious and communicating with them. The spirits of their land are feared, revered, loved and obeyed. I wonder at their intuitive intelligence, which is far more sophisticated than we, the denizens of a modern world, can understand.

A couple of days later I sit down to review Avantika's footage of Devta Rishi Vasishtha's visit to Bhrigu Lake. It had clearly been a long and rigorous trek, with the procession setting off early in the morning and only arriving at the lake the next day. The group was about fifty strong, with more men than women. Most of the men carried backpacks while some had heavier loads, possibly rations for the journey. Rishi Vasishtha's Goor, an old man with wispy hair, was barefoot.

The journey started out with the usual music by the bajantris but after a few hours, as the gradient became steeper and the terrain rockier, the musicians stopped playing. What was amazing was the dexterity of the palanquin bearers, for at times the incline was almost vertical, yet not once did the palanquin touch the ground. The bearers changed every half an hour, so that the pace did not flag. This particular pilgrimage was not an annual journey—it took place only once in about three to four years when the Devta expressed a wish to visit the sacred lake.

As dusk fell and visibility dropped, a few mashaals were lit, for the party needed to reach Pandu Ropa, a high-altitude meadow, where they would halt for the night. The Pandavas are said to have spent time at Pandu Ropa during their exile and the wild paddy that still grows in the wetlands here is believed to have been planted by them. Even from the footage, I can sense how cold it must have been at that altitude. When they struck camp, fires were lit, and a meal of rice and dal was served all around. Men and women gathered around the fire, singing and telling stories late into the night.

The next morning, the rath and its entourage set out for the last leg of the trek. The temperature had dropped and as an exception to the rule the Goor had worn a pair of sheepskin boots. Three hours later, as they neared the sacred lake, the musicians began to play, and finally the vista opened out onto a breathtaking sight—a mirror-like turquoise pool set in a bed of pristine snow, surrounded on three sides by the towering Pir Panjal and Dhauladhar ranges. Bhrigu Lake, where the great sage Bhrigu meditated, imprinting the spot with strong mystical energies. Such was the power of the spot that the Devta's entourage fell silent.

The rath was set down on the banks of the lake and prayers commenced. Avantika recounted how the fragrance of the smoking juniper in the dharj intoxicated as much as did the lack of oxygen at the altitude of 4300 metres.

Prayers over, the palanquin bearers lifted the rath and began walking towards the water's edge. Suddenly they gathered speed and entered the lake at a run, going knee-deep into the freezing water. The hanging draperies were immersed and a member of the Devloo began sprinkling the rath with water. And then it was done. The Devta had had his bath, recharged his energies and was satisfied.

Then it was the turn of the devotees to take a ritual bath. Meanwhile, the Goor went into a brief trance, allowing the Devta to communicate his satisfaction to the villagers. With that final rite, the matter was over. The villagers settled down to lunch by the lake before setting off for the trek back home.

Sitting on my balcony later, I gaze at the full moon, mesmerising me with its bright beauty. Tonight, she is adorned by wisps of wayward clouds that sail through the cool breeze, evoking images of animals and angels. Moonlight highlights the contours of mountain ranges set against silvery grey skies, a scatter of lights twinkling amidst their shadowy folds. I can hear the rush of the faraway river, the occasional bark of village dogs and whistling of leaves. I soak in the quiet beauty and peace, contemplating about the power of nature.

Suddenly, gusts of strong winds blow the leaves of the poplar trees aflutter, the pear tree thrashes around sending baby pears flying down the garden. I am yet unused to the inclement weather here. Within an hour a bright and sunny day could become grey, overcast with ponderous rain clouds. The wind picks up speed, door and window shutters bang shut. The tablecloth set atop the balcony table sails across it, flailing for a bit like a ballet dancer, before joining the shrouds of leaves, flower petals and baby pears and apricots on the grass. Soon enough there is a huge clap of thunder right overhead my cottage and I literally jump out of my skin. I run inside and watch lightning strikes on the opposite mountain slopes. The wind howls and the cottage shudders. The view from my bay window is quite frightening, although I always find it awe-inspiring to witness the ferocity and power of nature.

The spiritualised understanding of ecology and geography that is found so often in folk traditions is centred on the idea of oneness with nature, accompanied by a profoundly emotional register and deep reverence for the powerful and inscrutable facets of nature. This nature-oriented understanding is based on three widely accepted notions of immanence, namely, the sacredness of all creatures; the concept of interconnection—that the entirety of the living cosmos is linked; and, lastly, compassion—which values other lives like one's own because we as humans are answerable to those who are different from us.

21

Nature Spirits

I am completely intrigued by the concept of nature spirits! What were these spirit beings and their magical energies? Could the Goors actually communicate with them? I am eager to learn more, so once again, I dive deep into research.

What I discover is quite incredible. Belief in nature spirits is almost universal and found not only in indigenous cultures but even in most mainstream religions. Mythologies across the world abound with tales of supernatural beings or entities with subtle energies that are closely associated with the natural world.

Many ancient traditions understood this living quality of all of nature. Indigenous cultures of New Zealand, Australia, and South America, the ancient Egyptians, Kabballsts, Greeks, Hindus, Buddhists and the Norse have all contributed significant knowledge towards understanding the energy dynamics of our world and the universe. Within all these vastly varied cultures, there have been some evolved personages, visionaries such as shamans, mystics and priests who understood that there existed a subtle realm in nature, inhabited by conscious beings, broadly classified as nature spirits, with whom they could communicate.

The term nature spirits is really a general and an umbrella term, a bit like saying animal or plant. It simply denotes a being that works with the conscious and energetic side of nature. Just as there are billions of different species of plants and animals on earth, it is likely that there are at least as many different kinds of nature spirits.

Practitioners of pantheism, polytheism and shamanism share the belief that a nature spirit is an invisible being who is defined by its particular function within the natural environment of the earth. Such beings take form and work within the subtle energy fields of the physical world. They tie themselves to specific landscapes and to geographical features such as rivers, trees, even planets, and to species of plants and animals.

In the West, the first book to compile the different species of nature spirits and their unique characteristics into one compendium was *A Book on Nymphs, Sylphs, Pygmies and Salamanders*, published posthumously in 1566 and authored by Paracelsus, a famous Swiss physician, philosopher and theosophist.

According to Paracelsus, nature spirits are diverse elemental beings with bodies composed of finer kinds of matter, invisible to the human eye. He delineated these supernatural beings into four major elemental categories, examples of which can be found in cultures worldwide.

1. Earth: Earth spirits are beings that relate to rocks, stones, minerals, precious gems, hills and mountains, and are traditionally called "Gnomes". Gnomes are the spirits of the earth and are responsible for the growth and fertility of plants. They are small, earthy creatures that are often depicted as living underground or in caves. Another type of earth spirit is the "elf". Elves are also small, magical beings that are often associated with forests and woodlands. They are known for their wisdom and skill in crafts such as metalworking and weaving. "Dryads" are tree spirits that are said to inhabit specific trees and forests. They are often depicted as shy and elusive and can sometimes be helpful to humans who show them respect.

2. Water: Water spirits are connected to all waterbodies, but their presence can be felt in much more powerful ways in streams, rivers, lakes and the ocean. They are also known as "Undines", and include mermaids and mermen. In Celtic mythology, an "Each Uisge" is a dangerous water horse found in Scotland; the Nyx are shapeshifting water spirits in Germanic mythology who usually appear in human or horse form; "Naiads" are nymphs who preside over streams, springs, fountains and wells in Greek mythology.

3. Air: The spirits of the air are connected to all gaseous substances and are believed to be best sensed in winds and breezes. They are traditionally known as "Sylphs" and their male counterparts, the "Zephr". The perception of a fairy with tiny wings is a close approximation of how they are said to appear to children. These Sylphs are considered to influence the thoughts of people and have strong associations with art, the forest, and nature. Paracelsus theorised that the Greek "muses" were actually Sylphs! Other air spirits are Faeries, Griffins Gargoyles and the Pegasusians, the race of white, winged horses often featured in Greek mythology who we can call on for help. Egyptians worship "Amun" the God of creation and the wind; "Feng po" is the Chinese wind goddess and "Fei Lian" the Chinese wind god; the Japanese honour "Fujin" and "Shinatsuhiko", the wind gods; the Aztecs have several wind gods like "Ehecati" and "Tezcatlipoca".

4. Fire: Fire spirits can be found in volcanoes or in any form of fire, from candles to infernos. They are known as "Salamanders" and are said to be the most difficult of all the elementals to connect with. It is believed that Salamanders associate only with philosophers and adepts of the magical arts. Egyptian mythology eulogises "Ra",

fire God of the sun, light, warmth and growth; "Grannus" is the god of fire and the sun in Celtic mythology; "Apollo" is the god of the sun, "Hestia" the goddess of the hearth, while "Prometheus", god of fire, is credited with the creation of humanity from clay, in Greek mythology; Romans worship "Sol" as the sun god and "Vesta" goddess of the hearth and its fire; Hawaiian mythology worships "Pele", goddess of fire and volcanoes.

Rudolf Steiner, a spiritual philosopher, also makes a similar observation as he notes that nature spirits are intrinsically linked to the elements of earth, water, air, and fire. He points out that normal awareness understands the physical world through the senses, but there's a deeper realm where nature spirits operate, influencing the forces we see in nature. While science describes these forces based on surface-level experiences, to an occultist, they are merely illusions or maya, representations of the nature spirits at play. Beneath these illusions lies the true essence: the etheric body of Earth, where these spirits reside.

Just as Earth serves as our home in the cosmos, these entities inhabit their own realms within these elements. Their collaboration constitutes the etheric or life essence of Earth. These spirits play a vital role in nurturing the cycles of nature, facilitating the growth and decline of living beings, and breathing life into the entire planetary ecosystem. According to Steiner, the forces of nature, which we can observe like weather or the growth of plants, are also a kind of illusion that represents the spirits of nature. While what we see and understand through our senses may not reveal the complete truth about reality, these experiences can help us feel connected to a deeper, meaningful spiritual existence.

Steiner asserts that folk traditions about nature spirits stem from a spiritual reality, suggesting that ancient people, with their innate spiritual vision, were able to connect with elemental beings, which later transformed into the fairies and gnomes of myths and children's tales.

More recently, others have written extensively about nature spirits. In his book *Devas, Fairies and Angels* (1986), William Bloom, one of the UK's leading educators and a spiritual teacher, regards the fairy elementals in the same light as angels inhabiting what he calls the "Devic World". *Subtle Worlds* (2010), by David Spangler, a spiritual teacher since 1964, presents original research into our planet's subtle worlds.

According to Bloom and Spangler, Devas are the most evolved and highly conscious nature spirits, aligned with the flow and circulation of life and vital energies, as well as being the architects and artisans of form. They are custodians and overseers of natural energies and forces, such as electricity. In essence, Devas are the energy of life itself, vitalising all forms, including mankind. These entities are said to govern the inner intelligence of all nature, from the tiniest flower to the majestic cedar. These forces also give rise to natural phenomena such as storms, hurricanes or earthquakes.

Spangler writes, "An angel is a class of beings whose function is to foster, nurture and protect life and consciousness within the world. They are the gardeners of the interior life within all things. They assist us in remembering our oneness with the sacred. They empower and nourish the evolution of spirit; wherever consciousness is, there are angels."

While Devas are the architects of nature, nature spirits are the fieldworkers and construction hands. Nature spirits are the transformers of life, taking the raw, intense subtle energies coming from the higher-order worlds and stepping them down into forms that can be appropriated and used by the subtle bodies of physical entities, mainly plants, but animals as well.

According to David Spangler, nature spirits are said to share similar motivations as humans such as the need to survive, thrive, prosper, protect themselves, assist others, grow in self-awareness and learn to exist in cooperation with others. Like humans, they also evolve in consciousness. Once "Deva-hood" has been achieved, the nature spirits take on greater and greater responsibilities, looking after whole areas of land or sea and becoming responsible for groups of spirits, which are part of its retinue. There are Devas that look after towns and cities as well as tracts of the countryside. At the top of this metaphoric tree is the planetary Deva, which many people nowadays have come to call Gaia, our Earth Deity.

While indigenous belief systems intuited the spirit world, modern-day belief in the existence of nature spirits is based on the foundational understanding that, at its source, all energy is ultimately one. It is surmised that the one source has evolved over time into numerous specialised life forms, each of which developed in response to specific needs and experiences. As energy evolves down through the frequencies, from light to subtle and solid forms, life forms that are close to each other in energetic frequency, or consciousness, can see and interact with one another fairly easily.

Western religious thought, based upon Biblical traditions, regards nature as something created by God. If nature is sacred, it is because it is God's creation and not because it has intrinsic divinity of its own. This worldview made Christian traditions generally suspicious of nature gods and regard their worship as a form of idolatry. That is why they have historically rejected nature-based or pagan religions as unholy. However, several Eastern religions regard and worship nature as divine.

In the Islamic traditions, jinns, who are made up of fire, are believed to inhabit a parallel world which is not accessible to humans. However, they are often also associated with elements from nature. In most cases, it is believed that these spirits reside in lakes, trees, ponds, forests, streams, springs and wells. They, according to popular belief, are meant to be treated with respect and reverence. Any contamination of their residing places is considered sinful. There are also cases of possession by jinns in which the possessed have contaminated parts of nature that are otherwise considered sacred. Even though Islam is a monotheistic religion, it is not bereft of traditions such as these, which always hint at a mutual correlation between humans and nature.

The Hindu approach to nature is influenced by mythological and cultural narratives based upon the knowledge of the Vedas, Upanishads and Vedanta as well as Hindu devotional and ritualistic practices. The Vedas assert their authority over the higher transcendent cosmos, perceiving nature as a powerful entity that upholds and nurtures all forms of life. As per the Vedas, the ultimate truth, the supreme conscious force, assumes different inherent subjective forms to support the act of creation, revealing itself through the wonders of the natural world.

The Vedas pay tribute to nearly all elements of nature—earth, water, fire, air, storms, the sky, rain, forests, mountains, rivers, and a multitude of animals, birds, and reptiles. This reverence is so profound that it is often said that the wisdom contained within the Vedas was born from the nurturing embrace of Mother Nature herself.

This reverence for various elements of nature can also be seen in a Vedic invocation for cosmic tranquillity, aspiring for the seamless unity of the three eternal principles—God, nature and man:

> dyauh śāntirantariksam śāntih prthivī śāntirāpah śāntirosadhayah śāntih vanaspatayah śāntirviśvedevāh śāntirbrahma śāntih sarvam śāntih śāntireva śāntih sā mā śāntiredhi.
>
> Om śāntih śāntih śāntih
>
> May the sky be peaceful, may the midspace be peaceful, may the earth be peaceful, may the waters be peaceful, may the annual plants be peaceful, may the forests be peaceful, may there be peace and peace only, may such a peace come to me.
>
> *Peace, Peace, Peace.*
> (Yajurveda, 36/17)

According to Hindu thought, there is no separation between the divine and the world of nature. They are understood as being two aspects of the same reality. The cosmic reality is likened to the ocean, where nature or the manifest world is like the waves on the surface of the sea. Brahman or the un-manifest Absolute is like the depths of the sea, but it is all the same water in a single ocean. As the Yajur Veda states, "The natural world is a living, breathing entity, and every part of it is interconnected and interdependent. The Gods and Goddesses of nature are the guardians of this delicate balance, and it is our responsibility to live in harmony with them."

The informed Hindu perceives a divine presence within all forms of nature. The sacred presence of Brahman, or the Supreme Divine Reality, is what is called Ishvara or the "cosmic lord" in Hinduism. Yet it is also present in the soul or reincarnating entity, what is called the Jiva, our higher Self. And it is present in the world of nature, Jagat. God, Soul and the World are aspects of One Reality, but not in a limited way. Each share the entirety of the underlying reality. Each is sacred and holds the same deeper nature of Being, Consciousness and Bliss (Sat-chit-ananda).

Hinduism honours all the forms of the divine but also recognises the formless divine even beyond the creator, extending to the Absolute. Vedanta teaches us that this Absolute is the being, self and soul of everything animate and inanimate. It says our very Self is the entire universe and the entire universe dwells within us. To honour nature is to honour ourselves. Importantly, Earth is sacred as the very manifestation of the Divine Mother and worshipped as Bhumi Devi. In fact one of the reasons that Hindus honour cows is that the cow represents the energies and qualities of Earth, selfless caring, sharing and the providing of nourishment to all.

The concept of the family of Mother Earth in the Hindu culture is known as Vasudhaiva Kutumbakam. "Vasudha" means the earth; "Kutumba" means extended family consisting of human beings. This concept engenders that all human beings as well as other creatures living on earth are members of the same extended family of Devi Vasundhara. It is only by considering the entire universe as a part of our extended family can we respect, honour and care for all beings.

Approaching nature from this perspective, the worship of sacred mountains and hills, sacred rivers and lakes, sacred trees and groves, sacred flowers and grasses became common Hindu practice. Hindu thought embraces the divine as present not only in human forms but throughout nature, recognising its sacredness. This holistic view fosters a deep connection with nature, acknowledging the divine reality inherent in all things. It believes that the sacred exists in every form around us, including nature spirits, which are honoured as integral parts of the spiritual landscape. Each element, force and form of nature is believed to have dwelling Devas or celestial beings who preside over their functioning and evolution. Devas such as Brahma, Vishnu, and Shiva, form the Hindu trinity known as the Trimurti and preside over the functioning of the cosmos and the evolution of creation.

The *Samhitas*, the oldest layer of text in the Vedas, enumerate thirty-three Devas, eleven each for the three worlds. "Deities who are eleven in heaven; who are eleven on earth; and who are eleven dwelling with glory in mid-air; may be pleased with this our sacrifice." The Rig Veda venerates deities like Dyaus, the deity of the sky; Vayu, the deity of the wind and breath; Varuna, the deity of water and rain; Agni, the deity of fire; Indra, the deity of thunder; Surya, the deity of the sun, light and day; and Chandra, the deity of the moon and the night, who are responsible for maintaining the requisite balance in the functioning of all nature. Apart from hymns venerating aspects of nature, the Vedas also elucidate mantras to invoke the blessings of the five basic elements or the panchamahabhuta of nature: Akash or firmament, Vayu or air, Agni or fire, Apah or water, and Prithvi or earth.

In this rich tapestry of nature spirits within Hindu mythology, we see various spirits or deities associated with various elements of the natural world who assume a variety of forms and reside within nature's spiritual realm. These mystical beings embodying the essence of nature are respected and venerated in various ways. In fact, even today, Hindu ritual worship works with the forces of nature to bring a higher consciousness and energy into the world. Hindu pujas do this with special prayers and mantras, and offerings of subtle sensory essences like flowers, incense, ghee flames, special water or food and fragrant oils. These rituals invoke the Prana or the Spirit of the deity and allow the divine to enter into the form for worship, whether it is a statue or a natural object, so that the powers of the higher planes and worlds can have a place to bless us here on Earth.

Meera Baindur (2009), who specialises in environmental philosophy, notes that the notion of a nature that exists apart from humanity is largely foreign to many Indians, who tend to view the natural world through a human-centric and cosmic framework. People engage with and interpret their surroundings not just as they are but as they are perceived to be within these established worldviews.

In the heart of the forest, Vedic sages found inspiration in the interconnected dance of srishti and prakriti, drawing profound philosophical insights and spiritual nourishment from nature's creative embrace. The primary narratives in Vedic and Puranic texts and local oral traditions reveal a distinctly humanised perspective on nature in India. For instance, during the Vedic era, trees were revered as divine beings and likened to humans. The *Aushadhi Sukta* from the *Rig Veda* addresses plants and vegetables, exclaiming, 'O Mother! Hundreds are your birthplaces, and thousands are your shoots' (X.97.2).

Similarly, one of the verse from the *Bhagavata Purana* conveys this perspective as it says: 'One should look upon deer, camels, monkeys, donkeys, reptiles, birds and flies as though they were one's own children; what is that which distinguishes these from those?' (*Bhagavata Purana*, 7.14.9).

Nature is cherished as a nurturing mother, respected as a guiding father, and cared for like a treasured child. Its sacredness stems from humanity's reliance on it, which sanctifies everything, including individuals and the more fearsome aspects of nature like storms, earthquakes, and landslides. These natural phenomena are interpreted as manifestations of the gods, reflecting the principles that maintain the universe and the cosmic order known as rita.

In Hindu folklore, there are many different types of nature spirits, each with their own unique characteristics and abilities. One of the most well-known types of nature spirits in Indian culture is the Yaksha, who are supernatural beings associated with the natural world, known for their generally benevolent nature, though they can also be mischievous, unpredictable, and at times, even deadly. Renowned for their magical abilities and shapeshifting skills, they are often revered as protective or guardian deities of various natural spots, such as lakes, or wells. Yakshas are believed to be the attendants of Kubera, the god of wealth, and the Mahabharata mentions Yakshas as "spirits of the natural world, responsible for the abundance and prosperity of Earth".

Nanditha Krishna, an Indian environmentalist and historian, notes that the tree spirit, the Yaksha or Yakshi, is as old as the Indus–Saraswati civilization, which imparts a holy essence to the tree that shelters them. In India, the pipal tree, also known as ashvattha, holds the title of the most revered tree, believed to be inhabited by a spirit or Vriksha Devta. Throughout history, the worship of trees has been prevalent, especially in Hinduism, celebrated for both their life-sustaining fertility and also as homes to benevolent and malevolent spirits, compelling ancient peoples to honour them in hopes of harmony and prosperity.

It is believed that the veneration of Yakshas coexisted with the sacrificial rituals led by priests during the Vedic period. In fact, adorning the gates of the magnificent stupa at Sanchi from the third century BCE is a sculpture of Yakshi or Yakshini (female earth spirit) in the graceful three-bend pose (tribanga). As she stands beneath a tree, one hand playfully holds a branch while her foot brings forth its fruits, symbolising nature's fertility. Similar figures of female tree spirits can be found on the reliefs of the Bharhut and Amaravati stupas. The vrikshaka[1] or shalabhanjika[2] touches the tree—ashoka, amra, kadamba or champaka—with her foot for it to flower.

In a traditional ritual seen throughout West Bengal to Gujarat and Tamil Nadu to Bihar, villagers offer terracotta horses to their deities, believing that this age-old practice, reminiscent of the ashvamedha[3] ritual, will ensure a bountiful harvest, reflecting the horse's esteemed status as a vital protector of the community. The spirits, mainly Yakshas, who wander around the village outskirts and the sacred groves where people believe he still lives, mount the terracotta animals offered as a token of their devotion.

Another type of nature spirit is the Gandharva, supernatural beings that are associated with music and the arts, and often depicted as heavenly musicians and dancers. In Hindu mythology, Gandharvas are believed to be the attendants of Indra, the king of the gods. According to the Rig Veda, "Gandharvas are the spirits of the natural world, and are responsible for the beauty and harmony of the earth."

---

1 Vrikshaka: Tree maiden

2 *Shalabhanjika*: A woman or yakshi often depicted in Indian literature and art in a graceful pose bending down the flowery branch of the sal tree to pluck its flowers. The name comes from the Sanskrit word *salabhanjika* meaning "breaking a branch of a sala tree", sala indicating the sala tree (*Vatica robusta*) while bhanjika is derived from the verbal root *bhanj* which means to break.

3 The ashvamedha, an ancient Vedic rite, involved a royal horse roaming freely for a year to symbolise a king's supremacy; its successful completion, often culminating in a public sacrifice, elevated the king to the status of chakravartin and ensured the kingdom's prosperity, though not all rituals required the horse's actual sacrifice.

An important nature spirit is the Naaga.[4] In Hindu mythology, Naagas are believed to be the guardians of the underworld, and are associated with fertility and rebirth. According to the Mahabharata, "Naagas are the spirits of the natural world, and are responsible for the balance and renewal of the earth." Folklore also has it that Naagas can fake human form and many ancient tribes claim to be descendants of Naagas.

A further example of a nature spirit or a deity is Aranyani, the forest goddess, who embodies the spirit of the wilderness, celebrating the interconnectedness of all living beings. One of the most captivating hymns in the Rig Veda (X.146. 1–6) pays tribute to Aranyani, the mysterious spirit who relishes her solitude and embodies courage. The hymn comprises the following lines: "But Aranyani injures no one unless some other assails; feeding upon the sweet fruit, she penetrates at will. I praise the musk-scented, fragrant, fertile, uncultivated Aranyani, the mother of wild animals."

In the hymn, the poet wonders how she can traverse such vast distances from the comforts of civilisation without experiencing fear or loneliness. Though she remains unseen, her essence is felt through the soft chime of her anklets and her benevolence in nourishing both humans and animals alike.

Another one of the nature spirits are Apsaras, seductresses associated with beauty and grace. Vidyadharas are magicians associated with knowledge and wisdom; Kinnaras and Betalas are associated with music and dance, while Rakshasas, Pisachas are associated with darkness and evil. These nature spirits are often depicted as guardians, protectors, or celestial beings, and are sometimes worshipped as deities.

In addition to these specific types of nature spirits, there is a general belief in India in the spiritual power of the natural world. Many Hindus believe that the natural world is imbued

4 Naagas: Divine, or semi-divine, race of half-human, half-serpent beings

with a divine presence, and that nature spirits play an important role in maintaining the balance and harmony of the earth. As Swami Vivekananda once said, "The whole world is a living being, and every part of it is a living being, with its own life and consciousness."

Since the belief in nature spirits has been an integral part of religious history, mythology, folklore, legends and traditions of many cultures these spirits have been worshipped and revered for centuries and are often associated with specific natural features such as mountains, waterbodies, caves, trees and plants.

For instance, certain trees have been considered sacred in cultures across the world, because an important nature spirit or a tree deity resides in them. Deodar, a species of cedar, literally means "tree of gods" in Sanskrit, and in Hindu tradition is associated with Shiva, Parvati and Vishnu. To the Sumerians it was the "Tree of Life". The goddess of fortune and prosperity, Lakshmi, is found to reside within a tree, the sacred fig, or pipal (*Ficus religiosa*). In fact the three principal gods in Hinduism, Brahma, Shiva and Vishnu, all have associations with the sacred fig tree. The gular (*Ficus racemose*) also has associations to all three of these gods: the roots with Brahma, the bark with Vishnu, and the branches with Shiva. Vishnu is also associated with the banyan (*Ficus benghalensis*). Sacred forests, considered to be dwellings areas of diverse goddesses, abound all around India, wherein customary propitiation rituals are still conducted by the locals at specific annual celebrations.

In the Puranas, sacred geography intertwines the celestial with the earthly, where the *Sthala Purana* narrates cosmic origins, and the *Sthala Mahatmya* brings the sacred experience to life. In this belief, the landscape is shaped not just by its physical features—rivers, mountains, and forests—but also by the mystical spirits that inhabit them. Moreover, local narratives infuse them with meaning and bridge the sacred and the ecological in reverence for these extraordinary places.

Natural sacred places, marked by distinctive geographical features, are deeply revered and steeped in oral narratives. These stories known as *Sthala Puranas* weave a rich tapestry connecting the land (bhoomi) with a profound sense of identity, encompassing not only human-made structures but also essential elements like water, rocks, and trees. Unique local features are imbued with mythical significance through tales of divine journeys and events. Ritual practices, whether religious or social, continuously reinforce these narratives, giving each sacred site its own identity rooted in myth and history. These myths illuminate why certain places hold a sacred status along with the presence of ethereal beings, often reflected in their evocative names and the extraordinary events once believed to have unfolded there. These sacred sites, inhabited by the nature spirits, are often considered the ultimate destination for the devotees to easily communicate with the divine.

All around the world, there exist such woods, forests, rivers, streams, rocks, mountains, peaks, and trees that are deeply connected to ancestral spirits and divine beings. In India alone, the ENVIS[5] Centre, focused on the Ecological Heritage and Sacred Sites, has meticulously catalogued a remarkable total of 10,377 sacred groves across the nation.[6]

An essential part of nature worship includes the conservation of particular forest patches that are considered sacred to local deities or ancestral spirits. These spaces represent the spiritual and ecological values held by indigenous communities. The *Prithvi Sukta* hymn from the Atharva Veda expresses: 'Whatever I dig out from you, O Earth! May that have quick regeneration again; may we not damage the vital habitat and heart' (XII.1.35).

The reverence for natural sacred sites not only enriches cultural traditions but also plays a crucial role in conserving local biodiversity, as tribal healers, shamans, and priests passionately

5 ENVIS: Environmental Information System

6 N. Krishna (2015)

advocate for these ecosystems, believing that the spirits reside in untouched landscapes, swiftly transforming such plots into thriving, mature forests.

This intertwining of divinity and nature is a cornerstone of the Indian religious experience. Sacred groves protected by communities through ancient customs and taboos exemplify this connection. These patches of forest where local folk deities or ancestral spirits are venerated are overseen by religious bodies or dedicated management committees.

Across different states, the guardians of sacred groves take on varied forms—male or female, animal or ancestral—reflecting the ancient belief that deities and mystical spirits inhabit the very stones, trees, and wilderness around us, often finding their home in a secluded forest or beneath a solitary tree. For instance, in Himachal Pradesh, enchanting myths and legends surround sacred groves, or dev van, where the worship of deities like Bakhu Naag Devta and Ringarishi Devta protects these lush sanctuaries, prohibiting the cutting of trees and the removal of fallen leaves, ensuring the preservation of both nature and culture.

Similarly, in Rajasthan, sacred groves—known as vani, kenkri, oran—serve as reverent havens dedicated to deities like Garva-ji, Naraini Mata, Peerbaba, and Naharshakti Mata. Rajasthani Gujjars cherish a special tradition of planting and worshipping neem trees as the sacred home of god Devnarayan.

In Goa, the sacred groves, known as devrai, devran, and pann, serve as revered sanctuaries dedicated to deities like Durga and Rashtroli, where the indigenous tribes—Gavda, Kunbi, Velip, and Dhangar Gouli—celebrate their connection with nature by honouring sacred goats, banyan trees, mystical hills, venerable stones, and tranquil ponds.

In Madhya Pradesh, where tribals make up 19.9 per cent of the population, sacred groves called deogudi or sarna are protected by the reverence of local deities like Bursung, Pat Khanda,

Ganganamma, Mahadev, Bhandarin Mata, and Danteshwari Mata, for the tribes believe that neglecting these sacred spaces could unleash devastating natural calamities.

In Kerala, sacred groves known as kaavu or sarpa kaavu, such as Ayyappan kaavu, Sastan kaavu, and Bhagavati or Amman kaavu, are not only dedicated to their revered deities but also celebrate the tradition of serpent worship, with nearly all groves adorned with snake images, while those cared for by tribespeople pay homage to Yekshi and Vanadevata, the forest goddess and spirits.

In Puducherry, the sacred groves, locally called kovil kaadugal and Ayyappan kaavu, vary in size from 0.2 to 5 hectares and are dedicated to revered deities like Aiyanar, Poraiyatta Amman, Pachaivali Amman, Selli Amman, Kaliamman, and Maduraiveeran, inviting reverence and sanctity from the local community.[7]

This phenomenon of nature spirits and sacred geography spans other cultures too as we see the Dryads and Hamadryads of Greek mythology. According to Ovid, "Dryads are the spirits of the trees, and are responsible for the growth and vitality of the forests." In Japan, for example, there is a belief in spirits called kami, which are associated with natural features such as mountains, rivers, and trees. According to Shinto tradition, "Kami are the spirits of the natural world, and are responsible for the harmony and balance of the earth." Other examples are Kodama and Kurozome, the spirit of the *Prunus serrulata* (Japanese cherry); Metsaema, mother of the forest in Estonian mythology; Mielikki, goddess of the forests in Finnish mythology and Pi-Fang, a Chinese tree deity.

Interestingly, individual tree spirits can sometimes be persuaded to enter a cut stick, staff or wand and remain connected to it. Magic wands infused in this way allow an individual to maintain a more direct communication with this type of spirit.

Besides trees, flowers and herbs from around the world are associated with nature spirits and deities and have been used from

7 N. Krishna (2015)

ancient times. The lotus is considered sacred in Hinduism and is associated with Goddess Lakshmi, revered for its beauty and its role as a symbol of purity and enlightenment. Sage (*Salvia officinalis*) is considered sacred in many Native American cultures and is associated with the spirit of the sage plant, revered for its medicinal properties and its role in purification and cleansing. Ayahuasca is considered sacred in many South American indigenous cultures and is associated with the spirit of the ayahuasca vine. It is revered for its role in spiritual practices and its ability to induce visions and healing. The peony is considered sacred in Chinese mythology and is associated with the Goddess Xi Wangmu, revered for its beauty and its role as a symbol of wealth and prosperity. Lavender is considered sacred in many Mediterranean cultures and is associated with the spirit of the lavender plant, revered for its medicinal properties and its role as a symbol of peace and relaxation. The tulsi plant is worshipped in India as the earthy manifestation of Goddess Tulasi, an avatar of Goddess Lakshmi.

From time immemorial certain waterbodies around the world have been revered along with the deities or nature associated with them. For instance, the Ganga is considered sacred in Hinduism and is associated with the Goddess Ganga. She is revered for her ability to purify and cleanse. Therefore, her waters are often used in religious ceremonies and offerings.

Sikkim also boasts several sacred lakes that not only serve as the origins of the Teesta and Rangit rivers but are also revered as the dwelling places of local guardian spirits, including divine beings like devas, yakshas, naagas, and tantric deities, creating a mystical aura that captivates all who visit. In Egyptian mythology, the Nile is considered sacred and is associated with the God Hapi, revered for its ability to provide life-giving water and fertile soil. Lake Titicaca is considered sacred in Andean mythology and is associated with the Goddess Mama Cocha. The lake is revered for its connection to the spiritual world and its water often used in shamanic ceremonies and offerings.

In Shintoism, Lake Biwa is considered sacred and is associated with the Goddess Benzaiten, revered for her beauty and role as a source of inspiration for poets and artists throughout Japanese history. The Thames is considered sacred in Celtic mythology and is associated with the Goddess Sulis, revered for her role as a source of life and inspiration for the people of England. Lake Mansarovar in Tibet is considered to be one of the most sacred lakes and is associated with Lord Shiva.

Sacred mountains are an important part of many spiritual and cultural traditions around the world. They are associated with different nature spirits and are revered for their spiritual significance, as well as their natural beauty and ability to inspire awe and wonder. The reverence for these mountains reflects a deep connection and respect for the natural world and the spiritual power and significance of the environment. Mount Kailash in Tibet is considered sacred in Hinduism, Buddhism, and Jainism. It is associated with the gods Shiva and Vishnu, and is revered for its spiritual significance and its role as a pilgrimage site. Mount Fuji is considered sacred in Shintoism and is associated with the Goddess Sengen. It is revered for its natural beauty and is often depicted in Japanese art and literature. Mount Uluru in Australia is considered sacred in Aboriginal mythology and is associated with the ancestral spirits of the land, revered for its spiritual significance. Mount Olympus is considered sacred in Greek mythology, and is associated with the gods Zeus and Hera. It is revered for its importance as the home of the gods. Mount Sinai is considered sacred in Judaism, Christianity, and Islam. It is associated with Prophet Moses and revered for its spiritual significance as the site where Moses received the Ten Commandments.

Besides mountains, caves too are associated with nature spirits and deities. The Amarnath cave is considered sacred in Hinduism and is associated with Shiva, revered for its spiritual significance and often visited by Hindu pilgrims. Batu caves in Malaysia are considered sacred and are associated with God Murugan, revered for its spiritual significance. Waitomo caves in New Zealand are considered sacred in Maori culture associated with the spirit of the Cave God, revered for their natural beauty and their role as a source of inspiration for artists and tourists. Longmen Grottoes in China are considered sacred in Buddhism and revered for their historical and artistic significance.

All of nature is sacred, but certain places have, over a long period of time, gained a reputation for some extra quality or dimension, in some cases becoming centres of pilgrimage. It is a vibratory quality of the spiritual essence or consciousness of the particular place which provides the attraction. This is sometimes called the "genius loci", the presiding deity or spirit of a place. When sites take on the mantle of being sacred, human contact with these spiritual essences is established and forms of communication can take place. For instance, temples in India, Egypt and Greece are devoted to particular gods or goddess. Other natural sacred sites, revered as places of special spiritual power and worthy of reverence are Stonehenge, the Pyramids of Egypt, Machu Picchu, the Parthenon, the Great Serpent Mound, among others.

In the local folklore and legends of Himachal Pradesh, many stories and tales revolve around nature spirits and their interactions with humans. For instance, there are many tales of forest spirits who help lost travellers find their way out of the woods, protect or harm them. Vankhandini is the powerful goddess of the forest, with both a protective and destructive aspect. High mountain passes and inaccessible forests are her abode, as are cliff tops and craggy rocks. That is why she is propitiated and appeased before undertaking the treacherous crossing of a mountain pass or before cattle and livestock are taken to forests to graze. This goddess is represented by just vermillion-smeared stones and trishuls, symbolic of the earth force, set on high ground. Her powers, however, are immense. She can physically, emotionally and psychologically derange her victims, possessing them in gruesome ways. She requires appeasement with food and sweetmeats or the offering of a she-goat. Narsingh is a demon god who lives in a walnut tree, and Kailu, another demon, lives in the Kainth tree[8] and both require propitiation in different ways. Jalbataal and Jaljogan are water demons and Choupatiyas are the demons and gods of the crossroads.

Reverence for nature spirits highlights the belief in the interconnectedness of all living beings and the environment. Respecting these spirits is often seen as a way of honouring nature and maintaining harmony with the cosmos.

In his book, *The Maler: A Study in Nature-Man-Spirit Complex*, L.P. Vidyarthi, an Indian anthropologist, proposed the famous concept of Nature-Man-Spirit Complex in reference to the Maler tribe from Bihar, who believed in different types of spirits. In this concept, Vidyarthi emphasised the interconnectedness and interdependence of three elements—nature, man and spirits—which shape a specific culture and way of understanding life. In tribal India, the intricate bond between humans and nature fuels a deep belief in the supernatural, intertwining their social structures with ecological realities.

This connection often creates a delicate balance between respecting natural and spiritual forces. While some communities find their lifestyles rigidly dictated by these beliefs, others have adapted, demonstrating a remarkable resilience and ease in navigating the complex dance of man, nature, and spirit.

In our modern context, nature spirits are not a subject of scientific research, as they are supernatural beings that are not considered to be part of the physical world and because we do not possess the requisite sensory capabilities to know them. However,

---

8 The Kainth tree, scientifically referred to as *Pyrus pashia* and commonly known as Indian Wild Pear, is a small deciduous tree often found thriving along roadsides, near streams, in scrub forests and wastelands, reaching elevations of up to 2000 metres in the Western Himalayas.

recent research on the intelligence and communication abilities of plants and other living organisms suggests that they are not just passive objects in the environment but are active participants in the ecosystem. This research is often referred to as plant neurobiology or plant intelligence.

The deep intelligence that plants possess has been studied and elucidated by many prominent thinkers and writers and not just by scientists. Personalities like German polymath and writer Johann Goethe; George Washington, the first President of the United States of America; Masanobu Fukuoka, the Japanese philosopher; and Jagadish Bose, the first modern Indian scientist, have discussed how plants are highly conscious and intelligent entities. Plants have highly developed neural systems and they utilise neurotransmitters identical to those of humans.

That plants are conscious organisms, capable of information-processing, complex communication, and of having feelings, perceiving danger and pain, is a paradigm-shifting idea that leads to a larger, more profound understanding of the world we inhabit. The entirety of our environment consists of highly conscious self-organised systems which nest within other self-organised systems in a continuous and unbroken chain of complex relationships that we humans, characteristically, fail to recognise.

In many cultures where the link with nature remained strong, men and women who served as tribal healers, shamans and medicine people, had profound knowledge of the use of plants, trees and flowers singly and in combination, for various therapeutic remedies. These sacred medicines sometimes have complex recipes and effects which, indigenous healers or shamans claim, have been divined through communication with a plant or tree spirit itself.

In a 1950 letter of condolence to a grieving father, Albert Einstein, the greatest scientific mind of the modern age, wrote the following, "A human being is a part of the whole called by us universe, a part limited in time and space. He experiences himself, his thoughts and feelings as something separated from the rest, a kind of optical delusion of his consciousness. This delusion is a kind of prison for us, restricting us to our personal desires and to affection for a few persons nearest to us. Our task must be to free ourselves from this prison by widening our circle of compassion to embrace all living creatures and the whole of nature in its beauty."

This sense of harmonious holistic understanding and unity is what so-called "preliterate" societies understood so intuitively and readily and what is lost to our empirical proof-seeking modernity. And yet, it is only this connection with the secret and subtle world of nature that can save humanity as it teeters on the precipice of disaster. One doesn't have to necessarily believe in nature spirits, but such belief engenders an attitude of respect and reverence for nature, an attitude that, if adopted, could still rescue floundering humanity.

The shamans of yore and of today have been empowered to forge these spiritual connections with nature, connections that sustain and act as cohesive factors for entire communities. These societies, where nature or what the modern world calls "natural amenities" are seen as spiritual resources that help the local populations to connect with the sacred, may be wiser by far than the "developed" and "civilised" modern-day city dwellers whose estrangement from nature seems to be growing steadily and with increasingly tragic inevitability.

22
Kullu Dussehra

The medley of the mynahs chirp, the ravens cry and other twitters wake for pleasing morning music. Delicate flowers bob up and down in the breeze, scores of white butterflies dance between the pink hydrangeas and red poppies, while bees buzz around the marron hollyhocks and white lilies. Gentle breeze rustles through the willow trees and I can hear the melodious flow of the nearby brook.

I sit on the first-floor balcony of my cottage in Shanag village, gazing at the upper Beas Valley, over the orchards and fields towards the craggy mountains above the Solang Nala and the twin Gyephang peaks at its far end. This landscape, particularly when the mountain peaks are capped with sparkling snow, has been imprinted upon my mind's eye, never failing to imbue me with a sense of calm and solace.

I reminisce about the past year and a half spent researching, documenting and filming in the valley. My experiences and knowledge have expanded my perspective and introduced me to an entirely new worldview. And I am much richer for it.

These valleys of the Himalayas have for much of their history been secluded from most of the outside world by their geography and lack of proper roads. The earliest settlers here were pre-

Vedic tribals, who believed in animism. For them, these desolate mountains and thick forests were the abode of dangerous demons, devils and spirits, so they felt the need for divine protection. As earth and nature worshippers, they established shrines to nature spirits and local gods.

Over time, the people of this valley came to merge their local gods with the Vedic deities, resulting in the widespread worship of local animistic Devtas, alongside mainstream Hindu gods. They spun complex mythologies that fused the Hindu cosmology with their own myths of nature gods, blending identities and stories, and binding the community into a common perceived reality that pervaded the overall social consciousness.

The Devta belief system of Dev Bhoomi, with its mythic and magico-religious culture, has complex multidimensional layers. The village Devtas in Himachal Pradesh are not simply objects of worship. They constitute an institution that governs all social, cultural, moral, economic, religious and political life of the village folk, the wholesome expression of which remains alive and active even today in their everyday lives.

The Devtas of Dev Bhoomi are considered as living gods who are in constant communication with their people through their shamans, the Goors of the valley. These Goors are mediums, oracles, doctors, astrologers, counsellors, and practitioners of magic, and pretty much carry the whole weight of the community's engagement with their Devtas.

The myths and the legends of the Kullu Valley are mostly undocumented, passed down by word of mouth and experienced in its living traditions. People's beliefs are instinctual and experiential, rather than intellectual or philosophical. The emotionally alive culture of Dev Bhoomi has been sustained by their traditional Devta system of worship, healing and celebration, leading to a connected, rooted, mentally healthy and harmonious society.

My musings are interrupted by Meru. The valley has begun to gear up for its biggest annual celebration, the Kullu Dussehra, and today Meru is taking me to meet Raja Maheshwar Singh of the erstwhile royal family, who is central to these celebrations. We need his invitation and permission to film the renowned festival.

In most parts of India, Dussehra ends on Vijayadashami, the last of a ten-day-long festival period. But in Kullu, Dussehra celebrations begin on that day and their Vijayadashami is celebrated a few days later, following a period of festivities. Meru explains, "It is our belief that it is on Vijayadashami that Lord Ram and Lakshman invaded Lanka, and that Ravan was killed on a full-moon day. Now there is no full moon on Vijayadashami day, when the rest of the country celebrates it. Here in Kullu, Dussehra begins at that time and ends on the fifth day, which coincides with a full moon."

What is also peculiar to the Kullu Dussehra celebrations is the homage paid to Raghunath-ji or Shri Ram, the ruling deity of Kullu town, by all the Devtas of the valley. Over three hundred Devtas come from all over the valley and the adjoining valleys of Inner and Outer Saraj, Banjar and the Parvati valleys for this seven-day celebration. All the Devtas first head to the Raja's palace to greet him, as he is the royal representative of Raghunath-ji.

This custom was initiated in the seventeenth century by the rulers as a way of taming the local gods and nature spirits, who were symbolic of a more ancient and primitive religion than orthodox Hinduism. The only Devtas who are exempt from such homage are the deified sages, such as Vasishtha, who was Lord Ram's tutor, and Devta Jamadagni Rishi, who is a law unto himself.

On our drive to Kullu, Meru tells me a little about Raja Maheshwar Singh, the fifty-nine-year-old king, whose family had ruled the erstwhile princely state of Kullu since AD 1500. Singh has represented Kullu as a politician for over three decades, being initially elected to the state assembly when he was twenty-eight years of age. He has also served in both Houses of Parliament. Popular among the locals, he is seen as an important political voice in the state of Himachal Pradesh.

We reach the bustling town of Kullu in an hour. It is considerably warmer and noisier here, abounding in shops, traffic and crowds of people. We drive around the huge Dhalpur grounds which is where the Dussehra processions will gather. I see that a few colourful shamianas—festival tents, decorated with bright banners and flags—have been put up. Meru points to a large building alongside the tents, saying, "That's the Dev Sadan, which offers free accommodation to all the Devloo who will accompany their Devtas for Dussehra."

We take an uphill road to reach the palace complex at Sultanpur, where Raja Maheshwar Singh's ancestor, Raja Jagat Singh, had moved the capital from its earlier location at Naggar. We inch through the crowded bazaar to the palace complex. It is a low-key unprepossessing complex in a mix of Pahari and colonial styles. At one end is the palace entrance, where the words 'Raja Rupi Kullu' are painted in red and white on a tall archway. The Raghunath-ji Temple, which we would visit later, lies adjacent to the palace complex.

Meru parks his car in the courtyard, and we head towards the tall wooden doors set within the arch, which have images of Lord Ganesh painted on them. We walk through the doors into a large stone-cobbled courtyard. The two-storey palace lies before us, the stone buildings enclosing the courtyard on three sides. Wooden balconies wrap around both floors and wooden rafters helm the roof. Originally built in the early years of the seventeenth century, most of these buildings had been reduced to rubble by the earthquake in 1905. The present structures I see in front of me were rebuilt after that. We are welcomed in the courtyard by a member of Raja Maheshwar Singh's staff and led to an outdoor seating area.

Shortly afterwards, the Raja walks out from the doors behind us. He is a tall and hefty man, with a solemn face and an imposing moustache. He is dressed casually in a kurta-pyjama and a sombre-toned Kullu cap. He smiles warmly, completely transforming my first impression.

"Thank you for agreeing to meet me, Raja Sahib," I offer as we exchange a handshake.

"Well, royal titles and status have been abolished, so kindly call me by my name." Maheshwar Singh laughs, putting us at ease instantly. He asks me about the work that I have done so far, and questions me closely about my intentions and knowledge gained thus far. Having satisfied himself, Maheshwar-ji relaxes into answering my queries quite candidly.

"You see, I am the chief kardar of the Kullu Valley and have a special relationship with all the Devtas of the valley," he states. "The royal title was bestowed on my family by Hadimba Devi herself. My family traces its ancestry to the Pandavas and therefore we are related to Hadimba Devi."

Maheshwar-ji snaps his fingers and an attendant rushes to his side, bowing respectfully. After ordering tea and snacks for us, he tells us about his fascinating family history.

The Raja's ancestors, the Pal dynasty, ruled over Garhwal in the present-day state of Uttarakhand. However, after a fierce famine and an onslaught by the Gorkhas, the ruling family dispersed. According to known history, the kingdom of Kullu was founded in the first century AD by Behangamani Pal, who, it is speculated, came from Prayag, near Allahabad. At that time, it is said, the people of Kullu were suffering under the repressive regime of the Thakurs of Spiti, and rallied forces behind Behangamani Pal to overthrow the Thakurs and establish the first ruling dynasty of Kullu. The rule of the Pal kings continued till about AD 1450 with Raja Kelas Pal being the last in that line.

After him there was a long break of about fifty years during which it appears that the Thakurs and the Ranas might have captured power. After this interregnum, Sidh Singh, a descendant of the Pal rulers, declared himself the Raja of Kullu in AD 1500 and is recognised as the first of the Singh kings.

"My ancestor, Behangamani Pal, left our native place and came to Kullu, along with his wife, his purohit and his clan deity, Devi

Tripura Sundari," says Maheshwar-ji animatedly. "Shorn of his royal title, Behangamani Pal could only find employment with a kumhar, a potter, as his apprentice. Behangamani worked hard and transported the kumhar's wares around the valley. Once, during a journey to Banara village, he saw an old woman hobbling along the path with great difficulty. The old woman was practically crawling, and the sight filled Behangamani with great compassion."

He goes on after a brief pause, "Addressing the old woman as Dadi, Behangamani asked her to climb onto his back so that t he could help her get back to her village. The old woman agreed. Halfway through, the old woman asked him to take a break and change places. Behangamani was surprised at the woman's demand and tried to reason with her, but she was adamant. The old woman lifted him up effortlessly and began to grow in size. She grew so tall that she traversed the entire Kullu Valley in a few steps. Behangamani realised she was a powerful divinity. The old woman revealed that she was Hadimba Devi and that for his kindness, she would grant Behangamani the kingdom of Kullu. As long as he and his family continued to revere her, they would flourish in Kullu. So, Anu, that's why we still honour Hadimba Devi and consider her as our grandmother." Maheshwar Singh concludes his story, his voice quavering slightly with emotion.

He adds with great pride, "Apart from Hadimba Devi, the royal family has four clan goddesses whom we revere. Our main clan deity is Tripura Sundari Devi, whom our ancestor brought from our place of origin. We also put our faith in Devi Sharvari, Devi Docha Mocha, two sister goddesses who came from Tibet."

Maheshwar-ji is extremely knowledgeable about local lore and is completely steeped in the Devta culture. He informs me about his religious responsibilities as the King of Kullu, during the upcoming Dussehra festival.

"The royal family of Kullu participates in Dussehra, as representatives of Devta Raghunath-ji. In the sixteenth century, my ancestor, Raja Jagat Singh-ji, gave his kingdom to Raghunath-ji to rule. So, he is the king here and we as his primary servants follow his guidance in all matters. Our Dussehra is like the Kumbh Mela of all our Devtas. There will be over two hundred deities coming tomorrow to pay their respects to Raghunath-ji and I will receive them in this very courtyard. They come here every year to pay obeisance to Raghunath-ji, meet each other, share their happiness and sorrows with each other, give and take blessings. It is a hugely sacred festival for us."

Rajaji shares another interesting fact. "This festival of Raghunath-ji cannot start without the presence of Bijli Mahadev, as aspect of Shiva. Lord Rama and Shivji are very important for each other, so until Bijli Mahadev arrives, we do not put the idols of Raghunath-ji on the palanquin."

Bijli Mahadev comes along with his entire family—Parvati, Ganapati, Kartik, plus all the seven rishis and Narad Muni. Also, the rath of Bijli Mahadev stands right behind the palanquin of Raghunath-ji, as his protector, and remains stationed thus throughout the festival. Bijli Mahadev is an important Devta in the valley, and thereby hangs a tale. The story is told of an evil demon Kulant who took the form of a giant serpent and stretched its body across the Beas in order to block its flow and flood the village of Mathan in Lahaul-Spiti. Shiva's devotees appealed to him for help. The great god descended from his abode atop Mount Kailash and set fire to Kulant's tail. When the demon turned around to look at its flaming tail, Shiva smashed its head with his mighty trident. The mountain on which Kulant was slain took the shape of a serpent, and it is also said that Kullu derives its name from that of the demon Kulant.

After killing the demon, Shiva asked Indra, the god of all the Devas, to strike the mountain with lightning every twelve years, to remind his devotees of his might and protection. But not wanting his people to be harmed, Shiva would take the lightning strike upon himself in the form of a Shivling. It is said that true to the tale, the Shivling in the Bijli Mahadev temple is shattered by a lightning strike every twelve years and is thereafter mended by the temple priest using a paste of sattu flour and salted butter. Miraculously it is fully restored after every strike.

I ask Maheshwar-ji about the Goors of the valley. "A person needs to have great devotion in order to become a Goor, which is why many Deities do not have Goors at present. Our Devtas will not select inappropriate persons. Also, becoming a Goor is a lengthy process and involves several tests. Every deity has different rules for this." Maheshwar-ji explains some of the rituals and tests that a potential Goor needs to undertake, to prove himself capable. "The prospective Goor of Tripura Sundari has to go deep into the river and bring a rock from a place where the person can simply be swept away by a strong current. Once a Goor is approved, he is buried underground for a short time and then paddy is sown on top of him. This signifies his rebirth into a life that will be quite difficult. That is why it is not something everyone can or wants to do. It demands a lot of devotion. The Devta chooses wisely and if anyone pretends—and we have all heard of such cases—their lives are effectively ruined."

I question him about a Goor's divine possession trance—was it always the deity's words or was it sometimes a performance? Maheshwar Singh responds emphatically. "No Goors can be in trance or have the Devta within them all the time. But people keep asking questions of their Devta for a long time during a poochh session. That is why the Goor prays to the Devta that he may speak the deity's will correctly. It is certainly not a game of pretence."

Our conversation is interrupted by an attractive young man, wearing a beige silk kurta-pyjama, a blue sleeveless jacket and a bright Kullu topi. Maheshwar-ji introduces us to his older son, Prince Danvender, who has completed his higher studies in Delhi but has returned to the call of the land. Maheshwar-ji takes our leave, requesting us to continue our conversation with his son. I am absolutely delighted when he graciously invites us to his palace for the opening of the Dussehra ceremonies and gives me permission to film the entire festivities.

When I tell Danvender about my documentation of Dev Bhoomi and the Goors, his eyes sparkle. He endorses his faith enthusiastically, "Our Devtas are like our parents … our protectors. They have the final say on everything, including important decisions like marriage," says Danvender. "You know, even my bride was selected by Raghunath-ji, who chose her out of all the marriage proposals that were sent to my father."

Seeing my quizzical expression, he explains, "We put flowers representing each girl under a thaali in front of Raghunath-ji's idol, performed some prayers and covered the thaali overnight. The next morning, the chief pandit uncovered the thaali and checked it. Whichever flower had moved from its space would be the girl whom the Lord had accepted. So, obviously, I married Raghunath-ji's choice."

Danvender calls out to a staff member, who rushes indoors and comes out followed by an attractive young woman in a floral printed pastel chiffon sari. He introduces us to his charming wife Vibha and tells her about my filming. Vibha is as devout as her husband. "Yes, we have personally experienced miracles in our lives, through the grace of our Devtas," she says.

Danvender relates a miraculous experience. As the first in line in ascendancy, the prince needs a male heir to inherit his title. His first-born was a daughter. Though he and his wife were happy, a son is needed to assist his father in his sacred responsibilities, as only men are allowed to conduct the religious duties that the Kullu Raja has to follow. These duties and responsibilities are transferred to the male heir as soon as a king passes. Danvender pensively recounts, "We tried for several years to have another child, but were unsuccessful. We consulted doctors who could not help us. Then my father went around to all our clan Devis and other Devtas to pray for a male heir."

Soon Vibha became pregnant, but an ultrasound had inadvertently revealed that she was carrying another daughter! The prince explains, "Don't get me wrong, Anu-ji, we both feel that daughters and sons are equal, but I am bound by convention to provide a male heir. The family was despondent, but a few Devis and Devtas assured my father that I would get a son. We were puzzled. How was it possible, Anu-ji?" Danvender's eyes fill up at the memory.

"Then, what happened?" I have to ask.

"Well, this year I was miraculously blessed with twins ... A girl and a boy! Imagine that both the ultrasound and the Devi's verdict come out true," exclaims Danvender jubilantly. Both husband and wife smile broadly. "This is the power of our Devtas. They always take care of us," Danvender concludes emotionally.

Vibha adds, "Anu-ji, people in the valley lead simple lives which are conducted under the supervision of our Devtas. We do not do anything without asking them or without their approval. Whenever we have problems, they tell us the reason behind it and tell us what to do to overcome them."

After some more chit-chat, Meru and I take our leave promising the couple that we would be back the next day. As we drive back to Manali, Meru is reflective and shares something he has realised over the past eighteen months of filming. He says, "Anu, you know, since I have been visiting so many villages with you, I have reconnected with so many of my cousins and family friends. Now I have realised the value of going to festivals, staying with family members and having them come over to our place to stay."

The next morning, our first stop is the temple of Hadimba Devi. We walk into the temple compound which is buzzing with activity. Preparations are rife as Hadimba Devi's rath will begin its journey soon. Chunni greets me enthusiastically and informs me that the rath will travel in a huge procession of Devloo and other village folk, traversing twenty-four miles down the valley to the Ramshila bridge, which lies at the far end of the long Akhara Bazaar in Kullu. "We will camp the night there until tomorrow, when the Raja will send a formal messenger to the Devi inviting her up to his palace," he informs me.

There is a sizeable crowd of people in the temple compound. I am now acquainted with most of Hadimba Devi's Devloo and share pleasantries with them. The only one missing is Goor Tuleram who is nowhere to be seen. The musicians begin to take up their position in front of the temple. Mehar Singh, the bajantri, smiles at me. They begin playing a cheery rhythm while all of us wait. The lilting melody seems to mirror our feelings of anticipation.

Suddenly, Tuleram enters the temple compound with the Devi's rath right behind him. There is a collective cheer as the rath enters and the music becomes more upbeat. Tuleram offers flowers to the Joginis in the four directions and walks around the temple premises before heading to the tree of Ghatotkacha. Here, Tuleram stops and instinctively goes into a mild trance. The Devi tells her people that she is present and looking after them. His trance is over quickly and just as he sighs deeply, people crowd around the rath.

They make offerings to the Devi and seek her blessings. We watch the rath move out of the temple area and into the street where it is stopped by devotees every few steps. Both men and women are part of the procession, and I spot a few children too. As Meru and I follow the rath and the excited crowd, I recollect my initial quest during the Devi's birthday festival, in the month of May last year. It seems like my journey has come almost full circle.

As Hadimba Devi's rath makes its way slowly through Old Manali, Meru and I get into the car and drive to Pei village, our second stop of the day. The village lies close to the village, of Halan, home to the mandhar or storehouse of Devta Naag Dhumbal. He too is going to begin his journey to the Dhalpur grounds, and we have been invited by Goor Tej Singh to witness the send-off. We reach quite early and are told that we still have an hour before the Devta's journey begins. We mingle with the crowd and amongst the devotees present is Roshan Lal Thakur, an advocate. Mr Thakur is quite interested in my documentation, and as an ardent devotee of Devta Naag Dhumbal, wants to share many interesting facts about his Devta.

He tells me proudly, "You see, our Devta Naag Dhumbal has quite a reputation at the Dussehra grounds. He is known as a thanedar, as he recces the area and keeps the crowds in check when Raghunath-ji's palanquin moves through the grounds. Sometimes sticks have to be put around the area where the Naag Dhumbal rath is stationed on the grounds, as it is often known to start moving by itself. You know, in the olden times no one could photograph him. The picture would never be clear, and if someone got too close, the Devta's rath would rush towards the person and smash the camera."

Meru nudges me, cheekily saying, "Just as well you did not get permission to film him!"

As if on cue, the rath is taken out from the mandhar and those around us begin to cheer. The rath is adorned with numerous garlands. I notice a small round pole protruding from the top of the rath. Meru tells me this signifies the bent head of Devta Naag Dhumbal, marking the spot of his injury when he along with his brothers escaped the coals in their earthen pots as children, according to the Naag Devta myth. The bajantris play loudly as Tej Singh does a short aarti with the ghanti and the dharj. The mukhotas on the rath glint under the afternoon sun and seem to wear pleased expressions.

As Tej Singh completes the aarti, the rath moves to his side and then begins running down the path. Caught by surprise, Meru and I rush to keep up. The energetic Devta bounds off the cemented pathway onto the hillside and begins to rush down the grassy incline at great speed. I am amazed that the kahars manage to keep their balance running at such speed in a zigzag manner, and also fascinated by the agility of the men. Meru tells me that many Devtas prefer using their traditional routes from a time when there were no roads. We are unable to follow and take the road instead. The Devta is moving at a breakneck speed and by the time we reach the main road, his rath has already reached the first of many halts in this journey. A feast has been prepared here and everyone takes a short break to rest.

We are about to join in when I spot another procession coming down the road. It is Hadimba Devi's procession which has inadvertently caught up with us. Tuleram and Chunni are right in front of the rath. I wave to Chunni, and he smiles back. Almost instinctively I join in the procession, for I find that I have subconsciously adopted her as the patron deity of my project. The procession stops at a short distance, and I walk ahead to see why. I find four women wearing identical pattus in a chequered pattern taking the rath upon their shoulders from the kahars. In a full year of filming in the valley, I have never seen women carrying the rath.

I turn to Meru for an explanation. He grins at me mischievously, and reading my mind replies, "Well, rules are meant to be broken, right?" I am unconvinced, as so far as I have seen that the roles are very well defined in the Devta system. Meru is enjoying my confusion but then he relents and explains, "Anu, these women are from a particular family in this village who have been granted this right by the Devi to carry her rath." The women walk a short distance and then hand the rath back to the kahars.

As Devta Naag Dhumbal's rath nears Hadimba Devi's rath, both rush and tilt towards each other in their typical meet-and-greet fashion. People in the two processions also greet each other affectionately. Once the meeting is over, the processions begin to move towards their encampments where they will stay overnight.

We drive back to Manali as the soft light of dusk begins to settle in the valley. The skies are streaked with pink and peach and within a while purple shadows begin to envelop us. I am exhausted by now and decide to crawl into bed to have an early night, as I know that the next day will be a long and tiring one.

The third day of the Kullu Dussehra dawns bright, clear and warm. The gilded leaves of the poplar trees rustle cheerfully in the breeze, seemingly in celebration, and the chirping birds seem unusually animated. I'm excited to finally witness what many have termed as the "largest and grandest Dussehra celebrations in India". I dress traditionally for the day and don a festive red kurta. Meru too has discarded his usual T-shirt and jeans and worn a formal shirt over trousers, with his Kullu topi sitting jauntily on his head.

We reach Kullu town, passing a few processions of Devis and Devtas making their way to the Raja's palace. The Devtas' raths sparkle with their newly polished mukhotas, draperies of flashy dupattas and garlands of fresh flowers. The Devloos, carrying silver staffs and pennants, and villagers accompanying their Devtas are all dressed in their festive best. The bajantris play raucous melodies adding to the good cheer. It is only the Goors, walking ahead of each procession, who are wearing their understated shamanic cream robes. They are sombre and barefoot, holding their Devta's dharj.

It is a slow journey as we pass several other processions that have come all the way from Banjar and the outer Seraj regions of the Kullu district. I spot a different style of rath, circular, with masks on all sides as opposed to the petha rath that I see more commonly. Meru tells me that these types of raths are known as a khada rath or "standing palanquin" and are mostly found in the outer Seraj region.

"They have walked about sixty kilometres to get here," says Meru quite nonchalantly. We reach Rupi Palace and hear the familiar sounds of horns and trumpets emanating from inside. We enter the courtyard to vibrant scenes—raths of Devtas stream about, accompanied by their entire entourages. All of Maheshwar Singh's family members are present, dressed in festival finery, while many guests sit or stand along the three sides of the courtyard to witness this grand event.

Raja Maheshwar Singh stands at the far end of the courtyard, alongside an ornately carved wooden door, the Athara Kardu ki Padao, the door which is always open for Deities to walk in at any time of day to meet the king. Dressed in a red and gold brocade sherwani, a red pagri with a jewelled necklace and sarpech,[1] he looks every bit royal. His demeanour too is formidable and commanding whilst receiving all the Devtas, as the royal representative of Lord Raghunath.

Each Devta blesses the Raja, while their Goors wave their smoking dharjs around him, and the kardars garland him with floral wreaths. The Goors bestow felicitations in Kullvi, while the raths bounce and sway, tilting repeatedly towards the Raja. I observe the rath bearers closely and notice how each one seems to be trying to control the rath to become still, as the constant jumps of the wooden bars on their shoulders must hurt! Some of the Goors fall into trance which range from mild to medium. Meru tells me, "Each Devta is conveying a special message to Rajaji … some are just blessing him, while others have specific observations or requests."

The courtyard is a riot of colour, sound and giddy excitement as a steady stream of Devtas and their processions troop in and out. I notice that some of the raths have longer, silvery metal bars, which Meru informs me are distinctive of the Devtas from Banjar Valley. The Goors from Banjar too are differently attired, wearing dhotis and kurtas and carrying differently shaped dharjs.

I spot Vibha and walk across to wish her. She tells me about all the events that had taken place thus far. "We first performed the Kali puja, as Vijayadashami begins with a Shakti puja. We worshipped our clan goddess, Ugartara Devi, in the temple inside the house. Since then we have had a steady stream of Devtas coming to bless us. Most deities will also be visiting Raghunath-ji's temple and Rajaji will perform the puja there."

Of course, the most awaited event is the arrival of the Royal Grandmother, Hadimba Devi. While the rest of the Devtas are sent an invitation by the Kullu administration, the royal family

1 Sarpech: Also known as an aigrette, a decorative piece worn on the turban

personally sends a royal guard carrying a ceremonial staff to escort Hadimba Devi to the palace from the Ram Shila ground, where she has been stationed since the day before.

As we speak, Shuru Devi, one of the Raja's clan deities arrives. Hardayal is wearing his shaman's robe and a sombre expression, his hair loose. Shuru Devi's rath charges up to the Raja who holds on to one of the bars of the rath affectionately. Hardayal hands a few flowers to Rajaji, along with other offerings of silken cloth, dhoop or fresh grass, which is considered holy, and some token money. Suddenly Hardayal goes into a trance and begins speaking loudly and quite aggressively. His eyes flash, his body shakes uncontrollably and his thick, long, wavy hair flies about. Following his initial trance speech, Hardayal, or the Devi, conveys her insightful message which Meru translates for me later.

Devi Sharvari/ Goor Hardayal: I see that you are worried about the threat of terrorism in the country…

Raja Maheshwar Singh: Yes, Devi maa, we are your family … please protect us…

Devi Sharvari/Goor Hardayal: Do not worry, my son, there will be no terrorism in this valley … you may hear bad news from elsewhere, but I will protect you all and ensure that all is safe here…

Soon, Hardayal's trance is over, and his countenance abruptly alters, becoming humble again. Rajaji bows to the Devi's rath in visible gratitude. Sharvari Devi's rath and Hardayal walk up to where the rest of the royal family are standing and offer flowers to them as blessings before exiting the courtyard.

Suddenly, sounds of a commotion accompanied by loud resounding trumpeting reach us from outside the palace entrance. A palpable sense of excitement runs through the courtyard. Hadimba Devi has arrived. The Raja and other members of his family leave the courtyard and disappear somewhere. Meru says, "Rajaji will not welcome her as he does the other Devtas. Since Hadimba Devi is considered to be his grandmother, this palace too belongs to her. So, treating her like a guest would be an insult."

Hadimba Devi's procession walks in, led by Chunni, the kardar and Tuleram, followed by the Devi's rath, bajantris and other members of the Devloo. Tuleram is in his shaman's robe and his greying hair is plastered to his scalp, as he sweats profusely. His bare feet are dusty and calloused, testimony to his strenuous walk in the heat. The procession takes a round of the courtyard and then walks up the steps to the veranda and then goes inside into the large living room. The kahars place the Devi's rath inside and step out, leaving Tuleram, the pandit and the kardar inside.

I watch all this from outside the door of the palace. I soon spot Rajaji peeping from behind the carved wooden door at the opposite end. I expect him to walk in and greet the Devi, but instead he gestures to me to follow him. "Come and see the puja," he commands. Led by uniformed guards holding staffs, we walk through the door into a narrow lane. We pass a cow and goat shed and a small family temple of Ma Ugartara as we make our way out from the palace gate till we reach the Raghunath Mandir.

The entrance to the temple complex has a pagoda-style roof and the compound is crowded with devotees. Several ladies dressed in their festive clothes sit around singing bhajans. The sanctorum is a wide hall inside which the pandits, wearing white turbans and orange robes, are busy with preparations. Tiny golden idols of Raghunath-ji and his consort Sita Maiyya have been placed on a silver throne with garlands placed on it. Rajaji asks me to wait while he goes inside and changes into a red kurta and dhoti. The pandits gather around and begin chanting while Rajaji begins conducting the puja.

The puja promises to be an elaborate one, so I walk back to the courtyard to check out the action there. Meru, standing outside the living-room door, beckons me urgently. We peek in to see that the ritual to get Tuleram into a divine possession trance has begun.

I see Chunni ringing the bell while Tuleram, mumbling mantras, is bent over the dharj, inhaling its smoke. In a few minutes he begins swaying and I notice shivers run up his body. He leans back, his cap drops, and he plucks a hair from his head. Suddenly he jumps up and his body begins shaking. Chunni and the kardar remove his cloak and tie it around his waist, leaving him bare chested.

Tuleram rushes out of the living room, taking me by surprise and I jump hastily to one side. He stands on the veranda facing the huge courtyard which is full of people, and roars ferociously, sticking out his tongue, Kali fashion. His face is red, his eyes are huge and bulging and his expression is terrifying. This is the wildest and most spellbinding of Tuleram's trances that I have witnessed so far, and a hush falls over the courtyard. Tuleram strides out towards the carved door where the entire royal family have now gathered. Chunni places shiny dupattas taken from the rath around everyone's neck, while Rajaji holds the dharj and does an aarti of Hadimba Devi's rath.

As he does the aarti, the Raja becomes emotional and tears flow down his cheeks. Beside him, Prince Danvender, also overcome with emotion, begins crying profusely as he holds on to the rath. The ladies of the house then do aartis to the rath and make offerings to the Devi.

Tuleram who had been reciting the Devi's Bharata thus far, now begins to address the Raja as the goddess.

Goor Tuleram/Hadimba Devi: I am your grandmother … who gave you this kingdom…

Raja Maheshwar Singh: Yes, yes, Grandmother … this is all your benevolence.

Goor Tuleram/Hadimba Devi: And have I not protected you always and given what you want?

Raja Maheshwar Singh: Yes, Grandmother … you have always taken care of us … I beseech you to continue to bless us and the people of this valley…

Goor Tuleram/Hadimba Devi: Have faith, my child … know that I am always there for you…

This back and forth continues for a while like a dance, with Tuleram displaying a range of emotions as the Devi. He holds us all spellbound by shouting thunderously at times, shaking violently and sticking his tongue out or wheedling like a child.

Goor Tuleram/Hadimba Devi: My grandson … I have a request … I would like a jewelled headdress…

Raja Maheshwar Singh: Whatever you ask will be done, Grandmother.

Goor Tuleram/Hadimba Devi: I will ensure that all goes well in your festival … in the form of Kali, I will protect you…

Hadimba Devi's rath and procession now leave the premises with huge fanfare. This has been the most emotionally draining meeting for the entire royal family, most of whom are teary-eyed. As other deities walk in, their tears subside, and the Raja continues to greet them graciously and untiringly.

By teatime, as the sun's rays turn amber, the family retires indoors. Soon, the Raja and his son venture out into the courtyard after a change of outfits, this time wearing richly embroidered brocade tunics with brightly coloured turbans and jewels. Just then an old woman walks into the courtyard, leading a chestnut-coloured horse, which will lead the royal procession to the Dhalpur grounds. The Raja and the prince make their way to the Raghunath temple in absolute splendour. The procession is led by about a dozen uniformed guards holding staffs, pennants and giant ornamental umbrellas. With all the pomp and ceremony, it looks like a procession straight from their glorious past.

At the Raghunath temple, the idols of Raghunath-ji and Sita Maiyya are carried on a small rath by their pandits. The rath is a small, circular one with no masks but a golden egg-shaped filigree ornament. The pandits join the procession which moves through the narrow lanes of the bazaar, all the way down to the Dhalpur grounds. Meru and I run through the crowds, jostling and pushing people, trying to get ahead of the procession.

The scene at the Dhalpur grounds is magnificent. Thousands of people swarm the grounds and hundreds of raths are stationed at their designated spots along all sides. Some are still running around, meeting and greeting other raths, their colourful draperies waving in the breeze and their mukhotas gleaming in the setting sun. It is extremely noisy with sounds of dozens of bajantris playing and people screaming in excitement.

The procession moves towards a square wooden chariot, standing at one end of the grounds. This is a huge, ancient wooden vehicle covered entirely with yellow, green and saffron cloths. "This chariot has been in use for hundreds of years," declares Meru in an awed voice. The chariot has a pointed roof and large wheels beneath. Attached to all four sides are ropes which the devotees will pull to move the chariot. The pandits of Raghunath carry the idol inside the chariot and place it on a red velvet cushion. The Raja and his son stand at the helm of the chariot surrounded by the pandits. Several raths gather around the chariot, with the raths of Hadimba Devi, Sharvari Devi and Tripura Sundari stationed closest. The chariot is now pulled by a humongous crowd of devotees chanting "Jai Shri Ram" incessantly. The mood of the crowd is boisterous and euphoric.

Since I had known that it would be difficult to film this spectacle from ground level, we had earlier installed a jimmy jib fitted with a camera. I clamber onto it, displacing my cameraman, and take over the filming. From my perch I get a fantastic overview of the entire ground. The scene is breathtaking: the huge chariot is being pulled by hundreds of people, dozens of raths are rushing about, the bajantris are vigorously playing their trumpets and drums. A huge sea of people fills the ground and the adjoining buildings, immersed in the dance of the divine.

As dusk settles over the valley, bringing in a cool breeze, the raths return to their designated spots where tents have been erected to house the Devloo. The raths retire for the night after the evening aarti has been conducted. At one end of the ground, local musicians perform song and dance for an enthusiastic crowd. The numerous food stalls that have been set up alongside are doing brisk business, selling snacks, sweets, tea and cold drinks, while another line of stalls sell cheap trinkets, garments and other knick-knacks.

I take in all the bright eyes, smiles and easy laughter, marvelling at the scale of this festival. I am, unexpectedly, not in the least bit tired, nor is my crew. Adrenalin still pumps through us from our frenetic filming during the day and the exhilaration of this boisterous festival.

Suddenly my jimmy jib wobbles, and I look down to see Meru shaking the body of the jimmy jib, wildly gesturing for me to come down. Once finally on the ground, I see that Meru is hugely excited. He literally splutters, "Guess what, Anu?"

I stiffen in trepidation. Meru screeches, "There is going to a Jagti tomorrow! Rajaji just sent me a message. And he has given you permission to film it!" I look at Meru in amazement. He is all but doing an excited jig. I have never seen him looking so jubilant.

"But what is a Jagti, Meru?" I ask mystified. From his excitedly voluble and muddled explanation, I gather that a Jagti is a rare event, an assembly of the gods of the valley, called once in several years when an issue of great urgency arises. A Jagti can be called for by any of the Devtas and the assembly is generally held under the aegis of Raghunath-ji at his temple.

When a crisis that threatens the ecology, cultural purity or spiritual traditions of the valley occurs, the Dev Samaj convenes a Dev Sansad where the "upset gods" express their displeasure through their oracles and pronounce their collective verdict.

A Jagti is always called whenever the issue is a legal one. And whatever is decided by the Dev Sansad is accepted without question by the people of Kullu, for to not do so is to invite the wrath of the Devtas. For those who might contend that the Devtas are more a cultural force than a political one, these Jagtis are a case in point for the opposite idea.

And now I had been granted permission to film a Jagti! It was all so fortuitous! Caught up in Meru's infectious excitement, I prepare myself for yet another demonstration of the power of the Devtas.

The day of the Jagti is a warm one with a heat haze swirling around the mountain peaks. We are cooled by the breeze wafting up from the Beas as we drive alongside the sparkling river, en route to Kullu.

Meru tells me that last year, during the Dussehra celebrations, many Devtas had expressed a wish to convene a Jagti, as they had not had one in a long while. "Rajaji had promised to hold it during the Dussehra celebrations this year," he says.

As during the Dussehra celebrations, the Dhalpur grounds are buzzing with activity: pop-up shops are selling wares like knives, baskets, farming equipment, cosmetics, cheap jewellery, clothes, magical oils, sacred masks and temple paraphernalia. Food stalls are doing brisk business selling sweets, chaats and popular dishes like chholey bhature, rajma with rice, pakoras; drink peddlers sell local nimbu soda, aerated drinks and of course, chai. Locals, dressed in their most colourful, are out to celebrate and I am once again surrounded by animated faces, bright smiles loud chatter and laughter.

Further into the grounds, as far as I can see, are tents which house individual Devta's raths and their Devloos. The front flaps of the tents have been lifted up and I see hordes of devotees paying their respects to the Devtas, consulting the Goors or just chatting with the Devloo.

We wander through the melee, with me taking photographs and Meru chatting with acquaintances, until it is time for us to head for the Jagti. All the action will happen at the temporary temple of Raghunath-ji, which is a grand tent erected at the grounds. A large area has been cordoned off creating a compound.

We walk in through the temporary gate. The temple is housed in a red tent erected right in the centre of the compound. The idol of Raghunath-ji has been placed on a heavily decorated altar surrounded by his pandits. Dozens of Goors are sitting in a semicircle around the walls of the tent, according to what seems to be pre-decided positions. Meru informs me that the Jagtis are conducted with a certain discipline and according to procedures that have remained unchanged since days of yore. The Goors are seated and consulted in line with those methodologies.

This assembly of over a hundred Goors, with more walking in as we watch, is an incredible sight. Some are young, some old, some moustached, some bearded, some clean-shaven. Most of them wear their shaman's robe, although some have worn dhotis beneath. All the Goors have their dharjs placed in front of them, along with tiny piles of uncooked rice and flowers. They sit around, chatting amicably, waiting for the proceedings to begin.

We station ourselves at one end of the compound, where luckily, I find a large stone to perch myself on which gives me a vantage view. I scan the crowds of Goors looking for familiar faces and spot Tuleram and Hardayal seated next to each other in the centre of the front row of Goors.

Maheshwar-ji, dressed in a red kurta and dhoti, walks out of the temple tent along with Prince Danvender. He signals to the long lines of bajantris on either side of the compound, at which they begin drumming and blowing the horns. The pandits accompanying each Goor light up the dharjs and begin ringing the Devta's bells, while the familiar trance-inducing music rends the air. Soon the entire area is filled with thick, aromatic juniper smoke and the Goors begin to invoke ritual trance. Chanting mantras, they bend forward and inhale the smoke deeply. Plucking a hair from their heads, they drop their caps, which a member from their Devloo sitting behind catches. As the horns blare, the drumbeats quicken, and I see many Goors go into trance. Some tremble slightly, some imperceptibly, while others are shaking in various degrees of intensity. The ambience is surreal and intense. I feel transported to a different realm witnessing this mass divine possession trance.

In the distance, I see the silhouette of a figure jumping up and down frantically. As I zoom in my camera through the smoke, I see that it is Prince Danvender! He is shaking uncontrollably. He waves his hand and is handed a bottle of juice by an attendant. He takes a sip, while his attendant holds him from the back, seemingly trying to stop the jumping. I look at Rajaji, who is standing right outside the temple tent, to see his reaction. To my amazement, he too is shaking in a deep trance. He too is held by one of the pandits of Raghunath-ji. However, his shaking subsides soon, while Danvender continues convulsing ferociously, his attendant holding onto the prince's Kullu topi firmly. I look questioningly at Meru, and he shouts into my ear, "Prince Danvender is known to get into trances … but if his topi falls here, he could be declared a Goor, so that is why his attendant is ensuring that his topi doesn't fall off."

The ceremony commences with Maheshwar-ji consulting the Goors. He goes to each Goor by turn and questions him. Each Goor answers in his own peculiar way. The consultations are quick, and once a Goor has spoken as and for his deity, he hands Maheshwar-ji a few grains of the uncooked rice. Rajaji inspects the rice grains in his palm and nods. "To check if what the Goor has spoken is correct or not," Meru explains.

As Maheshwar-ji finishes with each Goor, a member of the Devloo immediately gets up and honours their chief kardar with a garland of flowers or a silken cloth around his neck. Meanwhile, Danvender has come out of trance and seems fully recovered. He watches over the proceedings, ensuring that everything goes smoothly. Three hours later, Maheshwar-ji finishes consulting all the Goors and the Jagti session winds down. The ceremonial horns are blown and the Goors begin to get up and leave to the sound of the drums. They head back to their tents.

Maheshwar-ji and Danvender head to their private royal tent for lunch and invite Meru and me to join them. The royal tent is a simple shamiana with a carpet and sofa, where the royal family gets to rest and have lunch. Maheshwar-ji is in a good mood, given that the Jagti proceedings had been completed successfully. Over a simple but tasty lunch of aloo puri, he tells me, "You are lucky to see this Jagti, this assembly of the representatives of our village Devtas. Last year, on the penultimate day of the festival of Dussehra, the Devtas had demanded a Jagti to communicate to us their will on certain important issues. So, we had promised to do it this year."

I am keen to know what the Devtas had conveyed to him at the Jagti. Maheshwar-ji takes a long sip of his lassi and replies, "Well, last year there was a major bomb threat to the celebration of the Dussehra festival!" Seeing my alarmed expression, Rajaji laughs, saying, "No, no. Nothing to worry about. Today the Devtas have unanimously said that they would guard Kullu from terrorist attacks and although there may be a few terrorist activities in the rest of the country, Kullu would not witness any. Our Devtas have assured me that as long as our Devta tradition remains and there is faith in the Devtas, they will protect us from all misfortunes."

Meru tells me about another Jagti that took place with several Devtas from Manali's upper valley in 2006. The government had sanctioned the construction of a large-scale project—a multi-billion-dollar Himalayan Ski Village Project, the largest-ever foreign direct investment in the tourism sector in India. The locals were divided about the project. Some sought personal gain by selling their land at premium prices, whereas others realised that locals may suffer and be marginalised by this project. A Jagti was called and the Devtas, through their oracles, unanimously rejected the project, asserting that such a project would damage the fragile ecosystem of the mountains and destroy many sacred spots. The state government was forced to scrap the project under pressure from local communities.

Maheshwar-ji nods in affirmation, saying, "Yes, our Jagti is a final order from our Devtas, and it cannot be ignored. It has to be implemented as commanded."

In many ways, my experience of the famed Kullu Dussehra with the royal family and the Jagti were the crowning moments of my eighteen-month-long sojourn in Himachal. Climactic in its colour, sound and opulence, and revealing in its intersectionality of culture and political power—for Maheshwar-ji is a parliamentarian of long standing—the Kullu Dussehra demonstrated the undiminished vibrance of the Devta system. The Jagti underscored the relevance of the Devtas in the modern context.

Epilogue

Once again, Meru and I walk down the familiar path towards the striking pagoda-roofed temple. The deodar leaves surrounding Hadimba Devi's temple glisten in the late afternoon sun.

It is May 2018, exactly ten years since I began filming my documentary on the shamans of the Himalayas at Hadimba Devi's birthday celebrations. We have chosen to come on the third day of the event, after the main festivities, to avoid the crowds that filled the previous two days.

There are still many people around, though most are tourists. The sprawl of festival stalls has significantly reduced from what it must have been in the previous days, though a few stragglers remain. We join the queue of devotees, lined up all the way around the temple to the front. "Coming full circle in more ways than one," I think to myself with a chuckle.

"What's the smile for?" Meru asks. I explain that I am struck by the symbolism of being at the same place and time from where I had begun my journey of exploration ten years ago.

"Ah! Yes of course." Meru smiles. "It's like the tenth anniversary of the *Shamans of the Himalayas*," he says, breaking into a laugh. "We must discuss it later."

As we inch slowly towards the entrance, I find myself reflecting on my journey—my search for self—over the past ten years. What had I experienced in the last decade? What had I learned? How had my primary concern—my physical health—fared? And how had I changed as a person?

"Anu, move." Meru nudges me, and I realise we have reached the doorway to the inner cave of the temple. After paying our respects to the goddess, Meru and I wander through the deodar grove in silence. I become aware that the ten years away from the world of Dev Bhoomi have sharpened my objectivity, while my personal evolution has given me deeper insight into its reality.

For me, Dev Bhoomi, with its traditional socio-religious culture, is a beyul—a part of "Secret India", a distinct alternative reality inhabited by those who believe. Dev Bhoomi is a magical bubble, one of many such unique bubbles in this country, each with its own mythology, way of life, and belief system. All of them are valid worlds of perception and cannot be judged by outsiders.

Intense engagement with Dev Bhoomi has brought me many personal insights and taught me several universal truths. I ask Meru a question I had posed ten years ago, to him and to others in the valley: "How is the faith quotient towards the Devta system in the valley today? Do you find that young people are moving away from the system?"

Meru thinks for a while before answering, "You know, Anu, about seven to eight years ago, it seemed that way … but somehow in the past few years the younger generation are getting more into it."

"So do you think the Devta system will survive the socio-economic pressures of the twenty-first century?"

Meru speaks confidently and with a huge smile. "Definitely, Anu! Our faith in our Devtas is extremely strong and still pertinent." He adds with a mischievous chuckle, "When you come here ten years from now … you will find the Devta system still intact."

As I marvel at Meru's conviction, we hear a huge commotion. "What's that?" I say, startled at what sounds like a roar of loud voices coming from the festival ground adjacent to the temple.

We almost run towards the festival ground, but as we draw closer, the roar diminishes considerably. We reach the festival ground to find a large group of about fifty to sixty men huddled around a few raths.

As we draw closer, two men come towards us and firmly order us away. One of them gestures forcefully with his forefinger. He says something curtly to Meru in Kullvi. Seeing that I am about to protest, Meru drags me to one side, whispering firmly, "Not now, Anu."

I refuse to leave the festival ground and before Meru can object, I clamber up onto the large concrete steps built at one end of the compound. Taking out my camera, I surreptitiously zoom in and focus the lens to try and get a closer look at what is transpiring amidst the crowd.

Meru clicks his tongue disapprovingly but says nothing. He has long resigned himself to my curious and persevering nature! Through my lens, I notice that there are perhaps five raths and that Hadimba Devi's rath is among them. I spot Chunni standing next to it. I see some Goors in their ceremonial short tunics. Standing around them are the Devloo and the Bajantris.

"There seems to be some discussion going on," I comment to Meru, who doesn't respond. While still staring through my lens, I ask him, "What did those men say to you?"

Meru's response almost makes me drop my camera. He says, "Tuleram's son Devi Chand has just been selected as the Goor of Hadimba Devi."

I am dumbfounded as my memory rushes back to the bright-eyed boy I had met ten years ago.

We find out later how the selection had happened. We are told, "During the course of the celebrations, the rath of Devta Shankh Narayan from the village of Nasogi suddenly went berserk and started darting around the field. After tracing a random path through the festival grounds, it came and stopped abruptly in front of Devi Chand who was standing amongst the onlookers. The rath flung Devi Chand's cap off and as it did so, he went into an involuntary trance. Following this episode, he was acknowledged by all as the Goor of Hadimba Devi."

I am still sitting on the steps, digesting this news, when we notice the crowd dispersing. We watch as a couple of raths and their entourages leave the festival grounds at the far end.

"Look, there are some people coming this way," Meru whispers. We observe a group of five men escorting a young man dressed in a Goor's cloak, though it's swathed in shiny fabric. Another shiny scarf is tied around his head. As they draw closer, I notice that the young man appears dazed, supported by his companions as he walks.

The group stops close beneath where we are sitting. Meru clutches my arm and whispers, "That's Devi Chand … Tulcram's son." I can hardly believe my eyes, for this tall and well-built young man with slightly long hair and a thick moustache looks nothing like the thin twelve-year-old boy I had interviewed ten long years ago. Seeing my disbelieving expression, Meru reminds me, "That was ten years ago, Anu."

As I stare in complete and unabashed astonishment at the completely transformed Devi Chand, he suddenly looks up at me. I am transfixed and instinctively nod to him. There is no response. Not even a sign of recognition. Devi Chand is not looking at me. He is looking through me with glazed eyes, lost in another world.

I lift my camera to take a photograph when one of the men notices and shouts angrily, "No photographs!"

I quickly lower my camera, while Meru raises his hands in a gesture of apology. The men return to the crowd, with four of them protectively supporting Devi Chand.

I murmur, "But, Meru, he told us he wanted to become a doctor … remember?"

Meru's response is firm, "Anu, you know very well that for us, the will of our Devtas is supreme and accepted by all. If the Devi has chosen Devi Chand as her Goor, he has no choice but to accept it with grace."

My journey certainly seems to have come full circle. Perhaps Meru is correct. The resilience of the Devta culture of Dev Bhoomi appears to have been demonstrated emphatically in the passing of the torch to Goor Devi Chand, son of Goor Tuleram. This enigmatic and wonderful belief system undeniably has deep and strong roots. It leads me to believe, and indeed hope, that it may successfully survive the relentless onslaught of contemporary culture and continue providing spiritual nourishment, emotional succour and community-connectedness to its generations of believers still to come.

Select Bibliography

Alter, A. (2008). *Dancing with Devtas: Drums, Power and Possession in the Music of Garhwal, North India*. Routledge.

Angelo, Jack, and Angelo, Jan. (2001). *Sacred Healing: A Soul-based Approach to Subtle Energy Medicine*. Piatkus.

Armstrong, K. (2022). *Sacred Nature: Restoring Our Ancient Bond with the Natural World*. Knopf Canada.

Baindur, M. (2009). 'Nature as Non-terrestrial: Sacred Natural Landscapes and Place in Indian Vedic and Puranic Thought'. *Environmental Philosophy*, 6(2), 43–58. https://doi.org/10.5840/envirophil20096213

Bande, U. (2006). *Folk Traditions and Ecology in Himachal Pradesh*. Indus Publishing Co.

Berggren, K. (1998). *Circle of Shaman: Healing Through Ecstasy, Rhythm, and Myth*. Inner Traditions/Bear & Co.

Berman, M., and Brown, D. (1999). *The Power of Metaphor: Story Telling and Guided Journeys for Teachers, Trainers and Therapists*. Crown House Publishing.

Berreman, G.D. (1964). 'Brahmins and Shamans in Pahari Religion'. *The Journal of Asian Studies*, 23(S1), 53–69. https://doi.org/10.2307/2050621

Biswas, A. (24 November 2020). 'The practice of shamanism and indigenous art of India'. *Karwaan: The Heritage*. https://www.karwaanheritage.in/post/the-practice-of-shamanism-and-indigenous-art-of-india#:~:text=They%20too%20believe%20that%20their,Rathvas%20and%20Sauras%20are%20made

Bloom, W. (1986). *Devas, Fairies and Angels*. Gothic Image Publications.

Boddy, J. (1994). 'Spirit Possession Revisited: Beyond Instrumentality'. *Annual Review of Anthropology*, 23, 407–434. http://www.jstor.org/stable/2156020

Bužeková, T. (2010). 'The Shaman's Journeys between Emic and Etic'. *Anthropological Journal of European Cultures*, 19(1), 116–130. https://doi.org/10.3167/ajec.2010.190109

Chaudhry, M. (2015). *Timeless Echoes: Writings on Kullu*. District Cultural Council and District Dussehra Committee.

Chaudhuri, S. (2008). 'Plight of the Igus: Notes on Shamanism among the Idu Mishmis of Arunachal Pradesh, India'. *European Bulletin of Himalayan Research*, 32, 84–108.

Chetwode, P. (1990). *Kulu: The End of the Habitable World*. Time Books International.

Choedon, P. (2021). 'The Nechung Oracle and the Construction of Identity in the Tibetan Diaspora'. *Asian Ethnology*, 80(2), 391–411. https://www.researchgate.net/publication/357685629_The_

Nechung_Oracle_and_the_Construction_of_Identity_in_the_Tibetan_Diaspora

Dalai Lama XIV, Bstan-'dzin-rgya-mtsho (1990). *Freedom in Exile: The Autobiography of the Dalai Lama*. HarperCollins Publishers.

Dandekar, D. (2018). 'Shamanism'. In P. Jain, R. Sharma, and M. Khanna (eds), *Hinduism and Tribal Religions* (pp. 1–4). Springer, Netherlands. https://doi.org/10.1007/978-94-024-1036-5_6-1

Dash, D.S.C. (2021). 'God, Man and Nature: A Vedic Perspective'. *National Journal of Hindi & Sanskrit Research*, 1(36), 99–102.

Dold, P.A. (2011). 'Pilgrimage to Kamakhya through Text and Lived Religion: Some Forms of the Goddess at an Assamese Temple Site'. In Hillary P. Rodrigues (ed.). *Studying Hinduism in Practice*, 46–61. Abingdon: Routledge.

Eliade, M. (1964). *Shamanism: Archaic Techniques of Ecstasy* (W.R. Trask, Trans.). Penguin Group.

Farmer, S.D. (2002). *Sacred Ceremony: How to Create Ceremonies for Healing, Transitions, and Celebrations*. Hay House.

Farmer, S.D. (2009). *Earth Magic: Ancient Shamanic Wisdom for Healing Yourself, Others, and the Planet*. Hay House.

Feinstein, D., and Krippner, S. (2006). *The Mythic Path: Discovering the Guiding Stories of Your Past: Creating a Vision for Your Future*. Energy Psychology Pr.

Frazer, J.G. (1922, 1989). *The Golden Bough: A Study of Magic and Religion*. Oxford University Press.

Harner, M.J. (1982). *The Way of the Shaman: A Guide to Power and Healing*. New York: Bantam Books.

Heaven, R., and Charing, H.G. (2006). *Plant Spirit Shamanism: Traditional Techniques for Healing the Soul*. Simon and Schuster.

Hodson, G. (1980). *The Kingdom of the Gods*. Theosophical Publishing House.

Ingerman, S. (2011). *Soul Retrieval: Mending the Fragmented Self*. HarperCollins.

Jerath, A. (1998). *The Splendour of Himalayan Art and Culture*. Indus Pub. Co.

Kakar, S. (1982). *Shamans, Mystics and Doctors*. United States of America: Beacon Press.

Kakar, S. (2003). 'Psychoanalysis and Eastern Spiritual Traditions'. *Journal of Analytic Psychology*, 48(5), 659–678.

Kapoor, R.L. (2003). 'What is psychotherapy?' Unpublished report, National Institute of Advanced Studies, Bangalore.

Kehoe, A. (2004), 'Eliade and Hultkrantz: The European Primitivist Tradition', In A. Znamenski (ed.). *Shamanism: Critical Concepts in Sociology*. (261–262). London: Routledge.

Kirmayer, L.J. (1994). 'Improvisation and Authority in Illness Meaning'. *Culture, Medicine, and Psychiatry: An International Journal of Cross-Cultural Health Research*, 18(2), 183–214. https://doi.org/10.1007/BF01379449

Kleinman, A. (1988). *The Illness Narratives: Suffering, Healing, and the Human Condition*. Basic Books.

Krishna, N. (2015). 'Sacred Groves: An Indian Heritage'. In N. Krishna and M. Amrithalingam (eds). *Sacred Groves of India: A Compendium* (pp. 71–79). Chennai: C.P.R. Publications.

Krishna, N. (2017). *Hinduism and Nature*. Penguin Books.

Laycock, J.P. (2015). *Spirit Possession around the World: Possession, Communion, and Demon Expulsion Across Cultures*. Bloomsbury Academic.

Mann, R.L. (1998). *Sacred Healing: Integrating Spirituality with Psychotherapy*. Blue Dolphin Pub.

Meadows, K. (1998). *Where Eagles Fly: A Shamanic Way to Personal Fulfillment*. University of California: Element.

Meadows, K. (2004). *Shamanic Spirit: A Practical Guide to Personal Fulfillment* (2nd ed.). Simon and Schuster.

Menia, T. (15 June 2022). 'Understanding the Shaman's Tribulations. Ethnography.com. https://www.ethnography.com/2022/06/understanding-the-shamans-tribulations/

Menon, I.V. (2015). 'The Shamanic Healing Experiences and Religious System among Uraly Tribes of India: A Sociological Analysis'. International Conference on Business, Marketing and Information System Management (BMISM '15), Paris (France). https://doi.org/10.15242/ICEHM.ED1115013

Metraux, A. (1977). *Le vaudou haitien*. UK: Gallimard.

Meyer, L. (n.d.). *Inuit Shamanism*. University of Texas at Austin. Retrieved 24 August 2024, from https://www.laits.utexas.edu/sami/diehtu/siida/shaman/inuit.htm

Müller-Ebeling, C., Rätsch, C., Shahi, S.B., Rai, M., and Gurung, I.D. (2002). *Shamanism and Tantra in the Himalayas*. Thames & Hudson.

Nath, R., and Prajapati, A. (2024). 'Understanding Vedic Texts through the Lens of Eco–Spiritualism'. *Obnovljeni* Život, 79(3), 281–294. https://doi.org/10.31337/oz.79.3.2

Nishimura, K. (1987). 'Shamanism and Medical Cures'. *Current Anthropology*, 28(4), S59–S64. https://doi.org/10.1086/203589

Oesterreich, T.K. (1966). *Possession, Demoniacal and Other: Among Primitive Races in Antiquity, the Middle Ages, and Modern Times*. University Books.

Paracelsus. (1941). 'A Book on Nymphs, Sylphs, Pygmies, and Salamanders, and on the Other Spirits'. In Sigerist, H.E. (ed. and trans.). *Four treatises of Theophrastus von Hohenheim, Called Paracelsus* (pp. 215–253). Baltimore: Johns Hopkins Press.

Pattanaik, D. (2008). *Myth = Mithya: A Handbook of Hindu Mythology*. New Delhi: Penguin Books.

Paxson, D. L. (2008). *Trance-Portation: Learning to Navigate the Inner World*. Weiser Books.

Plato (1952). *Plato's Phaedrus.* Cambridge: Cambridge University Press.

Pogačnik, M. (1997). *Nature Spirits and Elemental Beings: Working with the Intelligence in Nature*. Findhorn Press.

Purohit, S. (2002). 'Faith that works'. *Hindustan Times* (20 February). Lucknow Edition.

Rouget, G. (1985). *Music and Trance: A Theory of the Relations Between Music and Possession.* University of Chicago Press.

Schmidt, B.E., and Huskinson, L. (eds). (2010). *Spirit Possession and Trance: New Interdisciplinary Perspectives.* Bloomsbury Publishing.

Shabab, D. (1996). *Kullu: Himalayan Abode of the Divine.* Indus Publishing Company.

Sharma, B.R. (2007). *Gods of Himachal Pradesh.* Indus Publishing Company.

Singh, N. (2021). 'A Brief Outline on Shamanism: Its History and Beliefs in Current Times'. *Anthropology* 9:266. doi10.35248/2332-0915.21.9.266

Singh, U. (2004). *Between Worlds: Travels among Mediums, Shamans and Healers.* Penguin Books India.

Smith, F.M. (2006). *The Self Possessed: Deity and Spirit Possession in South Asian Literature and Civilization.* Columbia University Press.

Smoley, Richard, and Kinney, Jay. (2006). *Hidden Wisdom: A Guide to the Western Inner Traditions*

Spangler, D. (2010). *Subtle Worlds: An Explorer's Field Notes* (J. Spangler and F. Secrest, eds). Lorian Association.

Steiner, R. (1995). *Nature Spirits: Selected Lectures by Rudolf Steiner* (Klinker, W.U., ed).Rudolf Steiner Press.

Tedlock, B. (2005). *The Woman in the Shaman's Body: Reclaiming the Feminine in Religion and Medicine.* Bantam Books.

Thakur, M. (1997). *Myths, Rituals and Beliefs in Himachal Pradesh*. New Delhi: Indus Publishing.

Toy, A.D. (2012). *Nature Spirits, Spirit Guides, and Ghosts: How to Talk with and Photograph Beings of Other Realms*. Quest Books.

Tylor, E. (1871). *Primitive Culture: Researches into the Development of Mythology, Philosophy, Religion, Art, and Custom*. London: J. Murray.

VHAI (1991). 'India's Health Status'. New Delhi: Voluntary Health Association of India.

Vidyarthi, L.P. (1963). *The Maler: A Study in Nature-Man-Spirit Complex of a Hill Tribe*. Calcutta: Book land Private Limited.

Villoldo, A. (2010). *Shaman, Healer, Sage*. Random House.

Vogel, J. (1929). 'The Woman and Tree or Salabhanjika in Indian Arts and Literature'. In Konow, S (ed.). *Acta Orientalia*. (Vol.7: pp.202–209). Societates Orientales Batava Danica Norvegica.

Wahbeh, H. (2021). *The Science of Channeling: Why You Should Trust Your Intuition and Embrace the Force That Connects Us All*. New Harbinger Publications.

Winkleman, M. (2010). 'Shamanism and the Origins of Spirituality and Ritual Healing'. *Journal for the Study of Religion, Nature and Culture*, 3(4), 458–489. https://doi.org/10.1558/jsrnc.v3i4.458

Winner, E., and Rai, M. (2003). *World Shaman: Encountering Ancient Himalayan Spirits in Our Time*. iUniverse.

Witzel, E.J.M. (2012). *The Origins of the World's Mythologies*. New York: Oxford University Press.

Wolfe, A. (1988). *In the Shadow of the Shaman: Connecting with Self, Nature, and Spirit*. Llewellyn Worldwide.

Woolcott, V. (n.d.). 'History of Shamanism'. Retrieved 24 August 2024, from https://www.shamanicjourney.com/history-of-shamanism?amp=1

Acknowledgements

This book is the result of almost a decade of work. I began work on the documentary series *Shamans of the Himalayas* in 2008 and it took three years to complete the four-part series of forty-five minutes each. This series has been telecast on various international channels like Discovery, Gaia and is presently being aired on Amazon World. Due to the seminal nature of the work, it has also been screened at several anthropology/sociology departments of universities in India and abroad.

A few years ago, due to the heightened interest in the subject, I was persuaded to adapt my documentary series into a book. This adaptation has taken about four years to write, as I decided to expand the ambit of what was shown in the documentary. Therefore, I have a lot of people to thank for both the documentary and the book.

To begin with I would like to thank all the film crews who worked with me over five schedules of filming in the Kullu Valley. They are too many to name, but all are credited in the documentary series. However, I would particularly like to thank all my producers and assistants who worked with me on the ground research whilst filming and post-production.

As far as the book is concerned, I would like to begin by thanking my assistant director Avantika Sharma for the initial compilation of the documentary scripts written by me, plus having hundreds of interviews translated and transcribed.

I would like to thank Antara Datta, Ishita Pasricha, Bharti Motwani, Leela Carol and Deepti Nath for their copy edit of different segments of the initial three working drafts.

Thank you Merin Mani for working on additional research as well as copy editing the introduction, footnotes and bibliography.

A huge shout-out to Korak Ghosh for designing the book's cover.

I would like to thank my publisher Ajay Mago of Om Books International, and in particular Shantanu Ray Chaudhuri, editor in chief, for believing in this book and being hugely supportive through the process. Shantanu, I am grateful for your fine copy edit of the final manuscript.

Finally, huge appreciation and gratitude to Mehar Chand Thakur for his hard work and guidance and Antara for her invaluable support through the project.

Heartfelt gratitude to all the Goors, the people of the Kullu Valley and their Devis and Devtas for their gift of the documentary series and the book.